90

CHURCH

90 CHURCH

The True Story of the Narcotics Squad from Hell

AGENT·DEAN UNKEFER

2 4 6 8 10 9 7 5 3 1

First published in the UK in 2013 by Virgin Books, an imprint of Ebury Publishing

A Random House Group Company

www.randomhouse.co.uk

Addresses for companies within The Random House Group Limited can be found at
www.randomhouse.co.uk/offices.htm

The Random House Group Limited Reg. No. 954009

A CIP catalogue record for this book is available from the British Library.

The Random House Group Limited supports The Forest Stewardship Council (FSC®),
the leading international forest certification organisation. Our books carrying the FSC
label are printed on FSC® certified paper. FSC is the only forest certification scheme
endorsed by the leading environmental organisations, including Greenpeace. Our paper
procurement policy can be found at www.randomhouse.co.uk/environment

Text design and typesetting by carrdesignstudio.com
Printed and bound by CPI Group (UK) Ltd, Croydon, CR0 4YY

ISBN: 9780753540725

To buy books by your favourite authors and register for offers,
visit www.randomhouse.co.uk

CONTENTS

"The most successful federal law enforcement agency ever,
the Federal Bureau of Narcotics was populated by some
of the most amazing characters in American history..."

The Strength of the Wolf
The Secret History of America's War on Drugs

by Douglas Valentine

Publisher's Disclaimer

These memoirs are based on the author's best recollections of events in his life. Where indicated, the names and characteristics of some people have been changed in order to protect their privacy and identities. In some instances the author has recreated dialogue according to his best recollections and rearranged the details of events and chronologies in order to facilitate the narrative. Except in such instances the author has stated to the publisher that the contents of this book are true.

PREFACE

In 1930 the Federal Bureau of Narcotics was created primarily as an overseas intelligence operation with its agents often posing as CIA officials. It tracked the Sicilian Mafia who converted morphine into heroin then smuggled it in to New York City. The Bureau understood the magnitude of this evil, global plague of violence and death. However, it had less than three hundred agents worldwide to fight against the well-financed and well-organized Mafia that controlled the illicit drug trade with ruthless efficiency.

The Bureau's New York City operation was at the epicenter. Its headquarters was at 90 Church, an old post office in lower Manhattan. Only thirty agents were charged with the responsibility of making cases against organized crime. The bizarre and cunning way that they fought the Mafia to a standstill made them legendary. In 1968, at the most crucial point in its history, the Bureau was terminated. Two years later the Federal Drug Administration was formed with over four thousand five hundred agents but by then it was too late, the war on drugs was lost.

I was an undercover agent at 90 Church. I bought heroin, an absurd and dangerous job. I participated in many cases and had firsthand knowledge of others; however, this book is not just about my experiences. Nor is it an attempt to re-write history or lay blame or bestow glory, but simply to tell what it was like to work in an environment of desperation and madness.

To understand the agent's moral dilemma I have written a personal narrative. Because of the sensitivity of such activities, some of the events described in this book, including sequences, locations and other details, although inspired by real cases, have been changed. It has also been necessary to protect the identity of some of my fellow agents by changing their names and other identifying characteristics.

CHAPTER ONE

THE ROOKIE

DAY ONE

As far back as I can remember I had always wanted to be an FBI agent. I had never met an agent or a criminal, or even anyone who was victimized by a serious crime. But, like so many other things in my life that I could not explain, I just wanted to fight for *truth*, *justice* and the American way. This was Superman's creed from the opening of his TV show. It was such a silly combination of words that I was embarrassed to repeat them, but that was how I felt.

The FBI rejected me at the first interview. The two agents wore blue suits and had the same short haircut. They asked me questions like how much did I love my country and did I know people who were un-American? I answered as best I could. One of them referred me to a small agency that I had never heard of, the Federal Bureau of Narcotics. He said, "Their standards are very different." And after two short interviews they hired me. The two agents at the Federal Bureau of Narcotics were strange. One was wearing a T-shirt and the other was overweight. Talking to them was like meeting someone at a bar, friendly, saying whatever comes into your mind.

Only two months earlier I had moved from Ohio. I knew nothing about New York City. At about 5:00 on that drizzly morning in August 1964, I left my wife Daisy and my one-year-old son Mark sleeping and started walking to Manhattan to join the Federal Bureau of Narcotics. I was wearing a new gray suit, new spit-polished wing-tipped shoes, and was carrying a heavy briefcase filled with law books and manuals on self-defense. It never occurred to me that such a long walk might be a bad idea. The streets were wet and the buildings looked like abandoned sets from a black-and-white movie.

About six blocks from the Williamsburg Bridge, my right heel began to blister, and I started to limp. Suddenly I saw headlights charging directly toward me. A black Cadillac convertible was trying to run me down, swerving a few feet before it would have flattened me. I couldn't see the driver but I knew he did it on purpose. The car splashed through a large puddle, throwing muddy water on me from my chest to my ankles. I looked at my reflection in a store window. The suit looked wet but undamaged so I continued, limping from my blistered foot a little more with each step.

I tried to forget about the incident and was swinging my briefcase in cadence with my limp when the plastic handle snapped; it went sliding into the muddy street. It was too wide to carry with one hand, so I held it against my chest. Now limping badly and hugging my briefcase, I walked across the bridge with the hot, early morning traffic into Manhattan.

It was about 8:30 when I finally arrived at 90 Church Street. The Federal Bureau of Narcotics was on the top floor of an old post office, not far from Wall Street. Exhausted and sweating, I stopped at a coffee shop and sat at the counter. The waitress waved at her nose. "Gee, honey, I think you stepped in something."

In the men's room I looked in the mirror. My face and hands were dirty, and there was a black streak from my shoulder to my waist from carrying the muddy briefcase. My new suit looked like wrinkled pajamas. Blood from my blistered heel seeped through my sock, soaking the back of my shoe. Worst of all, now I remembered seeing a small mound in the puddle just before the Cadillac splashed me, which is why I smelled like dog shit. I washed my hands and face, tried to clean my shirt, but it didn't make much difference, everything just smeared. I looked like a dirty homeless bum and there was nothing I could do about it.

I was fifteen minutes late. Orientation had already begun. The receptionist ushered me into the office of George Blanker, Agent in Charge. He looked like the FBI agents who had rejected me, except his eyes were bloodshot, like my uncle who everyone said drank too much. There were two other new agents already sitting on the office couch. I squeezed in between them. In a condescending voice, Blanker was explaining what a dangerous job it was to be a federal narcotics agent, "We are soldiers on the front line in a war, out-manned and out-gunned. We are the only hope for saving America from a fate worse than any disease." The blue spider-web veins in his face glowed like a road map as he talked. "Drugs are the greatest threat to mankind, in the history of mankind, and it is up to *us* to save our country, us – just a handful of agents! Just *fink* of it!" His face swelled red with anger as he slurred, "*Fink of it!* Just *fink* of it! Only us to save America." He sprayed tiny balls of saliva as he pointed to the American flag. "*Fink* of it!" The three of us sat in a row, nodding, enduring the "Finking" spit shower. He retreated behind his desk, exhausted.

Then with new enthusiasm he flipped the switch of a tape recorder. From the sound of a dial tone we knew it was from a wiretap. At first the voices spoke in Italian, then, *"We're in America now, we should speak English. It's good practice."* There was a soft chuckle. Blanker told us that it was a major Mafia leader. *"Come to New York. I know we've talked about this before, but it's great here. The whores, the numbers, the rackets, the unions, it's wide open, it's America. In New York we don't fight, we work together. You have nothing to fear here, nothing to worry about. The police, they'll steal a hot stove, don't worry about them; just give them a little something. The FBI, the FBI are kids. They go home at five o'clock. They have nice suits, but they don't know what they're doing. You only have one thing to worry about: 90 Church. They are evil. They will fuck your wife. They will steal your mistress. They will take your money. They will lie in court. You never know who they are, but worse, you never know who they've got. If they get you, they will turn you into a rat. If they want you dead, they won't kill you; they'll make your best friend do it. They have no soul. Their slaves are everywhere, fucking and ratting on people. The agents of 90 Church are the most dangerous, evil people on the face of the earth."*

Blanker turned the recorder off and smiled with pride.

"I am proud of our guys. I am proud of this office. This is how we are feared by the dopers and the Mafia. You are joining a brave band of Americans and I wish you luck." Blanker waved us out. No one said a word.

We sat in the lobby for about a half hour, waiting to be told what to do next. I discovered a new problem; the hem of my right pant leg had unraveled and draped over my foot, completely covering my shoe. As I wondered how I was going to fix it, a senior agent greeted us and said that our first phase of training would be the pistol range. After pulling on his nose he said to me, "We will issue you a gun, which should be carried on your belt. You're not wearing a belt. Why don't you go and buy yourself one?"

I had only ten minutes to get to the firing range in the basement. I left the office, found a men's shop, grabbed a belt off the rack and paid for it. I limped back carrying it in one hand and holding my pant leg up with the other. Again I was late.

By the time I had convinced the security guard to clear me into the range, the other agents had received a revolver. The Range Master gave me a gray snub-nosed revolver in a holster. While everyone watched, I tried to put the belt on; it was too small. I pulled it across my waist to the first hole. It squeezed me like the end of a sausage. The holster and gun stuck out in front of my stomach. I could hardly breathe. I tried to hold my pant leg up, but the torn hem still covered my shoe and I kept stepping on it. I smelled like dog shit and was hobbling and sweating like a dirty, horribly wounded animal. I looked at my instructors, my fellow agents, and saw the disgust in their eyes. I hated myself.

That afternoon I was assigned to Group Two with two other new agents, Del Ridley and Jerry Ramirez. Our group had ten agents and the group leader was Agent Pike, a huge, fat, smiling German with big hands and crooked yellow teeth. Del and Jerry were each assigned a senior partner and given a desk, but Agent Pike said there were no senior partners available for me. He led me to a small table with a straight chair in the corner, away from everyone. I saw him go back into his office and talk to his secretary. He waved his hand in front of his nose as he talked to her.

Just when I thought things couldn't get any worse, Blanker's secretary brought in a large basket of fruit wrapped in red cellophane with a big sign, *Happy First Day*. "This has to be for you," she said. Then she placed it on the table in front of me and walked out shaking her head. My wife, Daisy, meant well. I looked over the red shiny wrapping, hoping somehow that no one had noticed this spectacle, but of course everyone had. They smirked at each other. Finally, Group Leader Pike came over to my table and told me to go home. I took the awful red basket and threw it in a trash barrel. The subway home took less than a half hour. Even strangers avoided me, preferring to stand rather than sit next to me.

Daisy was outside with my son Mark and saw me limping down the street, holding my pant leg up. "My God, what happened to you?"

I could not begin to explain. Daisy and I had only been married for two years, but had been together all through high school and college. We acted together in school plays and toured with a theatre group during the summer. She was my best friend, but now she couldn't do or say anything to help me. My greatest ambition in life – to fight for truth, justice and the American way – was over before it had even begun.

GROUP LEADER PIKE

The next morning I was on time. Pike and his secretary were the only ones there. Occasionally agents would come in briefly but ignored me. For hours I sat alone then finally Agent Pike came over to me. "At one o'clock let's you and I sit down with Agent George Blanker." I knew I was going to be fired. "Gee, um, did they issue you a gun yesterday?"

"Yes" I replied, trying to hide my disappointment.

He waved his big hand. "Well, can I have it? We just have to be sure it's registered, you know." I took my belt off and gave him the gun and holster. "Let's meet with George at one o'clock. Why don't you go to lunch now?"

The agents had come in and left with their partners. Everyone ignored me. I sat at my desk alone until finally at 1:00 Pike said, "Okay let's go have our little talk with George." I followed him through the halls to Blanker's office, like a bad student going to see the principal.

We waited outside Blanker's office, but I could see through the open door. Blanker was behind his desk, trying to calm two agitated men in wrinkled suits. Blanker called out to his secretary, "Is Agent Pike here yet?"

"Yes," she replied.

"Send him in."

I knew what was coming, but instead Blanker looked at me then said to Pike, "Who's this?" as if he had never seen me before. Before I could speak, he smiled, and said, "Would you please wait outside?" I returned to my seat outside his office.

I could still hear Blanker continue with the two angry men. "This is Agent Pike. He drives a government vehicle, a black Cadillac convertible." He read off a string of numbers. There was silence. Then one of the men said, "Were you at One Hundred Forty-Fifth Street and Lenox at about four-thirty a.m. Monday morning?"

Pike answered, "Yeah, I guess I was. We were working an after-hours joint, you know; we were there all night."

One of the wrinkled suits said, "There was a witness to a killing and an assault. A lady in a basement apartment got your license-plate number. Since the plate is confidential, it took us a while to track it. Were you there when someone was shot, then run over by your car?"

I heard Pike answer, "A drunk nigger tried to boost me off. He had a gun. I had to shoot him; he got in the way when I left. So what?"

One of the policemen said, "Well, okay, but why didn't you report this? Do you know the man is dead?"

"Well," Pike said, "it was me or him, the car wasn't damaged. I was going to write it up probably today, this afternoon. It happened very late. I was on my way home. I drove across the Williamsburg Bridge. It was after five in the morning."

One of the cops exploded, "You *shoot* a man on the streets of New York City, you *run* him over, you don't feel the need to *call* it in? Is this what you're saying? You fucking *kill* someone then drive away because your *black Cadillac* wasn't damaged? Jesus Christ! Is this your story? And you're a fucking *supervisor*?"

"Well, I should have gotten to it sooner," Pike apologized. "I'll write something up."

I heard Blanker say, "I'm sorry. I'll take care of this right away. Agent Pike is a Group Leader, he should know better. We're sorry about this and he'll do a report today."

The other cop was not satisfied. "This is bullshit. You can't treat us like this. This is not good for the Bureau either. Don't push yourself, George. Your guys have been crazy for a long time, but not this bad."

The two cops walked past me, shaking their heads as they left. Through the open door I saw Blanker turn to Pike. "Ted, this is not good. I can't believe this. I want a report on my desk in an hour.

These guys are really pissed. If this happens again, you're back in Chicago. Now get the fuck out."

Pike walked out, ignoring me, and went back to Group Two.

I just sat there staring at the odd assortment of pictures and awards that covered the wall. Besides the usual diplomas there were about ten strange plaques; each had a gun and a picture mounted on polished wood. There were different types of guns and next to each was a photograph of its owner, a smiling agent. A brass plate gave the agent's name followed by "killed while protecting his country in the line of duty" and a date. After about thirty minutes Blanker's secretary said, "Why are you here?"

I tried to smile. "I don't know."

She laughed. "Well, you're honest, that means you won't last in this office. Since you don't know why you're here, why don't you go back to where you think you belong?"

On the way back to Group Two I passed a large file room. Inside, seated around a table were a group of file clerks, fat girls with pimply faces and strange-looking guys so shy they wouldn't look at me. At the head of the table was what looked like a well-dressed teenager. He was making them laugh, but stopped when he saw me. He gave me a big smile and waved hello. This was the only friendly thing that had happened to me since walking in the door of 90 Church, and I was too stunned to wave back. For the rest of the day I sat at my little table, remembering what the cops had said about the black Cadillac convertible and Pike telling them how he "drove across the Williamsburg Bridge at about five in the morning". Incredibly, against all odds, it was Pike who had splashed dog shit on me and now by another weird twist of fate I had just escaped being fired.

That night I told Daisy what had happened. She laughed and pulled back her long brown hair. "Whatever will be, will be, we will face it together." She had said these same words before when she told me she was pregnant with Mark. We weren't married and she didn't care what other people thought. We would face it together.

DEWEY

The next day, the agents in Group Two were surprised to see me. I resumed my lone vigilance at my little table. Then the boy from the file room came in to see me. He was wearing a tailored sport jacket and bright tie. All the other agents were tall and serious, but he was much smaller and seemed to laugh at everything. His red hair was a mess, with a long strand covering one eye. With freckles and sparkling blue eyes, he looked like a kid ready to pull off all types of mischief. He was not carrying a gun, and I doubted that he was an agent. He introduced himself. "Hey, I'm Dewey Paris. I thought they fired you. Do you like sports? I'm giving two to one on the Yankees this weekend."

"No. I don't gamble," I said. "Yes, I'm still here." I hoped he felt sorry for me, but he didn't. He just walked out.

For the next three days I sat alone at my small table in the corner, even though there were two unused desks in the group. One desk was covered with notes and little piles of cash that agents would drop off or pick up. Everyone, including the two new agents, Del Ridley and Jerry Ramirez, continued to ignore me. Only Dewey remained friendly and waved at me every time I passed the file room.

Each night Daisy would watch for me to walk down the street

and meet me at the door with a smile. "Well, what happened today?" She would convince me that I was better than they were. She even predicted that someone, a veteran agent, would see my potential and make friends with me. "It always happens that way," she said. "Never, never, never give up."

She promised to send a big fruit basket to the office every day to move things along. This made both of us laugh.

After four days of the silent treatment I had had enough. I walked into Pike's office, "I want to make drug cases like the others, it's the reason I was hired. I'm as good as they are, I want a chance."

Pike rocked back in his chair and patted his huge belly. "You're an asshole, you don't belong here, you still smell like dog shit."

I gritted my teeth and stared back, waiting for him to fire me.

"Okay, we'll see, there's a case going down this afternoon. We'll see if you're as good as they are."

That afternoon Pike, Del Ridley, Jerry Ramirez, and a veteran agent named Ed Silkey met to discuss my first case. Pike told everyone that he had an informant named Buddy who had lined up a buy for ten thousand dollars for six ounces of heroin. It would take place this afternoon – and I was going to be the undercover agent. The plan was simple; I would take ten thousand dollars to a meeting in Harlem and buy the heroin. Del Ridley, Jerry Ramirez, Ed Silkey, and Pike would be on surveillance.

I could see the expressions on everyone's faces. No one believed that I was actually going to buy heroin. I had no training and was afraid and humiliated. I had no idea what six ounces of heroin looked like and was probably going to get myself killed, but I was never, never, never going to quit.

Pike smiled. "You can have your pick of anyone here to be close to you in case things go bad. You know what I mean." He waved to the three agents.

Agent Silkey shook his head. "Not me, I'm out of here. This is wrong, this is bullshit. I want no part of this. I'm on another case." He walked out.

Before I could say anything Dewey Paris came in. "Pick me, pick me," he begged, dancing around the room and raising his hand, "Pick me, pick me, pick me."

Pike exploded, "Get the fuck out of here, you little faggot."

Dewey Paris ignored him and stared at me. "I'm your friend, aren't I?"

I knew Pike was setting me up, so why not? My choices were two new agents or a file clerk. "I pick him," I said defiantly and pointed to the silly prancing teenager.

Pike turned red. "Okay, okay, here we go to Harlem with the asshole and the faggot. Come to think of it, it's the right combination."

On the way to Harlem, Pike and I picked up Buddy at a bar in Midtown. The informant was black, wearing a powder-blue suit with black trim. Buddy explained, "I met Harrison two nights ago at Small's. He got junkies in Brooklyn, near Coney Island. His connection's fucking him over real good. He needs to move more shit or lose the deal. He'll sell to anybody, believe me, you got dough, you got dope." The deal was simple: I would show Harrison the money and Harrison would show me the heroin then we would do the exchange on the street out in the open. Once the buy was made, Ramirez and Ridley would try to follow Harrison, but there would be no arrest. This was the first buy, and we needed to find the drug source.

We parked a block away from the meet. Buddy and I began walking down the street to the corner. I could see Pike, Ramirez, and Ridley following, but now more than a block away, trying to blend into the black neighborhood. Dewey remained in the government car, smiling and waving. Buddy and I waited on the street corner for about a half hour, leaning against the building and staring at people as they walked by. After a while I could no longer see any of the other agents. A black sedan drove past us and made a U-turn, parking about half a block away.

Buddy grinned; I knew that it was Harrison. A large black man with a red wide-brim hat got out of the car and began walking toward us, smiling. He shook Buddy's hand. Buddy introduced me as his friend who needed a new drug source. Harrison took a quick glance at me. "I don't have time for fucking bullshit. Do you have the money? I want to see it."

I pulled out bundles of hundred-dollar bills from my pocket and tried to show it to him without being too obvious. Harrison stared at the bundles, then took off his hat and waved it. "Looks good to me."

As Harrison was talking I saw a short man get out of Harrison's car. He carried his coat over his arm and walked toward us. I started to get nervous. "I've got the money. Where's the junk?"

Harrison laughed then handed me his hat. "Put the money in the hat." From inside his coat he pulled a chrome-plated revolver. Buddy backed away into the doorway of a barber shop. Then the short man flashed a sawn-off pump shotgun from under his coat. I looked desperately for the other agents, but they weren't there.

"Give me the fucking money, motherfucker," Harrison said as he cocked the hammer of the chrome revolver. My hand was shaking as I tried to hand him the money. I didn't know what else to do.

Harrison said, "If you're a motherfucking cop you're going to die."

Suddenly everything exploded in gunfire. Harrison was hit twice, dead center. I couldn't tell where the shots were coming from. His chest exploded – and his revolver went crashing to the sidewalk. The other man raised the shotgun directly to my face, and was cut down by three more rounds of fire: one to the neck, chest and chin. He grabbed at his face, which was covered with blood spurting everywhere. I tried to scream but I couldn't. I tried to run but I was frozen with fear. A third man, further down the street, began running toward me with a pistol in his hand, but suddenly he aimed away from me, across the street. He began shooting at Dewey Paris, who was running parallel, drawing fire to save my life. Dewey's left arm was raised straight in the air as he fired with his right hand straight across his chest and through the moving traffic. His target managed to get two shots off before Dewey, still running, brought him down. The black sedan, tires screaming, pulled away from the curb, charging Dewey, who was now standing in the street. In one quick motion Dewey reloaded his .45 and fired shot after shot into the windshield until it veered off and crashed – into a parked car, one car length in front of me. Dewey waved and gave me one of his big smiles, then jogged down the street, disappearing into a subway entrance.

Pike, Ridley and Ramirez surrounded me. The front of my pants were wet and warm. They pretended not to notice. Blood and bodies and car wreckage littered the street and sidewalk. People were running back and forth. I could hear the sirens, but my mind was frozen by the sight of Agent Dewey Paris's shooting rampage. The man I thought was a teenage file clerk had just shot the hell out of everything – and saved my life.

It's hard to tell your wife that after three days on the job you pissed your pants while a file clerk, who looked like a teenage kid, killed four people to save your life. My pants had dried before I got home so Daisy thought I was joking when I said I had pissed my pants. She waited for me to tell her more. When I didn't, the subject was postponed. After dinner I sat in the living-room chair and everything that had happened suddenly came back to me. I couldn't talk. I began shaking. Daisy could see something was wrong. She retreated into the bedroom and got Mark, who was sleeping. She gently rocked him in her arms until he awoke. She said to him, "Wake up, wake up, time to get to work." Daisy passed my son into my arms and went into the kitchen to clean up. My wife was beautiful and smart. She knew something terrible had happened, something so bad that talking about it would have to wait. I held my son in my arms until he fell asleep. The horrible reality of what had happened was now less important than my family.

THE REPORT

The next morning Blanker, Pike, Del Ridley, Jerry Ramirez and I met in a conference room. Pike pounded the table as he said to Blanker, "I want him brought up on charges. I want him *fired*. We had a good case going and he killed everyone. Four people dead, all of them shot multiple times. I can't even find him. You can't just kill people in the street and not report it. We're federal agents.

He's a psychotic killer. This has happened before. The Bureau can no longer tolerate him." Blanker nodded in agreement and looked down the table at all of us. "Write your reports up and I'll have him charged tomorrow."

I was tempted to remind Pike he had killed people in the street and failed to report it less than a week ago, but I didn't say anything.

After lunch Pike, Ridley, Ramirez, and Buddy the informant signed an incident report that said that Dewey Paris had panicked recklessly and caused the death of four dope dealers during an undercover operation in Harlem. The report named me as the undercover agent who agreed with the other agents. There was no mention of Harrison pulling a gun and threatening to kill me, or a man with a shotgun, or the charging car, or Dewey making himself a target to save me, or his spectacular display of marksmanship that I would never forget.

Pike put the report in front of me. "We were all there. We saw it. Sign it."

Last night I had cried in Daisy's arms when I finally told her what had happened. She had held me tight and said, "Fight for truth, justice and the American way."

Pike's face switched from a fake smile to a menacing glare. "This was your first buy. You were afraid. You didn't see things the way they were. We all saw it. You were in no danger. You don't have to sign the report...but if you don't, you should look for another job. Why don't you think it over? We can't let agents like Dewey Paris lose control and begin killing people, can we? He's done this very same thing before."

For the rest of the afternoon I sat at my desk, alone, staring at the report, which had an element of truth to it, but was grossly misleading and unfair. Even though it had everyone else's signature, I could not sign it. Daisy's words kept coming back to me. No one had seen or spoken to Dewey, but Pike's secretary said he would be in tomorrow for sure to pay off the winners of the baseball pool.

I went home at five o'clock. Lying on a report seemed to bother me more than seeing Dewey kill four people. Daisy understood it, too. "Once you begin lying, the whole structure will begin to crumble. If you lose your job over telling the truth you never had a real job in the first place." To distract me from all of this turmoil she put on sexy short baby-doll pajamas then smeared her lips with too much lipstick and painted her cheeks with rouge so she looked like an over-the-top street whore. I didn't feel like having sex anyway. It did make us laugh.

MICHAEL GIOVANNI

The next morning Dewey came in laughing and joking as usual. He laid out a stack of money envelopes on his desk; then left, announcing that he had an early lunch and was going to a basketball game in the afternoon. Pike waited for me to sign the report so they could fire Dewey. As I sat at my table a stranger walked through the door; he was unshaven, dressed in a black shiny suit and a floppy hat. His face was sunken and his eyes dark and beady like a snake. He wasn't very big, and he looked angry. He went directly into Pike's office. "Knock this shit *off*. It's *over*."

Pike slumped down in his chair and said, "What do you mean it's *over*?"

The man, raising his voice so everyone in the group could hear, replied, "Knock this shit off with *Dewey*. I just talked to Blanker. Change the fucking reports. You don't *touch* Dewey. Do you all hear? You know what Dewey does, everyone knows what he does. Do you understand? Change the reports and change them now." He walked past me then turned around and said, "Are you the agent that won't sign the report?"

Before I could nod yes, he said, "So you're the only agent here who stands up for the truth." He began to laugh. "So you won't lie on a government report." He laughed even harder and walked out.

Later I signed a new investigation report that said four drug dealers were gunned down in an attempted robbery and that the shootings by "various agents were justified."

I had confronted Pike and won with the help of a veteran agent just like Daisy said would happen. I had told the truth and gained the respect of my fellow agents. Gradually other agents introduced themselves. Besides Dewey Paris, there was Cleophus Brown, a black agent with a gold front tooth; Louie Gomez (Louie the G), a dapper Puerto Rican who carried an antique two-barreled Derringer; and Ed Silkey, who had refused to help Pike set me up.

Agent Johnny Greenway was the last to introduce himself. He was tall and wore cowboy boots with silver tips and a gray Western-style suit with a string tie. Strapped to his waist, cross-draw, was a chrome-plated six-shooter with a long nine-inch barrel. Of course he spoke with a Western drawl with plenty of how-dees and you alls.

My name now appeared on the roster as Michael Giovanni's partner. People would look at me and shake their heads. "You're Michael's partner? Do you even know who Michael is?" I had no idea, but assumed he was the stranger who had saved Dewey from false charges. Apparently everyone was afraid of him, including Pike.

For the next two weeks, I arrived in the morning and waited for Michael, who, if he came in at all, never arrived before 2:00 p.m. and then completely ignored me.

I had a lot of time to think. I kept remembering how strange my job interview was...especially in the last meeting with two agents, Colder and Wagner, more than two months ago. They started by telling me how hung over they were. Colder said, "God, I'm so hung over I can hardly see. Last night I met this girl, took her to her place and we fucked all night. I woke up this morning and didn't even know her name."

Agent Wagner laughed and told his story. "I got this broad on the side, goes for everything; you wouldn't believe the shit she does to me."

Both agents laughed together, then Agent Colder said to me, "You get the picture, don't you, what it's like on the street? Are you going to fit in? When was the last time you got laid? Tell us."

I was shocked that he would ask a question like that during a job interview. I wanted to answer. Daisy was the only sex I had known and she never took it seriously. When we made love she was always cracking jokes and laughing. But I couldn't tell them that so I said, "I'd rather not talk about my sex life if it's okay."

Both of the agents looked at me with disgust and changed the subject, but strangely one week later I got a letter informing me I was hired as a federal agent.

Jerry Ramirez and Del Ridley – the agents who started with me – were scheduled for training in Washington; I still expected to be fired any day since no one told me that I would be going with them. Also I had been given a lightweight aluminum gun. As Dewey

Paris explained, it was for agents who didn't really need one – like IRS agents. This reinforced my fears. I began to think that maybe, if no one noticed me, they would again forget to fire me and that sitting alone in the office day after day, pretending to be Michael Giovanni's partner, would somehow make me a real agent.

DARK SECRET

Eventually Michael did ask me to go to lunch. His idea for lunch was a hotdog from a vendor in the street. As we ate, he told me that this was the wrong job for me. "You're a smart kid, find something that will work for you; can't you see what's going on around you? Do you think Group Leader Pike can teach you to become a good agent?"

The question surprised me and I wasn't sure how to answer. "No. I don't think he can teach me anything," I answered. "I don't care, I want to be an agent and I'm not giving up. Maybe you or someone else can teach me. I see what goes on in the office." I told him the story about Pike and the two policemen. It made him laugh. For some strange reason, killing a man in the street, then running him over with your car, and forgetting to write it up seemed funny to me too. Michael returned to the subject of my career. "Give it up. Can't you see you're not cut out for this life?"

"Yes, I am. You don't know me. I want this job." There was a moment of silence between us. Then I asked, "Why did Wagner and Colder ask about my sex life during the job interview?"

Michael smiled. "It was a set-up question, standard for us. They try to get you to talk about your love life. If you're dumb enough to tell people who you're fucking in a job interview you're out, common sense."

I was surprised by the answer. "Why did they hire me, a nobody from Ohio?"

"Because you are impressionable, we can mold you into anything we want. Also you were an actor in high school and college. That's good for this job."

"What did you mean the other day when you said you know what Dewey does. What does Dewey do?"

"In case you haven't noticed, our job is to go into Harlem or wherever there are drug dealers and buy dope. Just like when Pike sent you uptown to get killed. What happened to you happens all the time. Dewey's a killer; he protects undercover agents, like he protected you. We need guys like Dewey to stay alive. The government doesn't care if you get killed or not. We're in a war."

Then Michael walked a few yards to the corner and pointed down the street toward the Hudson River and the New Jersey shore and said, "I've never been to Ohio. That's it over there, isn't it, across the river?" While still pointing at New Jersey he looked at me. "There are many terrible forms of addiction, all of them just waiting for you. If you become an agent you'll wish to God that you never left Ohio. You'll see. In the end you will become addicted to something just to stay alive and you will kill everything you love."

A week later, as I was leaving, Agent Michael Giovanni came into Group Two and asked, "Where are you going?"

"Home."

Without any expression he said, "You're my partner, you're going to work now."

Being Michael Giovanni's partner was more pointless than being alone in the office. He had me follow people for no reason. I followed a man until 3:00 in the morning, only to learn that he had nothing to do with anything. I think he made me do this for practice, but maybe just to wear me down. Once he said he was investigating a mob guy who I learned from the files had been dead for ten years. Yet every humiliation made me more determined not to give up, not to let Michael crush me. Week after week, I rode with him only to do his errands, get his lunch, park the car, get some coffee, call the office, get the car washed. I didn't even know when work began, or was over, nor could I name a single case we were working on.

My name was still not on the roster of the new agents scheduled to go to Washington for training, so my fear of being fired grew. The more despondent I became the more I wanted to give my life meaning and purpose.

While I waited for Michael's nonsensical orders, I roamed the streets of Manhattan every night with my cheap, lightweight gun and pretended to be hunting for drug dealers. To cure my frustration I drank. Every morning I smelled like liquor. I avoided talking about 90 Church with Daisy. My hung-over mornings at home depressed me and worried her. She would ask, "Are you sure you know what you're doing?" or "Why can't you talk to me?" I was slipping away into another world and didn't know how to stop it.

After about three weeks I had had enough. It was midnight and I was alone in the car outside a small restaurant in the Bronx, waiting for Michael, and as usual, I had no idea what was going on. The restaurant was closed and dark, except for a light in the back, which I assumed was the kitchen. Michael had told me to stay in the car: "Under no circumstance, come into the restaurant. This guy is very dangerous."

I sat there, thinking about the other times, being the butt of his jokes. I was never sure who to follow or watch on stake-outs. I stared at the small light in the back; all of a sudden I didn't care about what I was supposed to do. I left the car, walked down a small alley, and quietly opened the side door. There I saw a man wearing a waiter's jacket standing against the back wall, his pants down around his knees. He held a gun to Michael's head, which was buried in the man's naked crotch. In a panic to save Michael I drew my gray revolver and shot the man in the chest. The gun exploding in my hand made everything seem unreal. The man fell sideways, dropping his gun.

Michael jumped up, leaped forward, blotting the blood on the man's chest. "My *God*, my God! What have you *done?*" He wiped his mouth and looked at me, picked up the gun from the floor, and put it in his holster. He stared wildly around the room, then said, "Go to the car. Open up the trunk and bring my briefcase. *Hurry!*"

I stood there shaking and grunting. Eventually, in a trance-like state, I stumbled to the car and got the black attaché case from the trunk. When I got back, the man's pants were pulled up. Michael opened the briefcase, found a revolver in a plastic bag, and put it in the dead man's hand, squeezing the fingers several times on the trigger and barrel to be sure there would be fingerprints. He stood up. "You will do and say as I tell you. If you tell anyone what you saw, if you tell *anyone, ever*, what he was forcing me to do, that he had a gun to my head, you'll be dead. Do you understand? I must live with this, not you. If you tell anyone I will kill you."

When the police arrived, Michael was cold as ice. He explained that the dead man was a suspect in a big drug case, and that I, Michael's partner, had shot in self-defense. The cop found a gun and bag of heroin on the dead man.

In the car, Michael said, "I'm going to write this up and you're going to swear to it. You shot a drug dealer and saved my life, that's all." His eyes were red and teary. "Do you understand?"

The horror of it all put me into a trance. I didn't really know what he was saying. I had already seen four people killed in front of me, but this was different. Before it was like a bad movie. I was part of this, I was the one pulling the trigger. Michael drove to one of his bars and got out. "Take the car home; I'll see you tomorrow."

I managed to drive across the Williamsburg Bridge toward home, trying to pretend nothing had happened. Once across the bridge I pulled over and got out. Trembling, I leaned against the side of the car and threw up. Each time I wretched my guts I would look up at the cold blue night sky and it would make me do it again.

At home, Daisy woke up as I got into bed. "What's wrong? Are you okay?"

I had vomit all over my shirt and knew she could smell it. I tried to lie but I could feel her silence and her eyes staring at me through the darkness. I started to cry in short little squirts and puffs. "I killed someone," I gasped through the tears and snot running down my face. She didn't touch me; there was a long silence. Then I said again, "I shot him, I had to."

"What are you going to do?"

"It's all right," I answered. "Everyone will say I did the right thing. I'll be accepted now. I know now I'll be accepted."

"The *right thing*? Killing someone is the right thing to do to get accepted? I've tried to understand. You smell of booze every night and you say you don't fit in. You hate those people and yet you go to work every day to be part of them. None of it makes any sense. Now you kill someone to be accepted...I guess now you've got what you wanted. Tonight, finally, you've joined the Federal Bureau of Narcotics."

There was something else that she couldn't know. It was the terrible logic of 90 Church. I was beginning to like what I was doing. For now, it was something I had to hide so I could go on living.

The next morning my hand hurt from a cut that I didn't notice the night before. It was from shooting my cheap lightweight gun. The gun that Dewey had said wasn't any good for killing people. At the office, as usual, I sat at my little table, waiting for Michael. George Blanker came in to the group and put his hand on my shoulder. "Thank you, son. I understand you killed a dangerous drug dealer and saved Michael's life last night. Good for you. I know Michael will thank you, too."

In the afternoon I saw the report; it said that Michael and I were both interrogating the suspect. He had a criminal record. When Michael turned around, the man drew a gun from his pocket, and I outdrew him and fired in self-defense to save Michael's life. There was a picture of the dead drug dealer. He looked younger than me. This time, without hesitation, I signed the report even though I knew it was a total lie. Michael asked me what had happened to my hand. I told him it was from my gun. He didn't seem to care.

The next day there was a small box on my table. It was gift-wrapped like a box of candy, but when I picked it up, it was heavy. There was no note. Not even sure it was for me, I opened it. It looked like a .45 automatic; but much smaller. It was bright blue chrome, with white pearl grips. I took it down to the shooting range in the basement. The Range Master said it was a Walther PPK, expensive, reliable, and accurate. I shot about twenty rounds with it even though my hand still hurt. When I returned to my desk Michael was there and I said, "Thank you." He nodded once. Now everyone called me by my name and said hello and good-bye. Finally I was accepted, but it was an empty feeling.

Alone at home that night, I sighted down the shiny blue barrel and pretended I was shooting at drug dealers. The fact that I had killed someone and lied on my second federal investigation report was already a distant memory. I tried not to think about Michael or how much liquor it would take to erase the memory of that forced, perverted act from his already tortured mind. I was an agent now and that seemed more important than Michael's misery.

I tried to tell Daisy the same lie that was in the official incident report, how I saved Michael's life and became a hero. I know she tried hard to believe it. She wanted it to be true. Everyone lies about something; even my father lied to my mother about his secret love affair. I loved Daisy and we had never lied to each other. But this was something very different. Now things were changing. Daisy could never understand. I was an agent fighting crime. I was being trained by the best agent in the Bureau. I told myself that someday she would be proud of me and that would be enough to heal things. It wouldn't be fair for her to worry about the evil of my job. I had to lie to her. I had saved Michael's life and was keeping a dark secret; what difference did it make that I had lied on a report? Michael would always owe his life to me and protect me. I knew that someday that would be very important.

PEPPER

Now I was truly Michael's partner but even though I had been on the job for two months I did not understand any of his cases. One day as we drove through Greenwich Village, he told me to pull over. A Puerto Rican dressed in bright clothes, with lots of jewelry and a stingy-brim hat, came over to lean on the car. His name was Pepper. Michael told him to get into the back seat. "Pepper, I want you to meet somebody. Do you see this guy here in the front seat?"

Without looking at me, Pepper said, "How could I miss the fucking stiff?"

Michael chuckled. "This stiff is going to be your roommate. He's going to live with you for a while."

Michael reached over into my pocket and pulled out my credentials. "You won't need these. Go with Pepper. You want to be an agent, you want to understand drugs, go with Pepper. Live with him."

Before I could protest I was standing on the sidewalk with this stranger, watching Michael drive off. Pepper took me to his apartment in the East Village. The whole neighborhood was old, crumbling brownstones with people sitting on the front steps with nothing to do but throw things in the street. Pepper's apartment was in the middle of the block and very different. It was luxurious, with a remote-control lock on the street-level front door and expensive comfortable furniture. After he made me a drink he said, "If you want to learn, do as I tell you. First of all, take off your coat. You look ridiculous." He gave me one of his bright colored jackets. "You want to meet addicts? You want to learn about drugs? Do as I say. Otherwise, neither one of us is going to stay alive."

I would go home late at night and return every day to Pepper's apartment by noon. I met his customers. I saw how addicts lived and how they fed their habits. On an average, they stole two hundred dollars a day just to pay for their drugs. I watched them shoot heroin into their arms and their legs and thighs until their eyes rolled back. I saw girls, teenagers, whoring in the streets just to get a five-dollar bag of heroin. I saw one addict whose leg was so damaged that the skin fell around his ankle like a cheap sock, exposing meat and bone. I saw people covered with red and black sores shaking all the time, eating sugar out of the bag, stuffing it down their throats. I saw them lie and cheat each other, and steal from their families. I saw all of this because they came to Pepper with their pitiful stories, lies, and schemes. They came to us because they had to, because Pepper sold them heroin. He was good at it – no money, no dope, no excuses, no exceptions. If you were Pepper's customer your life was over, but you kept on living. Any decency you ever had just melted away, replaced by an obsession for drugs. Your only hope was to die as soon as possible to save your family and the people you loved. Decency and honesty became an ongoing con used to trick people. I could feel the sense of power Pepper had over their lives. It didn't disgust me like it should have.

Every day I watched the parade of dirty junkies coming and going to Pepper's fancy apartment as they spiraled down into hell.

On the afternoon of the fourth day, as Pepper was counting his money and arranging his bags of heroin, the buzzer sounded from downstairs. He walked over to the wall intercom. It said, "Open, it's Mars." Pepper backed away and stared at me, then rushed over to his desk drawer and pulled out a revolver and pointed it at my chest and in obvious panic said, "Put your gun on the table or I'll blow your fucking head off."

That all too familiar feeling of cold fear gripped me, I laid my gun on the desk and stammered, "Pepper, what's happening here?"

He put my gun in the desk drawer and walked back toward the intercom, pushing the button to open the door two levels down.

He wiped sweat off his forehead. "Mars, Mars La Pont, my connection. If they see a gun on you they'll kill us both. If you make one weird move then I'm going to kill you. Just be cool and we both may live through this. Do you understand?" He put his gun in his pocket and we both stared at the door.

There was a gentle knock. Two smiling black men entered and immediately looked me over. Both were well-dressed in leather and silk with expensive boots. One was huge, an obvious body builder. The other, smaller, covered with gold jewelry said, "Hey Pepper, who's the mope?" He was pointing to me.

"He's a runner, a little muscle, he's okay, I swear he's okay, Mars."

Mars stared at me and chuckled, then turned to Pepper while pointing to his huge muscular companion. "This here is Starbuck; *that's* what you call muscle. Pepper, if this mope of yours ain't okay you're going to be in the street down there without the benefit of the elevator." He looked at me then at Pepper. "I've got something for you and you'd better have something for me."

Mars reached down to his boot and pulled out a long white rubber tube and laid it on the desk. "Best shit in months, cut only once. Me and Starbuck can't keep it. Everybody wants some. Now where's my twenty grand?"

Pepper scrambled to his desk and began to stack money in piles, counting out loud while Mars looked on smiling. Then Mars pulled out a small leather pouch and poured white powder on the glass coffee table. With quick taps of a razor blade he scraped out four lines of cocaine. Then he rolled up a dollar bill. Starbuck was first; he sucked it up with a big gasp and rolled his eyes like a child eating ice cream. Then he pulled out a huge chrome revolver and pointed to me. I knew what this was all about. This was a test. If I didn't do this I would be dead in seconds. The sweat poured down my back as I sucked a line of cool burning cocaine into my brain. Starbuck put his gun away and gathered up the piles of bundled cash and put them in a black leather pouch he carried on his shoulder like a woman's purse. As the sweat continued to roll down my back the buzzer sounded again. Everyone turned and stared at it. Starbuck again pulled his chrome revolver ready to shoot it off the wall.

Pepper flipped the intercom button. "Who is it?"

"*Maureen.*"

"Not now, Maureen, I'm very busy."

"*Yes, now, Pepper, I was here earlier, there was no one home. Now, Pepper.*"

"Not now, Maureen. I said come back later."

"*Somebody's coming out, I'm in.*"

Pepper flipped the switch over and over, "Not now, not now." But the intercom was silent. He raised his hand to his head, "Jesus Christ, this is like Grand Central Station. She's on her way up."

After a few minutes there was a knock on the door. Starbuck holstered his gun and we waited for Pepper to open the door.

A beautiful white middle-aged woman dressed in a tailored expensive skirt and jacket stood in the doorway, a striking image of sophistication. She gave all of us a small nervous smile. "Oh, I didn't know you had company."

Pepper tried his best. "It's alright, they're friends, they're just leaving."

Mars grinned and ran his tongue over his lips. "My, my, my, look at them threads, designer for sure. Sweet mama."

Maureen tried to ignore him and said to Pepper, "I'm in a hurry, do you have what I want?" She fumbled for money in her designer purse.

Pepper sorted through the bags of heroin on the desk. "Sure, I've got it here for you. Here it is, let's settle up later, okay?"

Mars got closer, into her personal space. "I ain't seen such a pretty creature like you in such a long time."

She backed away. "Please, I came here to score. I don't want any trouble." She pulled out a wad of cash.

Mars laughed. "Trouble? No trouble. Pretty lady wants to score, big wad of money, my, my, my, got you a sweet little customer here, Pepper. Put your money away, today the dope is not for sale, no ma'am, not for sale. Not today."

Maureen stepped back. "Please, no, *please*."

Mars grabbed her purse and tossed it up in the air. Pepper caught it. "Not for sale. Not today. Tell you what, Starbuck and I want to play. We want to play with you."

As Starbuck smiled, her whole body began to shake. Pepper pleaded, "Please Mars, let her go, don't do this."

Mars's eyes grew wild. "Shut the fuck up. Here's the deal, white Scarsdale lady. Starbuck here and I are gonna go in the bedroom and party with you. Afterwards you can have all this dope free. Your money is no good today. What was your name?"

She was terrified, but managed, "Maureen."

"Maureen, I like that. Come on, Maureen, let's get it on."

Her whole body was sweating and trembling. She pleaded, "Please no, I just want to score...I have children, a husband, please, oh, *please*, no, oh *please*."

Mars smiled. "It's up to you, hot mama, if you want your dope."

The two black men went into the bedroom. Maureen was trembling out of control and began to cry as she walked slowly into the bedroom. Starbuck closed the door.

Pepper pulled his revolver from his pocket and pointed it at me. He whispered, "You say one word about this or try to help, I'll blow your fucking head off." He reached in the drawer and put my gun in his pocket, then motioned to the door, "We're getting out of this right now."

As we walked out, beyond the bedroom door we heard Mars say, "Leave those pretty shoes on. Starbuck's gonna give you a hot shot right in your pussy. You'll love it. That's it, hold still. Soon you'll be on your hands and knees barking, barking like a dog."

As Pepper and I walked down the hall toward the elevator, he handed me my gun. Then there was a loud, human cry; it was a sound that I had never heard before. I couldn't wait for the elevator, I ran down the stairs and out into the street to a cold but sunny day. There was a white Cadillac with gold trim parked in front of the apartment – a car I would never forget.

The streets of New York are always busy, millions of people with both joy and misery in their lives. No one could possibly begin to understand how I felt. Being afraid was the least of my feeling; the rape, the junkie's horror, the extreme hatred and desire to kill Mars La Pont, all swirled inside me like a toxic stew. As if this wasn't enough, my ticket to hell just got punched with a line of cocaine. I was scared, really scared.

After walking the cold streets of Manhattan for hours I checked into a cheap hotel and went to sleep, hoping it was all a bad dream.

The next morning I went back to the office, looking and smelling worse than my first day. Michael smiled. "Why don't you go home? You're going to work tomorrow. You've had enough vacation."

As I was leaving, I saw the list of agents scheduled to go to Washington for training the next week taped to the wall. My name was handwritten on the bottom of the list. I had made it.

I had spent the night without calling Daisy, so on my way home I bought her a black Yankees baseball cap. She had collected hats for years and wore a different one every day. It was late afternoon when I walked in and I surprised her. She was holding Mark. She looked at me holding her stupid little gift. Her face twisted to shock and tears as she backed up, and slumped into the corner, holding our son in one hand and waving me away from her with the other. I tried to explain where I was and why I didn't call, but she wouldn't listen. Eventually her anger lessened and I promised to call her the next time, no matter what.

That night again, I pushed all my feelings deep inside. I dreamed I was back in Ohio on our farm, driving a green tractor. I was pulling a large red mechanical rake that gathers up straw. Brownie, my Collie dog, was following, barking and running back and forth. He got too close to the rotating rake blades. As it pulled him in I heard the dog scream. It was her scream, too. I knew it very well and would never forget it.

CHAPTER TWO

THE SORCERER'S APPRENTICE

TRAINING

In January, six months after I had killed my first drug dealer and lied on a government report, Jerry Ramirez, Del Ridley and I went to Washington for training. We learned about heroin, self-defense, and drug laws. I began to understand the Bureau. Most of the drugs were imported from Italy and controlled by the five Mafia families in New York. The value of street heroin and cocaine varied widely, depending upon supply and demand and how much of it was diluted. To enforce narcotic laws, agents had to buy drugs from suspects at least two times to avoid a defense of entrapment. To do this, agents had to go undercover, and be introduced by an informant who would lie about who we really were. Making and using informants was the real industry of the Bureau. From its beginnings in the late 40's, the Bureau of Narcotics was not interested in making small arrests; it was just a waste of time and government resources. Its agents gathered information on big dealers and organized crime. The Bureau was dedicated to getting hard narcotics off the street, primarily heroin and cocaine and – if time permitted – marijuana. The objective was to take out the ringleaders, the Mafia wholesalers, any way possible. Despite the lofty goals of 90 Church, the agents had to make at least twenty new cases each month to continue to receive government funding. The agents handled this outrageous bureaucratic demand by making many small cases on lowlife junkies and pretending they were big investigations. I learned something else that explained why all the agents drove fancy, expensive cars: Cadillacs, Lincolns, and even sports cars. If the Bureau caught anyone transporting drugs or using their cars in any way to break the law, the agents would seize them and keep them, even if the suspects were found not guilty.

With only a handful of agents, the Bureau was overwhelmed; the Mafia had tremendous resources, financed with millions of dollars. America looked to this little agency to stop the horrendous flow of drugs that were killing people and causing so much crime. In New York City alone there were over twenty-five thousand known addicts robbing and killing people to support their hundred-dollar-a-day habits.

The Bureau gathered intelligence through an espionage network of criminals who the agents had turned into informants. Once a dealer was caught he had one of two choices: he could go to prison – in which case the agents would change the files so he would be labeled an informer and get murdered by the other inmates – or he could become an informant and set up his friends and drug connections. Now I understood what Dewey's ugly file clerks did all day. They were falsifying the records to protect informants or spiking the other files of criminals who did not cooperate.

In theory, if the defendant gave the agents enough information to make cases on other criminals, the Bureau would not prosecute his case and he would go free. In reality, he was never free again. He had to do anything that was asked by the agents, no matter what it was, including murder. The agents controlled his whole life. He informed on his friends, his drug source, and his family – everyone – in order to stay alive. Informants risked their lives every day and betrayed everybody. Agents held them in a deadly web of slavery. There was, of course, a bonus: the informant could return to a life of crime and drug dealing with the protection of the Bureau. For the first time I began to think about Michael differently. Michael didn't waste time chasing down drug dealers. He controlled his informants just like Pepper controlled his junkies. The informants did all the dangerous work.

After six weeks of training, I came back to 90 Church Street and to my own desk, but Michael was gone. Just like that, he had disappeared. No one knew where he was, or where to call him, and no one seemed to care. Only Pike offered a suggestion as to what had happened to Michael: "He's a boozer, he's on a toot, he'll show up. No big deal." Then he pointed his thumb to his mouth, the sign of a drunk.

I bought a shoulder holster. The gun hung close under my armpit with the barrel pointing out the back, not down, and since it was thin it was very well-concealed. I wore my new gun and pretended to be important. My partner was the infamous Michael Giovanni – if he ever came back.

GROUP TWO

After a week of waiting for Michael, I was teamed with Dewey Paris. Agent Greenway, the cowboy, told me that Dewey had been transferred from Naval Intelligence and had attended the University of Michigan. Dewey carried a dull black military-issue .45 automatic with bright red cherry-wood grips in a special holster that hung the gun down the center of his back. It was completely hidden so it never ruined the look of his expensive suits. Pike and all the other Bureau supervisors hated Dewey's gum-chewing, wise-cracking attitude, his obvious contempt for authority, and his total incompetence. They said he belonged in the file room with his ugly, shy, little friends. The supervisors were embarrassed to call him a federal agent. Dewey could not answer a single question, no matter how simple, about any case and he continually told dirty jokes to anyone who would listen. He had no friends and usually ate lunch in the file room, annoying his supervisors even more. Every day his desk in Group Two was piled high with messages, but they were all sports betting orders and nothing else. Dewey had saved my life. I didn't care what everyone thought, I liked him and he was certainly not what he appeared to be.

Dewey told me about some of the other Group Two agents. According to Dewey, Agent Ed Silkey could out-drive anyone; he was the best wheelman in the Bureau. Michael liked Ed for another quality: Ed liked to beat people up. His wife was a short, pretty Spanish girl who cheated on him all the time, eventually exposing her secret lovers to him with inevitable results. This kept Ed's tolerance for violence high. Ed always forgave his wife and she always came back to him, but there was a lot of emotional damage going on in between. Agent Louis Gomez, or "Louie the G," was obsessed with sex and he hit on every girl he met. Agent Gomez carried a switchblade knife most of the time because he thought carrying a gun sent the wrong message to dealers. Besides, his Derringer was so old it probably wouldn't fire anyway. Michael liked Louie's attitude.

Agent Greenway was from El Paso, Texas. He looked the part with his cowboy hat, cross-draw holster and nine-inch chrome Western-style six-shooter. I remembered a picture that Agent Greenway had on his desk, showing him standing in front of at least six dead people lying on the ground. I asked Dewey, "You know the picture on Greenway's desk – what happened?"

Dewey smiled. "You know, it's all about drugs and money. When Greenway was stationed in El Paso, his partner was killed. He was going to a ballgame with his kid and they just shot him."

"Who did? Who shot him, and why?"

Dewey shook his head. "On the border everything is for sale. There is nothing, and no one, that can't be bought and corrupted with drug money. They killed Greenway's partner because he made a case against some Mexican dopers. You see, in Mexico dealing drugs is a capital offense, so there are no arrests like there are in the United States. Every arrest is a shoot-out to the death."

"So what's with the picture?" I persisted.

"Greenway asked for Michael's help, which was a mistake. Never ask for Michael's help, never, never *ever*! Anyway, Michael wrote a memo to Greenway, telling him that he had a secret informant who knew people that were selling drugs on both sides of the border and he also knew who the killer was. Michael told Greenway to come alone. The memo said the informant would be waiting at a house just across the border. Greenway's boss and the Border Patrol agents went to the meeting and all hell broke out. Everyone was there. You wouldn't believe it – dopers, El Paso policemen, and even Federales. A gunfight broke out and lasted an hour. In the end they were all dead and there was no dope and no informant. Greenway dragged the bodies all together and took a picture of them with him standing over them. For certain one of the son-of-a-bitches killed his partner, and Greenway just likes to stare at all the bodies and wonder which one."

"I don't get it. Why were they waiting for Greenway? And what happened when there were no drugs or informant, when the agents just killed people?"

Dewey lit a cigarette. "Michael's memo gave them probable cause. Greenway's boss knew it was one of Michael's deals. They all fell for it. It's like Michael says, 'If you're guilty you believe the worst.' They were all there like Michael knew they would be. They were all guilty. It was a hell of a shoot-out. You see, Michael figured why would anyone go there in the first place and then start shooting if they were innocent? They transferred Greenway to New York City because there was so much heat. The Bureau finally realized the memo was bogus, and never said a word to Michael. And now guess what? Greenway is working for Michael and looking every day at the picture of dead bodies, wondering which one killed his partner. This is how good law enforcement works. Bring all the bad guys together and shoot them where no innocent people will get hurt."

Dewey said Michael used to be a schoolteacher who traveled Europe and Russia on educational grants to study subjects like politics, economy and crime. Then he found out the "educational funds" were really money from the CIA, who used his research to spy on foreign governments. He was the perfect spy because he didn't know he was a spy. Michael made a deal with the CIA, then something very bad happened. Whatever it was, Michael hated drug dealers and the government. Dewey said something funny about Michael: "If I were a drug dealer, I would look under my bed every night to see if Michael was there. Michael is worse than any boogeyman."

Being Dewey Paris's partner was worse than working with Michael Giovanni. Dewey did absolutely nothing. Our days were spent trying to raise money for his sports betting and in the evenings bouncing around Manhattan bars, trying to pick up girls. Dewey acted surprised when I asked where he thought Michael had gone; he laughed, "Michael's gone? How do you know he's *gone*? Just because no one has seen him doesn't mean he's *gone*. Michael doesn't go away, Michael is always here, Michael can never be gone and Michael can never be wrong, never gone and never wrong." Dewey Paris was never serious about anything until he pulled his gun. Then he was deadly serious.

STUCKEY

About a week later Michael came in the office. Except for the gift of my beautiful, blue, chrome-plated, pearl-handled automatic, he never expressed any gratitude to me for saving his life and keeping the dark secret of his forced fellatio. However, his attitude toward me began to change. When he came into the office he would ask how I was doing and try to find something for me to do, like look up names in a file or track down a phone number. I looked forward to seeing Michael because the other agents had started to avoid me again since I was not really part of any on-going investigations. Only Dewey with his constant stream of dirty jokes remained friendly to me.

Once again I became Michael's driver but now we would drink together late at night. I pitied him. I had Daisy; he seemed to have no one. He would rant on about his hatred of drug dealers and organized crime and the junkies, whom he called "people suffering from latent rigor mortis." Despite all the years of service he was still a low-level street agent, yet he pushed Pike and everyone else around. Every other Thursday night at about seven in the evening, Michael would drop me off to go home. I hoped he had a girlfriend and that they met on those nights for dinner.

But on one Thursday night, instead of dropping me off, we drove to the Heidelberg restaurant on 89th Street, on the Upper East Side of Manhattan. The Heidelberg catered to tourists. Loud and open, it wasn't the type of place we would normally visit. I followed Michael through a door to the back and up a flight of stairs to a small private banquet room. I had no idea what to expect when I saw agents from the office: Johnny Greenway, Dewey Paris, Ed Silkey, Louie the G, even agents from the other groups that handled the wiretaps and surveillance. From the looks on their faces, I was the last person they expected to see. Michael just said, "If he's with me, he's with me."

Then he waved me toward an empty chair and I sat down to my first real planning meeting. There were photographs and organizational charts of crime families and drug organizations on all four walls. I was surprised to see Dewey, with his know-nothing attitude, sitting next to Michael and in front of a large stack of files.

He shuffled them in and out of a suitcase on the floor. Dewey's hours and lunches with the Bureau's file clerks now began to make even more sense.

Each agent talked about his case and sought help from the others on surveillance, getting government money, research, wiretaps, and inside information on Mafia and drug dealers. Michael said nothing during the discussions; usually he just nodded or shook his head. We were served platters of Chinese food. Dewey told me later that their meetings were always catered; Italian, French, Chinese.

When the agents were done discussing their own cases, Michael talked about a case that he was working on. Despite the fact that I had been his partner for months I had no idea what he was talking about. He said that his informant, Charles Stuckey, would be negotiating a buy for a couple of ounces of heroin. Michael said he planned to requisition fifteen thousand dollars in government funds and suggested that Louie the G – the Puerto Rican agent – do the undercover buy with Stuckey. Michael assigned Ed Silkey, Dewey Paris, Johnny Greenway, and me to be the street team. Everyone sat around digging into bowls of noodles with chopsticks. As usual, Dewey made the first wisecrack. "I don't think we'll need a lot of surveillance since Stuckey will be selling and buying his own dope."

It got a short laugh from everyone except Michael, and I didn't get the joke. But it was clear no one was impressed with the case.

The next morning Dewey gave me the Stuckey file. Six months earlier Michael had set him up with an undercover agent for two buys of heroin. Stuckey was a drug dealer with a long history of arrests for numbers, assaults, and two prior drug busts. Now he was an informant. He had two clear choices: either work for Michael or go to prison for twenty years.

Eventually I met Charles Stuckey with Michael. Stuckey would have made a great salesman; he was well-dressed, and had a big smile. I liked him – his style, his confidence, and his interest in everyone he met. Michael introduced me as his "new partner" and told Stuckey to call me from now on.

Over the next several weeks Stuckey would call me to check out names in our files. We became friends as he tried to put together a heroin buy. Often, he would ask what I thought Michael was thinking. I always answered, "Honestly, I haven't the slightest clue."

Eventually Stuckey introduced Louie the G to his drug connection, a young black dealer from Harlem. The first $15,000 buy went like clockwork, but the dealer disappeared into Harlem and we lost him in traffic. The second buy was for ten thousand dollars and it went just like the first. We had a kilo of heroin between the two buys and it looked like a solid case, but we still didn't know the drug source. This bothered everyone except Michael. A week later agent Ed Silkey and I went uptown to arrest the dealer. We grabbed him around ten o'clock at night and took him back to the office. Silkey threw him against the office wall, almost knocking him unconscious, then ripped open his shirtsleeve.

That afternoon Michael came into the office and got into a heated conversation with Silkey and Dewey in front of Pike and Blanker. Dewey pointed his finger at Michael. "It's a fucking *set*-up. It's *Stuckey's* junk; I told you, you can't trust this asshole with a pack of cigarettes. Stuckey's double-crossing you, Michael – can't you see it? He sets these poor assholes up for a bust with *his* junk so he can walk free, deal drugs, and spend *our* money and kill people. This ain't the way it's supposed to work." Pike and Blanker nodded their heads in agreement. I was shocked to see Dewey betray Michael in front of Pike and Blanker and the other agents.

Michael didn't say anything at first, letting Dewey calm down. Then he said, "I trust my informants. Stuckey wouldn't do this. Give this asshole you busted last night to the cops, put him in the system. Don't offer him a deal and make him serve the time. It'll be good for him." Dewey, Blanker and Pike just shook their heads in disgust over how badly Michael was handling the case.

Michael and I met with Stuckey, who seemed in good spirits – smiling and talkative as ever. He even brought his teenaged girlfriend to the meeting and bragged to her about his government friends and Mafia buddies. Stuckey asked us how the case went and Michael looked at him and said, "The boys think it was your junk. Did you set this man up?"

"How could you *say* that?" he said indignantly. "I would never do that to you, Michael. You've been good to me, and I'm gonna see my way out by being good to you. I don't care what they say. I didn't set him up. It was *not* my dope."

This satisfied Michael. He smiled and patted Stuckey on the back, but even I could see that the guy was conning Michael.

At our next meeting at the Heidelberg, we ate Italian food. Michael stunned everybody. "I'm going after Tommy One-Finger." Tommy "One-Finger" Carpini was a member of one of the five crime families. He got his name because the little finger on his right hand was missing. He worked as an entrepreneur for the Mafia, financing everything from numbers to restaurants to drug deals. If you needed money you went to Tommy One-Finger. He would set you up with money and become a partner in whatever illegal activity you had in mind. Since Tommy used mob money, he could never lose. If anyone defaulted on the loan they would die in the street. Michael explained that Stuckey had made a new friend inside the Mafia who introduced him to Tommy One-Finger. Stuckey and his new friend were going to ask Tommy One-Finger for a loan of fifty thousand dollars for a drug deal. Michael was going to ask Pike to match it with another fifty thousand dollars.

The next day Dewey stormed into Pike's office with Stuckey's file. With all of the agents listening he said, "You've got to be fucking kidding! These people wouldn't let Stuckey wipe their ass. Stuckey doesn't have the balls for this! Don't you see? How can you approve the money for this case? It's all going to come down on Michael. Don't you see how wrong Michael is?"

Pike smiled. "It's Michael's ass. He trusts this guy. I'm going to give him the money. Stay out of it. If it fails, Michael goes down with the case."

Later Michael and I met with Stuckey at a bar in Midtown. He was more than a half hour late, but oddly the waiting didn't seem to bother Michael. When Michael laid out the case proposing two $50,000 payments, Charlie lit two cigarettes in a row, trying to give me one. He started to sweat. Charlie knew if he lost Tommy One-Finger's money in a drug deal he would be killed. Michael assured him that things would be okay and put his arm around him. Looking straight into his eyes, Michael said, "Charlie, I promise you two things: one, this is your last case, you will be free from 90 Church, and two, you will not have to testify in court."

Stuckey took a deep breath, put out his cigarette, and looked at me with renewed courage and a big smile.

With these new developments we scheduled another meeting at the Heidelberg and ordered steak from Gallagher's. Michael outlined his plan. The drug dealer was Lewis Turko, a big-time international wholesaler to the Vito Genovese crime family. Turko had sold drugs to Tommy One-Finger before, with success. Turko trusted Tommy and knew he would be sending couriers. The deal would be for six kilos of pure heroin, for a total of one hundred thousand dollars cash. Stuckey would get fifty thousand dollars of mob money from Tommy One-Finger and be Tommy's courier. Stuckey would then introduce Turko to an undercover agent – Dewey, who would pretend to be a courier for another buyer supposedly recommended by Tommy One-Finger – who would put up another fifty thousand dollars. But that payment would actually be government funds. Everything seemed simple, perhaps too simple.

With Pike's approval, Michael requisitioned fifty thousand dollars cash from the Bureau to be used as an undercover buy. Michael laid the cash out on his desk, called me over and said, "This is stupid. Look at that money. These are new, large-denomination bills. Take the money and go to different banks along Wall Street, break up all the hundreds into twenties, fives, and tens. Don't draw attention to yourself. This has to look like drug money."

I spent the afternoon going from bank to bank along Wall Street, changing the money and making up stories why I needed small-denomination bills. When I got back to the office I bundled all the money in rubber bands. Michael put the cash in a green gym bag, then Dewey, Michael, and I drove to meet Stuckey at a restaurant in the Bronx. Stuckey had a black leather attaché case filled with cash from Tommy One-Finger; all new twenty-dollar bills bundled neatly in green-and-brown bank wrappers. Dewey took the gym bag and Stuckey carried the briefcase and went to a private health club in Midtown to show Lewis Turko the one hundred thousand dollars. After seeing the cash Turko agreed to sell six kilos of heroin.

The next night Turko would bring the six kilos to a bar in Times Square. Stuckey and Dewey would meet him and each give him fifty thousand dollars. Stuckey's hands were shaking and he kept repeating, "They're going to know it was me. Please, Michael, don't do this, don't do this."

I felt sorry for Stuckey; he was being pulled into something very dangerous.

Michael led him over to the corner of the restaurant and when Stuckey came back he seemed to be calmer. Michael grabbed the black attaché case from Stuckey and gave it to me. Then he told Dewey to give me the gym bag with the government money in small bills.

"Here," Michael said to me. "You're in charge of all the money. Don't lose it, and don't spend it. I don't trust Dewey. He ratted me out to Pike, tried to fuck up the case! He's a disloyal cocksucker." Then he squeezed Charlie's face with both hands as if he was joking. "And I don't trust Stuckey here. He may not come back with it." He smiled at me. "You're the only one I trust."

When I got home that night I opened up the black briefcase and the green gym bag and stared at the money. I had never seen one hundred thousand dollars in cash before. I showed it to Daisy. We knelt in front of it, first touching the Mafia's new money, all twenty-dollar bills in brown bank wrappers neatly stacked in the attaché case, and then the Bureau's dirty small bills bundled in rubber bands and piled loosely in the gym bag. The money didn't seem real. There was no excitement in touching and seeing it. Before we went to bed Daisy said, "I feel disgusted for being interested in seeing drug money. It makes me feel dirty." The gym bag and attaché case sat on the coffee table all night, like Monopoly money after the game was over.

The next night we met at the office and Blanker came in to wish us all luck. Dewey was wearing a body wire. Stuckey looked pale and nervous; his hands were shaking and he kept staring at Michael. Michael pulled me aside and with a big smile said, "I'm afraid Stuckey might bolt. I'm gonna take both the gym bag and suitcase to the meet. Stuckey will not run without the money."

Michael drove the lead car by himself, carrying all of the cash, followed by Stuckey and Dewey. The rest of us trailed in a caravan of four radio cars to meet Turko at a bar in Times Square. Turko would have a suitcase with the drugs. Dewey would give Turko the green gym bag of old bundled money and Stuckey would give him the black attaché case filled with the new, bank-wrapped twenty-dollar bills from Tommy One-Finger. A simple exchange in a busy place.

Michael pulled over to the side of the street to meet Dewey and Stuckey for a last-minute pep talk and to give them the money. Five government automobiles lined the street a block away, all listening in on Dewey's body wire.

Michael handed the black attaché case to Stuckey and the green gym bag to Dewey, and the two of them started walking down 42nd Street toward the bar. But, less than half a block away, just as everyone except Michael had predicted, Stuckey panicked. He ran down the street with the black attaché case. Within seconds he was out of sight into a subway entrance. There was no use chasing him. Michael jumped out of the car and ran up to Dewey. Over Dewey's wire you could hear both of them talking on the radio. Michael said, "Dewey, you got to do this alone."

Dewey answered, "Pike and I told you about this asshole, Michael. You wouldn't listen. Pike is right. You don't know what you're doing. Pike said this is a set-up, now someone is going to get shot. Make sure Silkey is close to me with his pump if things go bad. I'll make the buy for half."

Dewey walked into the bar and Michael got back in the car and spoke calmly to everyone on the radio. "The informant is gone so we don't have to protect anyone's identity now. There's a change of plan; Dewey will make the buy for half the dope, just three kilos. Follow Turko to the car; let him drive off, then pop him carrying the other half of the dope. We'll have him on tape for a major buy and we'll get him for possession of the three kilos. We'll get our money back, the Bureau will have a new car and we'll get six kilos off the street."

Less than fifteen minutes later, Dewey came out of the bar carrying a small suitcase. He stopped on the sidewalk and rubbed the back of his head, the signal the deal had gone down. Five minutes later Turko walked out of the bar, carrying the green gym bag, and went across the street to a parking garage.

Pike was right beside him when the valet delivered Turko's white Mercedes. He drove west on 47th Street toward the Hudson River. Then all traffic stopped. Two government cars in front of Turko blocked the street. There was a chorus of car horns. Agent Greenway got out of one of the cars and started yelling and waving his hands at the other cars while he made his way to Turko's Mercedes. Agent Silkey got there first. He smashed the passenger-side window of Turko's car with the butt of his pump shotgun and pointed the barrel at his head. Greenway dragged Turko from the car and threw him on the street. Turko started to get up and pulled a black revolver from his belt. Greenway dropkicked him with his cowboy boot and kicked the gun out of his hand. Silkey handcuffed him and dragged him to the car. It was all over, within minutes. An hour later Lewis Turko sat in the Bureau's conference room, sweating, with his hands cuffed behind his back, staring across the table at Greenway, Silkey and myself. The green gym bag was on the table.

Lewis Turko was about forty years old and despite being very rich he dressed like a janitor in wrinkled pants, scuffed shoes, and an old faded shirt. He sat calmly without saying a word. We smiled at him and waited. Finally, Michael walked in.

"Hi, Lewis. How are you?" Michael said. "I only got a couple questions. Who broke the window on my new white Mercedes? And gee, Lewis, what have you got in this green bag here? Could it be three kilos of junk and fifty grand? Tell me it ain't so."

Michael dumped the money out of the gym bag onto the table – all new bills, bank-wrapped in neat bundles. It was the mob money.

Turko just stared at the piles of new twenty-dollar bills bundled neatly with brown bank wrappers. Then Dewey walked into the conference room. Turko jumped up and yelled, "Say nothing no matter what they do, say nothing!"

The whole room, except Turko, erupted in laughter. Finally Michael said, "I see you've already met Agent Dewey Paris. He has a suitcase full of heroin, heroin you gave him. It's all on tape. They're going to find you a toothbrush and put you up for the night, and I'm going to file the papers on my new Benz."

Turko stopped staring at the money and looked at each of us

and said, "You don't know what you are doing here. Take the small fish, that's our understanding. You don't know who I am. I swear by my Christ that I will destroy every one of you for what you are doing to me. The Genovese family will never forget. You will all feel their revenge."

There was a surprised long silence, then Dewey reached across the table and twisted Turko's nose until it bled.

Turko, with his hands cuffed behind him, stood up and roared like a wounded grizzly bear.

The revised plan was just as good as the original one; in fact, it was much better. Everyone except Michael knew that Stuckey didn't have the courage to go through with it anyway. But now Stuckey could return the money to Tommy One-Finger and say that he had no part in Turko's arrest. He would be safe – maybe even a hero – for backing out of a drug set-up and saving the mob's money. Stuckey had conned Michael and would go right back to selling drugs and conning more people.

Michael was only credited for making the right decision when the case began to fall apart. The only thing Blanker said to Michael was that he was lucky, and that in the future he should take Pike's orders and work harder to control the cases. Pike was actually disappointed that the case got turned around and ended so well.

The next morning the Bureau held a press conference. It was one of the biggest cases of the year and the evidence was overwhelming. Lewis Turko was part of the Vito Genovese family engaged in worldwide criminal activities. Pike took the credit and did all the talking, along with Blanker. The six kilos of heroin, the money and the green gym bag were all laid out on the table. An enlarged photograph of Turko and a chart of the Mafia's family tree was mounted on an easel. Blanker never mentioned Michael, and laughed with the reporters as everyone gathered.

But now I realized there was something very wrong about the money: it was the crisp new twenty-dollar bills, bundled in brown-and-green bank wrappers! Before, it was in the black attaché case, but now it was in the green gym bag. I had overlooked it the night before when Turko was staring at it on the conference table. This was Stuckey's mob money from the black attaché case, *not* the small denominations I had laundered and should have been in the gym bag! As I wondered how the money got switched from one bag to another I felt a sinking premonition of things I didn't want to know. I walked back down the hall, hoping to find Michael, but he had already left the office. On my desk was a pink phone-message slip for me. It was a call from Stuckey, received by the agent on night duty at the office. The message read: *Where are you? Hurry up; I want to get this over with.* The time was 1:30 in the morning – an hour after Stuckey panicked and disappeared into the subway at Times Square, carrying the attaché case filled with Tommy One-Finger's new money...that was now on display in the conference room!

As I stared at the strange phone message the phone rang. I took a call for Michael from the NYPD. They had found a body in the trunk of a car at 145th and Hudson River. It was Charlie Stuckey.

Agent Silkey and I drove uptown immediately. The crime scene was roped off with yellow tape and Stuckey's car sat in the center of the barricade under the highway overpass. They had already taken Stuckey away; it was obvious what had happened. There was blood inside the trunk, and there were six bullet holes through the trunk lid.

I looked down and saw a lollipop lying on the ground, covered by hundreds of tiny brown ants. I thought it was an important clue; maybe the killer had been sucking on the lollipop. I showed Silkey but he just laughed. "Lollipop, lollipop, what are you, fucking Sherlock Holmes? What does a lollipop have to do with anything?" He stepped on it. It stuck to his shoe.

Silkey asked the cops if they had tossed the inside of the car. The lead detective replied, "No. We show him listed with you guys so we called you. He got whacked last night at about two a.m. The watchman in the building over there heard the shots, he even called it in. But you know shots in this area happen every night. We were too busy. Our patrol found him this morning and called you after a check of his driver's license. There's no doubt he's your man, Charles Stuckey."

Silkey and I walked up to the side of the car and looked in. We both saw it at the same time and stared at each other: the attaché case was in the back seat!

Through clenched teeth, Silkey whispered, "*Get the fucking money, leave the case, stuff it in your shirt. I'll keep them busy.*"

He turned and walked toward the cops and soon they were huddled in a circle laughing at Silkey's jokes.

I unbuttoned my shirt, got in the back seat, and popped the gold latches of the case. Inside was a phone book! A phone book and nothing else. I walked over to where the cops were still laughing with Agent Silkey and signaled him to get back into our car.

"No money, just a phone book," I said.

Silkey pounded the steering wheel. "What the *fuck*, it was never our case, but shit we came close to making a few dollars! When Michael's running things there are *always* dead bodies and missing money, every time something, always very weird."

As we drove back to the Bureau, I kept thinking about Stuckey's phone message; why was he waiting for me? Now I began to seriously wonder about the money. None of it made sense. I was the only one who had custody of *both* the gym bag and attaché case until I gave them to Michael.

Then we walked into Group Two and learned that Tommy One-Finger was dead, killed along with three others – all mob hits. Now I knew why the money was switched. Turko and his Mafia friends recognized Tommy's new twenty-dollar bills on the conference table, then again on the evening news and in press photos. Since it was Tommy One-Finger's new money that set Turko up for the bust, Tommy had to be in on the set-up. Tommy had paid for it with his life. Everybody was happy. The Bureau had an airtight case and no one cared about Stuckey. He wasn't needed. All the other mobsters were blaming and killing each other. Icing on the cake.

Michael wouldn't talk to me about how the money got switched or about the lollipop I saw on the ground where Stuckey got shot, but Michael did feel sorry for Stuckey. He even asked Pike to initiate a special investigation to find Stuckey's killer.

Everyone celebrated one of the biggest cases in the Bureau's history. But I still had questions. How could Stuckey, a two-bit con artist, talk his way into one of the biggest Mafia moneymen in New York City? Did he have inside help? How did the mob money get switched? Besides me, Michael was the only other person who handled the money. Did he switch it when he carried both the gym bag and attaché case from the office to the meeting in Times Square? Could Michael have predicted what would happen if the money was switched? How did Stuckey end up carrying a phone book? Why didn't the killer take Stuckey's briefcase? Did the killer already know what was in it? Who told Stuckey to wait for me? Was someone setting him up to be killed? Why wasn't Michael mad at Dewey for complaining about the case to Pike? Why would Michael ask Pike, who is the dumbest supervisor in the office, to investigate Stuckey's murder? Most of all, what happened to the fifty thousand dollars I had laundered? I was ashamed of my thoughts...Michael was the best agent in the bureau and everyone knew it. Dewey had said Michael was "never wrong." I told myself that I was lucky to be his partner. I would never betray him like Dewey did. I wanted to learn from Michael.

I kept my questions to myself – I didn't want to ruin the case with accusations that I could not prove. Also, I had signed an investigation report stating that I had sole custody of all the money prior to the buy. Worse, the phone message would only implicate me in Stuckey's killing. Finally, Stuckey was killed – more than fifty blocks uptown – at the same time all the agents were in the office talking to Turko.

Turko's Mercedes was now government property. An agent who made a big case got a bonus of being allowed to drive any car that was seized. However, Blanker wrote a memo to Michael, saying that he wanted the Mercedes for himself. Michael just threw the memo in the trash, had the window fixed, and tossed me the keys! It made being Michael's driver more fun.

One night about two weeks after the Turko case I drove Michael uptown to the Tremont section of the Bronx to meet an informant. The whole area was deserted and looked like it had been bombed. Most of the buildings were dark, roofless shells. I knew from the neighborhood it would be one of his secret meetings. Michael told me to wait in the car while he met the informant on a dark street corner.

I watched in the rearview mirror as the two men met in the shadows of the streetlight and I remembered the two promises Michael had made to Stuckey, "This will be your last case and you will not have to testify." I could see Michael talking and smoking a cigarette. I watched the bouncing little orange dot as he laughed and waved his arms. The other man kept pulling at his mouth; he was sucking a lollipop.

FIRST CASE

The dinners at the Heidelberg remained confusing to me, and yet, in hindsight, they should have been the easiest to understand and explain to Daisy. The meetings were discussions about what was true or false, which lies should be believed, who could be trusted, and how much support should be given to active cases being conducted by the Bureau. At various times, agents argued who should or should not be reported as the source of information. I knew these decisions meant life or death to someone in the street. Pike and the other supervisors didn't really care about the safety of the agents and were too dumb to control complex investigations. I understood what Turko meant when he said, "Take the small fish, that's our understanding." In order for 90 Church to survive as a government agency each group had to make at least five cases each month. It was easy to make the cases against junkies. The Mafia would not retaliate against the agents as long as we just took the "small fish." It was easy to understand why the agents needed to conspire amongst themselves to plan cases. But there was also a conspiracy within a conspiracy. Sometimes, like the Stuckey case, things appeared simple but were not.

To Daisy, the meetings seemed just a waste of time, a place to complain about the job and work up enough courage to be disrespectful and disloyal to Blanker, Pike, and the other Bureau supervisors.

Daisy came to accept the late hours, the smell of booze, and my growing fits of depression. But she still wondered why the Bureau would tolerate people like Dewey who did nothing except bet on sports, and why no one could see that Michael was an alcoholic. I twisted my stories to convince Daisy that everything was as it should be, and that I had finally become a federal agent fulfilling my lifetime dream of fighting for truth, justice and the American way. For a while, at least, she was proud of me. But I knew, sooner or later, she would not understand.

About a month after busting Lewis Turko I went into one of the interrogation rooms. When I turned the light on, I saw a man standing in the corner. "Leave the lights off, asshole, and get out." He was very handsome, dressed in a plaid suit with patent-leather shoes and an open silk shirt. He stared through the darkness at me like a nocturnal animal.

Michael said, "That's Danny Cupp. You don't want to recognize him in the street." Danny had a reputation as a skilled informant. I'd seen his name in many reports, including being a source of information on Turko.

I wanted to be part of the war, work with people like Danny Cupp. That night I asked Michael to help me become an undercover agent. He laughed. "No, you don't. Booze, money, and women will get you. You don't want to die that way. You think it's dangerous in the street, with people shooting at you? You don't know what real danger is. There are worse ways of dying than from a bullet."

I didn't understand. "I'll take my chances. I want to work undercover."

Later that evening Michael and I were driving uptown on the East Side of Manhattan. He told me to pull over to let him out. "Give me your gun and your credentials." He said.

Not knowing why, I handed them over. Then Michael dug into his pocket and pulled out a wad of cash. "You want to become an undercover agent? Okay. Here we go. You'll do exactly as I say." He counted out five hundred dollars and stuffed it into my coat pocket.

"I want you to go out and make a case. I want you to find a drug dealer and I want you to get him to sell you heroin or cocaine, no pot. It's very simple. Take this money and go into those bars and spend it. Spend every dime of it before you go home tonight; don't go home until you spend it all. Do not buy transportation, do not buy food, do not buy any tangible product. This money must be spent on booze and fucking women, or whatever it takes to find a dealer."

I looked at him. "What if I don't find anybody tonight?"

Michael smiled. "Every night from now on – with the exception of Sunday – I'm going to drive you to this corner and give you five hundred dollars and you're going to spend it just like you are tonight, until you find a dealer or he finds you. Or you die a drunk. Or you give up and quit. Now get out."

That night and for the next two nights I went to places like Friday's, The Dove, or Maxwell Plum's, but they were filled with people just having fun, young ambitious executives and pretty girls with hang-ups about food and the stars. I would buy them a drink and they would buy me a round. Nothing happened except that I got drunk and made a lot of innocent, nice friends. Finally, I found a place called the El Hambra. The people at the bar had droopy eyes and looked at me with suspicion. I bought everyone a round and no one returned the favor. I knew I was in the right place. I closed the bar down and then someone took me to an after-hours club. By five in the morning, I had spent the five hundred dollars and was so drunk I couldn't stand up. I was lucky to get home, but I had made progress and planned to return.

I was thankful that the next day was Sunday. Daisy had planned to take our son, Mark, to Candlestick Lake Park about fifty miles north of the city. She had talked about this picnic for a week. We had the usual hotdogs, chips, blankets, and a grill. Daisy found a grassy picnic area next to the lake. I was so hung over that the drive from the city exhausted me. Daisy played with Mark while I lay on a blanket, trying to fall asleep, but the world kept spinning around every time I closed my eyes. By noon Daisy had cooked the hotdogs and prepared lunch, but I had no appetite. Mark gave up trying to play with me and I finally fell asleep.

A commotion, and Daisy screaming, "My *God*, no!" woke me up. Mark had slipped off the bank and fallen into the lake. I tried to get up, but I was too dizzy so Daisy had jumped in after him. The water was only waist-deep near the shore. By the time I staggered to the edge of the water, Daisy had Mark in her arms and was wading up through the mud. She got to the shore and I helped them back to the blanket. Mark was fine, he was just shaken up and crying. Daisy was covered with mud. She had lost a shoe. She sat on the blanket, holding Mark and staring at me.

Then she began to cry, which also made Mark cry louder. "You don't give a shit about us. You're too drunk to save your own son. You think you're a big-shot undercover agent. We're just in the grandstands to your work and in the cheap seats."

My hangover was so bad that I couldn't say anything back. After a while they both stopped crying and Daisy just looked at me with a cold stare. Then she said, "There's no room anymore for Mark and me is there? What's in your mind right now? Drug dealers, Michael, Dewey? Tell me, because it's not us."

"No, that's not true. You're all I think about."

The lie stunned her. She began packing up everything and stuffing the bags and grill in the car. On the way home she never said a word. She just sat in the car with the mud drying on her legs and looked out the window. I did care, but she was right; I wasn't thinking about my family.

I kept thinking about the El Hambra bar. I was thinking how I would show Michael and all of them I could be like Danny Cupp. I would show Michael and all of them I could do it. They'd forget about how I had pissed my pants. I was not going to be the office joke forever.

On Monday night Michael drove me to the same corner, counted out another five hundred dollars and told me to get out. Normally, I drank vodka and 7-Up, but after a while the sweet soda made me sick, so I just drank straight vodka. After two more nights of this, with no luck in meeting a drug dealer, I was thrown out of the El Hambra. I had laid my head on the bar and fallen asleep.

I was already known as a big spender so the next night they let me back in. I made a friend, Elliott Goldstein, a talkative young advertising executive. He was involved with a girl who lived in the area and made friends easily. Elliott kept visiting the men's room. We had a good conversation and I kept buying him drinks. We talked about sports, girls, booze, work, everything.

Finally, he said, "Do you want a line?"

I knew what he was talking about. "Yes."

He reached into his pocket and slid a small glassine envelope across the bar. "Here. This is for you."

I went into the men's room, but put the envelope in my pocket and came back, pretending to wipe my nose. "Thanks, Elliott."

The next morning I gave Michael the envelope. "See, I made my first case."

"You idiot, he *gave* you the drugs! You're as guilty as he is. You're supposed to *buy* the drugs. You didn't give him any money."

The next night Elliott introduced me to his assistant, who introduced me to one of her girlfriends from the same ad agency: her name was Ricky, a redhead with brown freckles, very pretty. Her whole personality seemed calculated to please me. She had no opinion or desire of her own. Ricky was like a bowl of peanuts on the bar – help yourself, they're free, no obligation. It was the first time I cheated on Daisy. It wasn't easy or fun. I didn't love Ricky. I was on the job. It didn't seem to count. Like a lot of things going on in my life, I buried the guilt by justifying it as part of the war on drugs. The four of us partied for the next two nights. I bought the drinks and Elliott gave everyone coke to snort. I would go in the men's room and pretend to use it. I was actually having a good time.

On the second night I asked Elliott, "Where do you get the snort? I can't let you keep giving them to me for free. Let me buy some."

"I've got a friend in Queens, he owns an Italian restaurant. Well, it's really a pizza parlor. He says he knows John Ormento, the mob guy. But, look, no way am I gonna sell you nose candy. I'll give it to you, but I'm not going to take your money. I'm not a dealer, just an ad exec."

"Then this party is gonna have to stop. Come on, be a friend and let me pay for some."

I spent one thousand dollars on the first buy. Elliott said he had never done anything like this, and took no profit. We all partied on. We went to the Tropicana and Basin Street, and I picked up every tab. Finally, I persuaded Elliott to sell me two ounces of coke for two thousand dollars. Again, he said he hated doing it but he would do it for me and make no profit; after all, I was his friend.

Two nights later, Dewey Paris and agent Johnny Greenway conducted surveillance while I paid the money to Elliott. I felt pretty good about myself. I gave the evidence to Dewey and said, "My reward for making this case will be that I can stop drinking myself into a stupor every night."

Dewey laughed. "This is bullshit. This is *training*. This is not a major case. This guy is a meatball. We can't use him; he's a waste of time. Michael will give him to Pike to play with."

"He's going to lead us to someone big, I know it. His connection owns a pizza parlor in Queens. This could be a big case." I wasn't going to let Dewey or anyone else take away my accomplishment. "Everyone has to start some place." I began to think that Dewey, who had never made a case, might be jealous, Elliott was a drug dealer, and I was making truth out of all the lies I had been telling Daisy.

In the office the next day, Michael typed out the report with the fastest two-finger pecking I had ever seen. It said that I drank no liquor of any kind during the investigation and the purchase of drugs by government funds was for the first buy and $5,500 for the second buy. I signed the report even though the first buy was only $1,000 and the second was $2,000. What difference did it make? Selling coke is illegal; price has nothing to do with the crime. I compared all the money Michael had given me and the real cost of the coke that I bought from Elliott, and it matched. My travel expenses were the maximum $20 a day and I was issued a government check for $160. Why not cover my liquor expenses by inflating the cost of the drugs? It all seemed to make sense.

Weeks later, as I passed one of the interrogation rooms, I saw someone I thought I recognized; I wasn't sure at first because his face was misshapen, puffy, round, and red. There was blood trickling from the side of his mouth. It was Elliott, sitting in the dark. Pike had beaten him. Elliott was now an informant. His advertising job was now a hobby; his *real* job was to find the dealer uptown who sold him the drugs and to turn him over – and that would only be the beginning. Pike wanted Elliott back on the street, doing drugs and finding drug dealers. Elliott just looked at me with a blank, unbelieving stare. I walked away from a man who had only wanted to be my friend.

A LESSON

My progress did not impress Agent Michael Giovanni. He asked me if I had second thoughts about continuing to be an undercover agent. I didn't. Then I asked Michael if he had put any other agent through this $500-a-night routine to find a drug dealer.

"Yes. Dewey, but he only lasted one night." Michael laughed.

"That son of a bitch Dewey, he took the five hundred dollars and gave two hundred to the beat cop to help him find a dealer. Then he bought a hundred dollars' worth of coke and gave the *cop* the collar! Then the son of a bitch pocketed the rest of the money and went home. You can't trust that Dewey, you can't train him either, he's very tricky." Michael began laughing even harder. "He went undercover and got himself a drug dealer in about two hours and stole *my* money."

My training continued a few days later when Michael took me to a dry-cleaning shop in Harlem to buy clothes. He wanted me to look like a drug dealer. The clerk waved us on into the back room. Michael asked my size and picked out four suits, all of them shiny mohair, black or gray, all dark colors. I put one of them on, along with a bright shirt, no tie, and my wing-tipped shoes. I looked ridiculous. Michael dug into his pocket and paid five one-hundred-dollar bills for everything and we left.

As we walked to the car Michael looked at me. "Well, you're almost there. Let me tell you a few things. You must look at people. Look at them hard. Never talk first, never interrupt. Let them talk; find out what they have to say. Look *at* their eyes, but never *in* their eyes, or you'll get fooled. Do they stare back at you, or look down like a liar? Look at their hands, their fingernails. They'll tell you if they're self-confident. Truly dangerous people are always self-confident. Their hair and what they're wearing will tell you if they believe in their own future or if they're just a stupid junkie on their way to hell. You can always tell when a man is carrying a gun just by looking down at his pant cuffs and his shoes. If he's wearing a gun, one pant leg will droop more than the other. Not one thing, but many things together, will tell you if a man is lying. You must be able to *feel* if someone's lying to you. After a while you'll *know*. Knowing when people are lying will help you to lie better. Never be afraid to lie, it's what you do. Lie all the time; lie to everybody, it's good practice. Truth is not important. Your lies are your reality and the world you live in. The most important thing to remember is that criminals think the worst about everything and everybody. They think everyone is just as bad as they are and out to get them. If you remember this you can always outsmart them.

"Another thing, carry lots of cash – flash it, show it off. Someday it will save your life, because people don't think straight when greed sets in. Greed makes them forget all the things that are important – like not getting caught." Then he chuckled. "But soon you will learn that money will have no value to you. Spending your life trying to get money is silly."

Then he got serious again and said, "One other thing, very important: dangerous people always smile when they talk about serious things. Never, *ever* trust a smiling face; it could cost you your life someday." He rubbed his chin. "Dewey smiles, doesn't he? But Dewey is a psychotic killer. That's why he smiles. You must do everything he tells you to do if you want to stay alive."

TRUST

It was now winter again. I had been an agent at 90 Church for more than a year and a half. I got a thousand-dollar raise, which was less than an ounce of heroin cost and what was spent every night on our junkie cases. Pike told me to work with a hippie-turned-drug-dealer. His name was Calvin. One of his customers turned him into the Bureau. Cleophus "Cleo" Brown, a black undercover agent, bought two ounces of heroin from Calvin. He was not really considered a major dealer so we turned him into an informant. At first he was afraid, but I touched his forehead to mine, hugged him, and looked straight into his eyes and said, "I will protect you." I won his confidence and we made our plans.

My first question to Calvin was who was his source? His answer stunned me; it was Pepper's connection, Mars La Pont. We met Mars the next afternoon, at a dark, quiet bar in the Village, not far from Pepper's apartment. Calvin told Mars I had spent time with him in the West Street penitentiary and was his new partner. It took a few minutes, but Mars remembered me and Maureen. He smiled, "Oh yeah, pretty, pretty woman, Scarsdale. We made her dance and crawl. Starbuck bought her from Pepper, made her work for her dope."

"What happened to her?" I asked.

"She cut Starbuck then she do herself. Too bad, good cunt, good money."

Mars seemed okay with me at first then got skeptical as we began negotiating for a buy of heroin. He said he had also been in West Street too and remembered the never-ending choice of either potato salad or coleslaw. It was either potato salad or coleslaw at every meal, even breakfast. I laughed and agreed. I could feel the friendship and connection with Mars. This was my second undercover buy and I was good at it and getting better. Mars said he would make arrangements to deliver an ounce of heroin for three thousand dollars. He told me to meet him at Calvin's apartment the next day at four o'clock. I agreed, and said I would bring the money. I felt good about the deal and was going to get revenge for Maureen by sending Mars La Pont to jail.

It was extremely cold in New York that week. That afternoon

Daisy had called and said there wasn't enough heat in our apartment, so I went home early to buy an electric heater and look after her and Mark. Daisy was pleased that I came home and it broke a period of silence between us. At about 8:00 that evening Calvin left a telephone message for me, saying Mars La Pont wanted to talk to him and that I should call him back. He wanted me to be there at the meeting. I was too busy trying to repair my relationship with Daisy to return his call.

The next morning, I picked Michael up and told him how well things went the day before. Today I would be making a buy of heroin. I told him about Mars La Pont's initial suspicion but then us bonding over choosing either the potato salad or coleslaw while in jail. Michael turned to me and said, "Three meals a day, seven days a week, three hundred sixty-five days a year, West Street Penitentiary serves potato salad. No coleslaw *ever*. No choice."

I tried to call Calvin, but there was no answer. Finally, around noon, Dewey and I went to his apartment. No one answered the door, but Dewey slipped the lock with a special hook made from a putty knife. I searched the apartment while Dewey went to the kitchen to find something to eat.

I found Calvin outside on the fire escape; they had taped his wrists spread-eagle on the steel railing. Something was stuffed in his mouth and covered with tape. They had ripped his shirt and pants off and pulled his underpants down around his ankles. Bound to the railing, cold and naked, they had thrown water on him. My innocent hippie friend who trusted me sat in a pool of gray ice frozen blue. His wide blank eyes stared at me. Dewey climbed out through the window, eating from a box of cookies, and said, "Jesus Christ, what a way to go. He's a fucking popsicle.

It must have taken him hours."

I just stared back into Calvin's eyes. I had never seen a look like that before, a blank dark stare. This was my fault; he was dead because of me. I said I would protect him. I told Dewey I would get Mars for this. "How could they do this to someone?" I asked. "How can we just do nothing?"

"Well," Dewey replied, "just think what you were planning to do to Mars."

No one cared about Calvin, or the smiling Mars La Pont, but I did. There was death, misery, and shooting every day. I had tried to ignore it since my first day on the job. I was too worried about fitting in, trying to be an agent. Everyone knew Calvin's death was not my fault – and after all, it was part of being a narcotics agent. But the next day in the office I asked Michael for his help. I wanted to get Mars La Pont.

"Why him?" Michael asked.

"Because he killed my friend and sells dope to innocent people."

Dewey roared with laughter, Michael rolled his eyes and said, "To each in their own time."

CHAPTER THREE

THINGS ARE LOOKING UP

LISA MARIE

Spring came early and I had been an agent for almost two years. Every night I made small buys of heroin from junkies, which did nothing to stop the flow of drugs into New York City, but it did give the Bureau an acceptable case count to justify its existence.

Daisy didn't know what to think of my new clothes and renewed confidence. In fact, I had even developed a routine. At least two nights a week I would be home for dinner. The rest of the week she knew to expect me home very late and drunk.

Mark turned four and we had a party for him: balloons, little friends and a big white cake. It was all terrific, but somehow I felt like a guest. I sat and watched, not really part of anything.

I had not made a major case on my own. My first encounter with Mars and snorting a line of cocaine was an insignificant memory. My real passion was to bring Mars La Pont to justice for killing Calvin. It turned my desire into an obsession.

From conversations overheard in the office I knew that some of the agents had an ongoing poker game somewhere in Queens. One night Dewey asked me if I wanted to play. I told him I wasn't very good at cards, but would like to go anyway. He said that the game was always played at the "clinic."

I assumed that the clinic was a medical facility; instead we drove up to a house in Forest Park, Queens. I recognized Michael's white Mercedes parked on the street.

"This is a clinic?" I asked. "It looks like a house to me."

"It's a clinic," Dewey insisted. "It's the Bureau's clinic. It's a medical rehabilitation facility for addicts."

"From what I've seen at 90 Church, a morgue would be the closest thing to a medical clinic that the Bureau would run for addicts."

This made Dewey laugh as we walked up the front steps and entered the two-story house. The inside foyer was completely dark but I could see a light coming from a room off to the left down a hallway. As we walked I heard the rattle of chains. I heard someone call my name in a friendly tone: "Hi, how are you. I'm so glad you came."

Out of the darkness appeared a figure and the sound of chains being dragged on the floor. In the dim light I could see a face covered with long horrible scratches. I stared into the bloody face – and recognized Pepper, the Puerto Rican I stayed with in Greenwich Village to learn about drugs. He extended his left hand to me. His handshake was cold and wet. His right hand was handcuffed to a chain, which was locked to a radiator on the far side of the room. Through the darkness I could see an old couch and a small bathroom in back. From the way he looked Pepper had been chained there for days.

Michael, Silkey, and a stranger sat around a card table in a room further down the hall. A baseball game on TV created a weird, ordinary, background noise. The stranger had a pale, unshaven face, long teeth with a pointed chin, and scraggly hair. Despite his unkempt personal appearance he was wearing a starched dress shirt with a bright silk tie. Dewey introduced him as Kyle, a police detective from the Queens precinct. He was also a member of an elite Task Force investigating organized crime. He looked like a huge rat posing as a human by wearing a shirt and tie.

Pepper could stretch his chain to watch the game as he sat on the floor. As we played cards and laughed, Dewey would yell out to Pepper, "Talk to me, baby, talk, or you'll spend the next two weeks right where you are. No candy for you unless you're good. You love candy, don't you? Tell me you love it. Talk to me."

Now I understood the clinic. While the agents played cards they'd ask Pepper questions, then look at each other for a consensus on the value of the information. Pepper knew the only way to go back on the street to his precious fix was to provide enough information to buy his release, and every day without his heroin his torture grew worse.

Pepper rambled on about his drug connections and old news that was of no interest to anyone. Then he began listing the names of his customers. Every once in a while Kyle or Silkey would stop him and ask him to talk more about one of his junkie friends. Finally Pepper pulled taut on the chain and lay in the floor in a fetal position. The game and the jokes around the table continued while he lay on the floor, crying like a baby and scratching himself bloody. Accustomed as I was becoming to life on the street, the oddity and the pitiful sounds of excruciating pain coming from the other room – from someone I knew – unnerved me.

Eventually Pepper started to talk about a female junkie. She had her own money, dressed well, and drove a new car. Still no one showed any interest, even when Pepper said he thought she had mob friends.

Finally Michael said, "What's her name, Pepper? What's her name?"

"Her name is Scalopinni. Lisa Marie Scalopinni. No, wait, maybe it was Scarluci."

Everyone froze. Kyle looked at Michael and Dewey. Dewey laid his cards on the table, got up and walked into another room. I knew he was calling the office to talk to one of his file clerks. He came back within a couple of minutes.

The card game continued. Pepper crawled off to a dark corner and I could hear him crying softly and thumping his head against the wall.

Fifteen minutes later the phone rang. Dewey left the table to answer it. When he returned, he reached into his pocket and pulled out his keys. He unlocked Pepper's handcuffs. Then he went over to a wall cabinet, opened up a drawer and handed Pepper a manila envelope. Pepper's hands were shaking and covered with blood as he tore it open and dumped the contents on the table: a knife, wallet, money, and several bags of heroin. There was also an eyeglass case. I knew it contained needles and drug paraphernalia. Pepper grabbed it first, still on his hands and knees, and crawled to the bathroom and closed the door.

After about ten minutes he came out, walked down the hallway and out the front door without saying a word, like nothing had ever happened.

The moment Pepper walked out the door, the card game was over. Kyle, Silkey, and Michael looked at Dewey. Finally Kyle said, "You've got to be fucking kidding."

Dewey shook his head and stared down at the table. "It's Domenic's kid. It's his daughter."

Michael looked at me and said, "Tomorrow morning you're moving back in with Pepper." Everyone around the table laughed – except Kyle, who didn't understand the humor.

Dewey looked at Michael and said, "What do you want to do here?"

Michael rubbed his chin, "We need to think this out. The first step is that Pepper has to get a new drug connection." He put his arm around my shoulders. "And here it is."

I had no idea what they were talking about; they all smiled and chuckled.

Michael went on. "You're the new drug connection. Move in with Pepper. Let him introduce you as his connection. You're going to be a drug dealer. Lisa Marie is a junkie. She betrays everybody. Let nature take its course. She'll betray Pepper and want to deal directly with you" – he extended his hand like a claw and snapped it closed in a tight fist – "then we'll have her. With her we'll have the old man. My God, Domenic moves millions of dollars in drugs each year. He is part of the Magaddino family."

Dewey said, "We need a gypsy."

"Yes, we need a gypsy," Michael agreed, "and with her we can even get papers. This could go big. We have to go on record as soon as possible. There will be no deals."

On the way home, I was too embarrassed to ask about the "gypsy" but Dewey explained that the clinic was a house seized by the government in a drug case years ago. Not only was it a good place to play poker, it was also a safe house to hide people. He said, "It's a good place for junkies to talk, particularly when they've been 'rehabilitating' for a few days. You'd be surprised what you can learn. I think it does them good to be away from the street and drugs. Don't you?"

In my mind's eye I could still see Pepper's bloody face ripped open by his own fingernails. I wondered how many other junkie informants had been "rehabilitated" at the clinic.

After explaining the case to Daisy and promising to call every night I moved into Pepper's Village apartment the next day.

Like clockwork, that afternoon Lisa Marie called and wanted to make a score. Pepper told her he didn't have any drugs but that he was going to meet his connection in Midtown. Lisa Marie said she wanted to meet his drug source and score before everything got sold off to other customers.

That evening I met Pepper and Lisa Marie Scarluci in an upscale bar in the Upper East Side of Manhattan. Her appearance was not what I had expected. Thin and rather homely, her long nose had a crook at the top like many ethnic Italians. She let us know she had her father's affection. Lisa Marie had only one fault: she loved to party. She had progressed from pot to cocaine and now to heroin. Her drug habit embarrassed her to the point that she scored from Pepper, rather than getting it from anyone in her father's circle, to keep it secret from her family.

For the next two weeks Dewey instructed me on exactly what to say to Lisa Marie when Pepper and I met with her, usually two or three times a week. At first I told her that I was living in Baltimore but staying with Pepper for a month or so. Then I told her I respected her father even though I really had no idea who he was. I said someday I hoped I'd do business with her family. Just as Michael had predicted, Lisa Marie Scarluci eventually betrayed Pepper and told me not bring him to our meetings. Lisa Marie was lying. Pepper was lying. Dewey was lying. I was lying. There was no room for the truth anywhere and it was all going to get worse.

MOON

Domenic Scarluci was the topic at the next dinner meeting at the Heidelberg. Not only did he control a huge drug operation, he also ran numbers, prostitution, hijacking and murder for hire. He lived in Queens, as did many of the other Mafia families. His three-story house was walled in with tight security, and he had good relations with the local police to ensure his security and privacy.

The Scarlucis were very close to the Charles Moon family, another Mafia group, who sold heroin supplied by Domenic Scarluci. Charles Moon had a son, Bobby, who did most of the legwork for his father. Bobby Moon was a childhood friend of Lisa Marie's, and provided security for the drug deals. Bobby had killed at least eight people for the Columbo family. He was a gun for hire and his family was proud of him.

Dewey presented the case. His background information on the Scarluci and Moon families was very professional, with files, family trees, enlarged photographs, and copies of earlier surveillance reports. Dewey even had the dinner catered by the Crescent Moon Café on Broome Street in lower Manhattan, a restaurant owned by the Moon family.

Dewey explained that in the first phase of the operation I would continue to develop a relationship with Lisa Marie, and Kyle would get a gypsy into Scarluci's home.

I soon found out what a gypsy was when Dewey placed a metal container about the size of a cigar box on the table. It was a small tape recorder with a sound-activated microphone that could record conversations in a room, and on the telephone line. Once installed, you could call the phone number that was being tapped and activate the machine so that it rewound and played two hours of its contents back over the phone at a high speed in a matter of minutes. The receiving tape recorder would then be played at a slower speed so it could be understood. It was simple, brilliant and cheap to make, but crude compared to the equipment used by the FBI and CIA. It was called a gypsy because it was illegal. If the Bureau had to explain where it got its information the agents would have to claim that it came from an informant who was a 'gypsy' and could not be located to testify.

Michael ended the dinner presentation by warning everyone that, except for Kyle, we could not trust the NYPD. Furthermore, the case was confidential and not to be discussed with anyone at 90 Church until we had a plan of action. Once we had information from the illegal gypsy we could use it as probable cause to obtain a legal warrant. Lisa Marie would be the major source of information.

Getting the gypsy placed at Scarluci's home was easy, but a little brutal. Dewey set up 24-hour surveillance at Domenic's home. We soon learned that there was a live-in maid so the house was almost always occupied. The only exception was twice a week when she left the house to do grocery shopping.

A few days later, the maid, an elderly woman, was mugged on

her way to the grocery store. She was taken to the Queens precinct to look at photographs of possible suspects. While she was there the police found her purse in a dumpster several blocks away from where she was robbed. Kyle personally returned the purse and apologized for the loss of her cash, and her black eye. However, everything else was still in the purse – keys, wallet, etc.

I recognized Dewey's work. One of Pepper's junkie customers had mugged the old lady and then given the purse to Dewey, who was waiting in front of Domenic's house. With the maid's keys they had no problem getting in and in less than a half an hour had screwed the gypsy underneath Domenic's desk in his study, and jacked into the desk phone. Afterwards, Dewey put the keys back in the woman's purse and threw it in a dumpster one block from the grocery store. Kyle told his beat cops to be sure to search all dumpsters in the area. The purse and keys were easily found.

Every day we played the recordings back at the poker table at the clinic, but never discussed them in the office. Domenic assumed that the phone lines were always tapped, so none of the telephone conversations were incriminating. The recordings of live conversations inside Scarluci's study, however, were astounding. In one conversation a dealer pleaded for his life. Apparently he had skimmed some drug money. Domenic forgave him, but told him never to do it again. Later that same day, Domenic could be heard ordering the man to be killed. Two days later the dealer's body was found in the East River.

Charles Moon visited Scarluci often and they could be heard laughing about Charles's son, Bobby, and how good he was at beating and killing people. They hoped he could build a good "crew."

One of the most chilling conversations on the tapes was a presentation by a drug dealer who wanted Domenic and Charles Moon to give him two kilos of heroin on credit. The dealer explained his program for high-school girls: he would give them free marijuana and then let them snort coke. Once the girls liked the coke he would pretend he was out of coke and tell them they should try heroin. Once hooked on heroin he would have the girls raped to destroy their self-respect. Then they would turn tricks for a fix of heroin and pay back everything. The plan was so outrageous it was almost comical, but they were serious. None of this was of any interest to Michael or Dewey until Charles Moon mentioned the name "Edmond Manchester," who would bring in a new shipment of heroin in the next few weeks.

During this time my relationship with Lisa Marie improved. Pepper would give me the heroin and she would always buy two or three small bundles of heroin. Each time she would pretend that this was her last buy. She tried to be nice to me and sometimes even brought me little gift bags of cocaine. I wasn't addicted from the first time I used coke and a lot of time had passed, so I would let her see me snort it. Whatever doubts she had about trusting me were gone.

As usual, each time Dewey had something new for me to say to her. It was information meant to build her confidence in me. Once Dewey had me tell her that I knew about a certain robbery in New Jersey. I called the heist very well-handled, and said her father should be proud. Another time I told her that I was glad that a drug shipment had been completed; and later I said a certain dealer deserved to get thrown in the river, since everyone knew he was stealing from her family. Lisa Marie was impressed that I knew so much. She never once gave me any information on her father.

After about three weeks of being Lisa Marie's connection I was surprised to receive a memo of commendation from George Blanker on the excellent work that I had done to develop new cases on organized crime. I was asked to stand up at our Monday morning meeting while the agents gave me a round of applause. Blanker explained that I had recruited a secret informer who was leading us to a major investigation of two Mafia families. Like many times in the past, I was too embarrassed to admit that I didn't know the bigger plan, but just followed instructions. As usual Dewey and Michael were not even mentioned.

Later, Pike told me that he got a court order for a wiretap on Domenic Scarluci's phone based upon the information I had received from Lisa Marie, which established probable cause. Now I began to understand that it was the gypsy providing the information that Dewey passed on to me to impress Lisa Marie. Lisa Marie simply confirmed it – but Dewey wrote reports saying it was *coming directly from her* and she was the reliable source named to obtain the wiretap warrant.

The legal wiretap was necessary, but had limitations since it only recorded phone conversations on Domenic's private phone line, not what was happening inside Scarluci's study. But we were now able to "legally" explain everything.

Once I arrived early to one of my meetings with Lisa Marie and saw Domenic Scarluci for the first time. She was walking down the street holding onto the arm of a gray-haired, well-dressed gentleman. It was difficult for me to imagine that such a friendly-looking man could be the cold-blooded killer and Mafia leader whose voice I had heard so often on the tape, chilling me to the bone.

I also began to wonder if there was any difference between Pepper and me selling dope.

Finally I questioned Dewey. "This is not right. I'm selling drugs to Lisa Marie, and Pepper is selling drugs in the street. What's the difference?"

He laughed. "First of all, you're selling Pepper's drugs to Lisa Marie, it's not your drugs, and secondly, if you get popped it will be your first offense, so you won't get any time."

I didn't laugh. "Dewey, this is not how we're supposed to play the game."

Dewey stopped smiling. "*Game?* You think this is a fucking *game*, a game with *rules*? You heard Domenic and Moon on that tape with their game plan for high-school girls. What kind of game was *that*? Where are *their* rules? New York City alone has over twenty-five thousand dead people running around stealing and killing innocent people – and worse, making more dead people by infecting them with drugs and getting them to do the same thing. This is not a *game*, this is a *war*! We're fighting an enemy worse than you can possibly imagine. They only care about killing and stealing and forcing others to do the same. We're not fighting for America's soul, we're fighting to survive, and if we don't win now, what do you think the future will be like?"

I thought a few minutes, then said, "Yeah, you're right."

MANCHESTER

That evening we ate French food at the Heidelberg, and for the first time, no one talked business during dinner. The case had become extremely serious and confidential. Michael waited until they served dessert and all the waiters had left the room before turning the meeting over to Dewey.

Dewey held up a photograph of a middle-aged man who looked like a schoolteacher wearing a tweed jacket and bow tie. "His name is Edmond Manchester."

Some of the agents began to clap.

"Edmond Manchester lives on the West Side, Eighty-sixth and Amsterdam. We have him on a legal tap with Scarluci. The paper supporting his warrant is solid. We are taking this case to court."

Again there was a round of applause for Dewey. I sat there pretending that I knew what they were talking about.

"Scarluci is arranging for Charles Moon to buy ten keys of smack – top grade, pure quality – for two hundred and fifty thousand dollars. Tomorrow we'll review the information from the wiretap with Pike and Blanker, and begin a twenty-four-hour surveillance on Edmond Manchester. Based on the information we have now, it will take a few days for the Moon family to put together enough money for the buy. Interpol and the Bureau's files have no criminal record of Manchester, only that he pretends to be a second-rate international jeweler."

Michael explained that an investigation of this magnitude would draw a lot of attention and, unless the buy went down next week, our plans would leak to Scarluci or Charles Moon.

The next day Pike and Blanker beamed with pride over the news of Manchester. They congratulated me and patted my back again, never once mentioning Dewey or Michael. Pike actually believed the only thing Dewey did was to type my investigation reports, and he even suggested that if I wanted to get a new partner he would okay it. The Bureau supervisors did not think it was ludicrous that I

– a novice agent with no previous experience with organized crime, and with less than two years on the job – would be in charge of a complex case that was going to bring down two Mafia families. No one seemed bothered about this except me.

Two days later the call came. Dewey summoned Silkey, Michael, and me over to a quiet corner in the office. "Here's the deal. Last night Scarluci called Manchester and told him they were ready to move ahead, and that he should put the product out for display today. Manchester is going to front the drugs and we know it's going to be this afternoon. We've got to be on him. Ed, you lead the surveillance. Don't lose him. Everything is at stake."

Ed Silkey and I drove immediately to the West Side and parked outside Manchester's apartment. We waited for almost two and a half hours. Finally Manchester came out carrying a small suitcase, and hailed a cab.

Silkey yanked the car in gear and spun a U-turn, pulling out in front of two cars, ignoring their blowing horns and screeching tires. He was four car-lengths behind Manchester's cab, going south, when the traffic stopped for a red light, but Manchester's cab continued on. Silkey downshifted, pulled up on the sidewalk and pushed the accelerator to the floor. The car fishtailed down the sidewalk, smashing garbage cans and scattering pedestrians, before careening back into the street, through a red light. We were now only three cars behind, but I was sure I'd be dead in just a few minutes.

Silkey seemed completely oblivious to the turmoil and wreckage he was leaving in his wake, but my arms were locked straight out in front of me, hard against the dashboard, and I chanted over and over, "Please, God. Please, God." I expected to see Silkey calmly light a cigarette as he dashed through another red light, narrowing the gap to one car-length.

We followed Manchester to the Port Authority. He got out and paid the cab. Silkey stopped the car and we followed on foot. Manchester strolled through the Port Authority crowds to a bank of lockers next to the ticket counters. He placed the suitcase in one of them, pocketed the key, and walked back the same way he came in.

I got the locker number. Silkey put his arm around me. "Good work."

Pike set up a 24-hour surveillance on the locker, but we had to know what was in the suitcase. Based upon the wiretap information and the surveillance, Pike got a search warrant for the locker and at about midnight, when the huge terminal was almost empty, the Port Authority Police opened the locker for Dewey, Pike, and myself. We took the suitcase to 90 Church to examine its contents. There were not ten, but eleven kilos of pure, snow-white heroin. There was a bonus kilo. Each bag was carefully wrapped in clear cellophane and taped.

While Pike and Blanker watched, Dewey and I marked each of the kilo bags with special ink that could only be seen with an infrared light. Dewey explained, "Now we have the evidence marked, we return the heroin to the locker, to see who comes to pick it up."

Trying to get control of the case, Pike told Dewey: "Continue the twenty-four-hour surveillance on the locker. I'll have two agents relieve you at eight tomorrow morning. Don't take your eyes off it for a second."

The next day I saw Dewey in the office around noon. He was clean-shaven and laughing with the other agents as usual. He certainly didn't look like he'd been up all night on surveillance at the locker. Later in the afternoon we went to the Port Authority to check on the second surveillance team.

When we got there Dewey told the agents to take thirty minutes off for dinner and that he and I would take over.

Dewey left for about ten minutes and came back with a Port Authority policeman who opened up the locker. Dewey was now carrying the suitcase of heroin, which he then placed in the empty locker. Dewey thanked the policemen as they walked off.

"My God," I said to Dewey. "I thought you put the dope back in the locker last night! These guys have been watching an *empty locker* all day? You've had the heroin all this time? Are you *crazy*? What if someone had come to pick it up?"

Dewey just shook his head. "Yes, I took it home with me. I couldn't sit around in a bus terminal all night watching a stupid locker. I had things to do last night. Don't say anything, Pike would get mad. Pike doesn't like me...he thinks I don't follow orders very well." He started to giggle. "You know I try hard to please Pike, don't you?"

SWINDLE

The next day some astonishing developments emerged in the case. First, at 8:30 the next morning a young man arrived at the Port Authority locker and picked up Edmond Manchester's suitcase. The team followed him to Charlie Moon's house in Queens. I learned later that the legal wiretap had intercepted a message giving instructions on how to pick up the locker key, and where to deliver the suitcase. Later the surveillance team followed another courier, who delivered the two hundred and fifty thousand dollars from Moon's house to Manchester's apartment.

Pike and Blanker wanted to arrest Charlie Moon and Edmond Manchester – they had solid surveillance on the drop, the pick-up, and payment to Manchester – but Michael objected. He argued that there was no hurry to make an arrest; we needed to know who else was involved, we should wait to see what Manchester did with the money, and whether or not Charlie Moon tried to sell the heroin to his friends. Pike agreed, but when Dewey asked him to continue 24-hour surveillance on the lockers in the Port Authority, he refused, calling it "stupid"; why watch an empty locker? The drugs were already gone. I thought it was a dumb request too. Dewey kept arguing they may use the same locker again. I had enough experience working with Dewey to know that, somehow, this was going to end very badly.

That evening Michael convened a dinner at the Heidelberg. We had Nathan's hotdogs with potato knishes, brown mustard, and sauerkraut, with draft beer. Dewey played a tape from the legal wiretap. The first part of the tape was not relevant. Then came the bombshell. It was a phone call from Charlie Moon. Charlie told Domenic Scarluci that he had received the shipment of "gems" and that there were more than he had ordered. He was grateful, but the quality was bad. The value of the gems was "not as good as it should have been. In fact the diamonds should have been perfect; instead they were of questionable quality and only worth half as much as what he had paid."

Domenic was shocked. "That's impossible," he argued. "I've worked with Edmond for years. This is not possible. Please remain calm and I will straighten it out."

Next came a phone call to Edmond Manchester. Again Domenic pretended to talk about gems. Manchester insisted that the gems were absolutely perfect. He would have an independent appraiser look at the diamonds to assure their quality but he was certain it would be straightened out. However, there would be no refunds at this time, and if the quality of the gems was indeed poor he would make it up on the next shipment. Domenic was not pleased. When the tape ended, Michael looked at Dewey and started to laugh, then he said, "Good work." Dewey smiled and answered, "Under your command, my captain." Michael started laughing again as he walked out of the room, ending the meeting. I smiled and pretended to know why Michael was laughing, but I had that sinking feeling again.

THE DRUG DEALER

A few days later I got a phone call from Pepper telling me that he had set up a meeting with Lisa Marie at a small restaurant in Little Italy. On the way, Dewey told me to ask Lisa Marie if she wanted to buy eleven kilos of high-quality heroin for seventy-five thousand dollars. "Tell her it's in a locker in the Port Authority and you'll front the dope but only if you can see the money first. Tell her it's from the same connection her father uses."

I was astonished – but there wasn't time to argue with him. I got to the restaurant a half hour late. Lisa Marie was already through her second drink and visibly angry.

"Where the *fuck* have *you* been?" she demanded. She had never sworn before and had always spoken in a dignified, calm manner. I reached into my pocket and pulled out the three bags of Pepper's heroin and discretely passed it over to her across the table, covering my hand with a napkin. She took the bags and slid them into her purse and handed me fifty dollars. Her attitude became friendly and she handed me a gift bag of coke. We sat in a corner booth and both snorted a pinch.

"I find myself in a very unusual situation," I said. "I have more smack than I know what to do with. I have recently come into a quantity of excellent heroin. I want you to consider buying it."

She was shocked. "You've got to be crazy. I don't do things like that. I only buy for my personal use."

"That's too bad. You have no idea how much money you could make. I can offer you a terrific deal." Then I leaned close and said, "I have eleven kilos of heroin. I will sell them to you for seventy-five thousand dollars. They're in a locker at the Port Authority. When you raise the money I'll give you the key to the locker. I know who you are and I trust you. Besides, we're dealing with the same people who work with your father. I'll front the dope; you just bring me the money first so I can see that you're for real."

She looked at me like I was crazy. "I'm leaving. I don't know what you're talking about. I want nothing to do with this."

As she started to get up, I said, "If you change your mind, call Pepper's apartment. He'll know where to find me."

Lisa Marie walked from the restaurant without even a glance back. I sat there in silence with my drink until Dewey came and sat down.

"I just tried to sell evidence in a major case to a junkie for seventy-five thousand dollars," I said. "I don't have the heroin, the drugs are gone; they're at Moon's house. None of this makes any sense. Why am I pretending to be a major drug dealer?"

Dewey smiled. "Why not? You've been selling her heroin for a month now. What's the difference, a couple of bags, a dozen keys, so what?" Dewey was never serious about anything so I couldn't tell if he was just fooling around with Lisa Marie or had a serious plan.

We went to the clinic almost every night to listen to the tapes from the gypsy. The latest one began with Lisa Marie's voice. *"Daddy, I have to talk to you."*

"Please, Lisa, not now, I'm awful busy."

"Papa, it's very important. I know something that you should know, and we should talk now."

After a brief pause Domenic said, *"Okay, darling, what is it?"*

"Daddy, a man has offered to sell me eleven kilos. He wants seventy-five thousand dollars. He knows me. He knows you. He knows the people you work with."

There was a long silence, and then Domenic said, *"My God, what's his name? What are you saying?"*

"He didn't give me his name. He only said he'd show me the goods and that it was in a locker at the Port Authority, eleven kilos, and he wants seventy-five thousand dollars cash."

"My God, at the Port Authority lockers? How do you know this man? What is his name? How could he find you? How could this be? This is not possible!"

"He was introduced to me by my friend, Pepper. He lives in the Village. He sold some pot to some of my friends at parties."

"People who sell pot at parties to pretty people like you do not sell kilos of heroin! What are you doing, Lisa?"

"It's nothing, Papa. It's under control. I'm okay. What should we do? Are you interested?"

Domenic responded coldly, "Yes, call your friend. Make

arrangements. First we'll see the heroin, then we'll make arrangements to pay him. As soon as you can make the deal I'll have the money available. I have it here, but I want you to have some help in dealing with him."

"How about Bobby? I've already told him. He was even going to put up some money."

"Yes, Bobby can help you. Now leave me alone. I have a few phone calls to make. Go make the arrangements, get back to me."

After a few moments, Domenic called Charlie Moon. *"Charlie, you were right. Edmond has got to go, and he's got to go today, right away. Lisa Marie has been approached to buy the other half of our gems. Manchester is definitely behind it. The son-of-a-bitch is even using the Port Authority lockers. He even wants to do the switch there just as soon as she can deliver seventy-five thousand dollars. It's fucking unbelievable! Lisa Marie wants Bobby to help her. I think that's a good idea. Edmond has cheated us, there's no doubt, and he must be dealt with. No mercy. This is personal."*

And then Charlie Moon's voice: "Let's do it right away. We've got to send a message here. I can't believe this fucking rat. I'll send some others to take care of Manchester. Let's make sure that we clean everything up. I'll make some phone calls; meet you at the club in two hours."

Dewey turned off the recording and everybody stared at each other. Michael started laughing so hard a tear ran down his cheek. "Let's not get excited. Now's the time to hold back, it's time for us to wait." Michael then looked at Dewey. "I think it's time Edmond Manchester joined the team, don't you?" Then Dewey and Michael started laughing together.

NEW FRIENDS

I knew Dewey took the suitcase of heroin overnight and created another eleven kilos of heroin, but only half as valuable. Michael knew Charlie Moon and Scarluci would not be fooled with the poor quality of the first buy and would come after Manchester for cheating them. Lisa Marie had now confirmed Manchester's "treachery" and sealed his fate with two crime families. I remembered what Michael had said about criminals: they always think the worst about other people.

Dewey and I drove to Manchester's apartment building. On the way, I radioed the office and learned the make and plate number of Manchester's car. Dewey showed his credentials to the doorman and said we were going down into the basement garage to check on some cars.

We walked around until we found Edmond Manchester's black Cadillac. Then Dewey used the house phone by the elevator to call Manchester. He told Edmond that he was a fellow tenant and that he had backed into his Cadillac, and asked him to come down to inspect the damage.

Within a few minutes Manchester was walking through the dark garage. Dewey and I hid in the shadows. We had brought a portable tape recorder with us and, as Manchester searched for the caller, Dewey turned it on.

Manchester stood in silence as he heard Domenic's voice on the tape: "*Edmond has cheated us, there's no doubt. He must be dealt with. No mercy. This is personal,*" and then Charlie Moon's voice, "*Yes, I agree. Let's do it right away. We've got to send a message here. I can't believe this fucking rat.*"

Dewey held his mouth to keep from laughing and played it again. Edmond still couldn't see us. He just stood there in the dark. Finally Dewey said, "Don't be afraid. We're your friends. We're not going to hurt you. We're from 90 Church. We've come to help. We like you. We are your new friends."

Edmond Manchester turned white. He stood silent, shaking with fear from either what he had heard on the tape – or Dewey's sympathetic, soft voice telling him we were from 90 Church. I wasn't sure which. Then Dewey stopped laughing, "Let's go upstairs to your apartment and get to know each other better."

The three of us took the elevator to Manchester's penthouse apartment. Manchester sat silently in the living room, staring at the floor while Dewey went into the kitchen to open the refrigerator. He yelled to me, "Start in the bedroom, search everything. Do you want a ham or turkey sandwich? He's got both, but only white bread. Take your time, I want to check the ball scores on TV."

Manchester lived alone, but I could see from the personal items in the bedroom and bathroom that he had girlfriends. There wasn't anything unusual in the drawers and closets, just clothes, all very expensive. The next room was his study, and there piled on the desk were stacks of bundled money. "My God," I yelled to Dewey in the other room, watching TV. "*Look* at this!"

"I don't have to," he yelled back. "I know what you found. Damn it, Michigan is losing."

Edmond jumped up. "That's not *my* money! You can't prove anything. That's *your* money! You're just trying to frame me. *You* put it in there!"

Dewey started to laugh. This even made me laugh. At least one hundred thousand dollars on Manchester's desk. Dewey looked at the money, went back into the bedroom and returned with one of Manchester's suitcases. He held onto the sides of the suitcase, and used his handkerchief to open the two locks. He told me to stack the money inside. Then he said to Manchester, "You're right, Edmond. This isn't your money. We'll take it back where it came from. It was a cheap trick to frame you. I'm sorry about that. However, if this ever goes to court, you can explain how you got this money in the first place, but you and I know it's never going to court. You're going to work for us now, because if you don't" – Dewey started laughing again – "I think you get the picture...We're going to have a lot of fun together. Don't you see that? We want you to continue doing exactly what you're doing. You're just a sewer pipe and we're going to protect you. Don't worry about Moon and Scarluci. They're just a bunch of loudmouth guineas. Now, why don't you get a good night's sleep and we'll talk again in a few days. We're your new best friends. Oh, one other thing; give my friend here your passport. You won't be needing it. By the way, who does your suits? Nice tailoring. Weave isn't worth shit, but nice lines."

Dewey took off his jacket and wrapped it around the suitcase. He carried it out of the apartment and loaded it in the car trunk, still wrapped in the jacket. I knew this wild ride was not over yet.

SWITCH AND RE-SWITCH

The next morning Dewey and I stopped by the Port Authority. He had the suitcase we took from Manchester's apartment and carried it into the same bank of lockers that Manchester had used before. Again carrying the suitcase wrapped in his jacket, Dewey put it into an empty locker and threw me the key! I remembered

Dewey pleading with Pike to continue the surveillance on the empty lockers. Dewey knew Pike would think the idea was stupid and would refuse; now it was the safest place in New York to hide drug money. Over one hundred thousand dollars now sat in a Port Authority locker, the last place anyone would look for it! In fact, the only place that agents were told not to look!

When we got to the office Dewey told me to requisition seventy-five thousand dollars in government funds for a buy of heroin from Lisa Marie. Nothing made sense. The plan was supposed to be for Lisa Marie to pay *me* seventy-five thousand dollars. Now everything was upside down again. Was I selling or buying the heroin that I didn't have?

Around noon Pepper called to set up a meeting with Lisa Marie at the same Midtown bar where we met last time.

Late in the afternoon we stopped by Pepper's apartment and picked up a few bags of heroin for Lisa Marie. I gave Pepper thirty dollars, which made me laugh as I thought about all the drug and government money around me – the seventy-five thousand dollars in government money in Dewey's briefcase and over one hundred thousand dollars in the locker. On the way to the meeting Dewey gave me my new instructions: "Lisa Marie will want to see the heroin first; give her the key to the locker so she can see the eleven kilos of heroin."

I lost all sense of reality. I looked at Dewey as if he was crazy, but then it came to me. *Now* I understood, Dewey had made *another* switch; there was no money in Manchester's suitcase when we put it in the locker this morning. Now I understood why Dewey wrapped the suitcase in his jacket and held it by the sides. It was to avoid adding his fingerprints. The suitcase in the locker now contained the new eleven kilos of heroin that Dewey made when he cut the original eleven kilos of pure heroin in half. I still didn't understand why I had gotten the seventy-five thousand dollars in government funds. It would be pointless to ask. Dewey never gave anyone a straight answer. I just did what Dewey told me to do, and knew that he was being directed by Michael.

At the meeting, Lisa Marie led the conversation. "We have given your offer of eleven kilos a lot of thought, and I've raised the money. I don't know you, but I'm willing to give you a chance. If the drugs are as good as you say, then you will be paid. If they're not, I'll return the drugs. You said you'd front the drugs, I want to see them now before I pay you a dime."

I reached in my pocket and handed her the locker key and her little bags of heroin. "Port Authority, the locker's on the north side of the ticket booths. Oh, and the bags of junk are on me."

She stuffed the heroin bags in her purse and reached under the table for a black attaché case and placed it in front of me. In the middle of the crowded bar I opened it and saw stacks of bundled, new, hundred-dollar bills. Lisa Marie looked into my eyes and said, "This is your deal. You've been kind to me. At ten-thirty tonight meet me in front of Halburton Trucking, on Ashton Avenue in Queens. It's just a couple of blocks from my house. Take Queens Boulevard, it's easy to find. I'll be there with this money. You come alone and I will be alone." Again she looked straight into my eyes and said, "I trust you. You won't hurt me." She smiled and kissed me on the lips, and walked out the door, carrying both the black attaché case filled with cash and the key to the locker at the Port Authority.

That night, to kill time, Ed Silkey and Dewey and I had dinner in Little Italy. I called Pepper to tell him to join us, but he didn't answer. This concerned me since he was expecting my call. About nine-thirty I drove Dewey's car to meet Lisa Marie. Dewey and Silkey followed. We got to the Halburton Trucking Company about fifteen minutes early. I told Silkey and Dewey to park a couple of blocks away. I didn't want Lisa Marie to be suspicious and the two of them made me worry about Lisa Marie's safety.

I stood on the dark street, remembering all that had happened, the look in Lisa Marie's eyes, the smile, the trust, the gentle kiss on the lips – and I began to wonder what I was doing. Now I was selling heroin to the Mafia. None of this made sense, and I began to think that Dewey was truly crazy, and I was going to end up in jail. Then Lisa Marie's dark BMW turned the corner. It drove past me, up the block, turned around, came back past me and disappeared around the corner. I saw it turn around again and come back rolling to a stop in front of me.

I couldn't see who was driving, then the car door opened. It was not Lisa Marie, it was a man about my age, good-looking, his hair combed straight back in a ponytail. He wore a dark sport coat and white silk shirt with an open collar. He smiled, and his smile scared me, "Lisa Marie asked me to deliver something to you. The junk is terrific." He started walking toward me, carrying a shopping bag. He repeated, "Lisa Marie wanted me to give you this." As he started to hand me the shopping bag the street erupted in gunfire. The first bullet hit him in the chest and the second nicked the edge of his chin; bullet after bullet began striking him so hard that he began to wave his arms. His face was twisted as he tried to scream, his hands came together as if in prayer, and then another bullet hit him and jerked him up in the air. His white shirt turned mostly red with huge polka-dots.

So many bullets came that the sounds blended into one loud roar.

Horrified, I began to imitate his macabre motions, waving my arms like his and twitching my head back and forth as the bullets struck and jerked him around. We danced together for what seemed like minutes, until he fell down at my feet. I stood there wondering why I wasn't hit, with so many shots fired right in front of me. I couldn't believe I was still standing. Out of the darkness I heard Dewey's voice: "Toss the car, Ed."

They had killed the man in a barrage of crossfire. Dewey walked over to the body and flipped it over with his foot and stared at the dead, handsome, young man. Kneeling down to get a closer look at the man's face, Dewey said with a smile, "Hi, Bobby. This was for Pepper."

I was shaking, but finally I screamed, "How could you *do* this? He was *giving me the money*. We had a *deal*. He was buying our heroin! How could you *murder* him?"

"You shouldn't be selling heroin," Dewey answered with his usual sarcasm. "It's against the law. When will you ever get that straight? Drug dealers sell heroin, not agents."

Without looking up, Dewey turned the shopping bag upside down. A revolver with a black silencer rolled out – and nothing else...no money.

"How did you know?" I asked.

"I told you before. What did you think? She's a junkie. She betrays people. That's what junkies *do*. Why would she meet you here in a dark, empty street to give you money she already showed off in a crowded restaurant? Besides, she sent Bobby here. He's a stone-cold killer, works with Joe Valachi. Besides, Kyle left a message after your meeting this afternoon. Somebody took Pepper for a ride. They tied him up and threw him out of a car on the Jersey Turnpike. It broke his neck. Who do you think did that? Who got him into that car?"

Then I heard Silkey say from inside the BMW, "Jesus Christ! Guess what we got – eleven kilos of heroin!" He held up Manchester's suitcase that Lisa Marie had taken from the locker at the Port Authority and, without saying another word, Silkey held up Lisa Marie's black attaché case containing the seventy-five thousand dollars that her father had given her. Silkey put the money in the trunk of Dewey's car. He left Manchester's suitcase of heroin in the back seat of Lisa Marie's car where he found it. Silkey radioed the NYPD and soon squad cars surrounded the area.

It was just another drug buy gone bad: Bobby Moon, a well-known killer, carrying eleven kilos of heroin, which he had gotten from Manchester, now trying to sell it to a federal narcotics agent for seventy-five thousand dollars of government money. Fortunately the surveillance team stepped in just in the nick of time, before it turned into a robbery-homicide. The Bureau got a new BMW, got its seventy-five thousand dollars back, seized eleven kilos of heroin and got a hit man off the streets. Manchester and Lisa Marie's fingerprints would be on the suitcase containing the heroin, and my reports, written by Dewey, described the negotiations with Lisa Marie and how I had requisitioned the government money for the buy, which was now safely returned to the Bureau. Meanwhile, the money Lisa had raised from her father's Mafia friends to buy their own eleven kilos of heroin was still in the trunk of Dewey's car.

THE FIGHT

In the office everyone treated me like a hero. It certainly looked like that on paper: I had developed the informer, gone undercover and set up Bobby Moon, seized eleven kilos of heroin, and saved the government seventy-five thousand dollars. Pike decided to execute the warrant on Charles Moon's house immediately. He called Kyle to tell him the Bureau was going to Moon's house, and asked him to coordinate the raid with the cops. Dewey said he had a dentist appointment and couldn't go. I didn't go either. Pike said it would be best if I was not involved in the search. The agents and Queens police broke down Moon's door and found the original eleven kilos of government-marked heroin in his basement, plus three more kilos and a cutting-and-bagging operation. They also found over a hundred thousand dollars in drug money. Charles Moon and his wife had learned only hours before that their son had been killed trying to sell drugs. Moon's wife was crying so hard she threw up on one of the cops.

That evening Michael, Dewey, Kyle, and Silkey met at the clinic. Stacked on the table was over one hundred thousand dollars from Manchester's apartment and Lisa Marie's seventy-five thousand. Dewey had already begun dividing it into small piles. Michael began talking about how we would now use Manchester, not only here in the United States, but overseas as well. Scarluci and Lisa Marie would come next. Michael believed we could turn Scarluci, especially now that we had his daughter.

Around 8:30 Kyle walked in the door wearing a raincoat to hide his uniform – police dress blues with a tie, badges on his chest and silver bars on his shoulders. He had been at a city function and had left early to join us. Michael looked at him and said, "Make any new cases lately?" Kyle showed his horrible rat grin of long white teeth. Dewey, Michael, and Silkey laughed, as Kyle sat down and looked at the piles of money. Dewey pointed to a small stack that he was making on the table and said to Kyle, "This one's yours" and he pushed it toward him. Kyle stared at the small pile of money and his face clouded up. "I don't want your filthy drug money," he said, and threw one of the bundles of hundred-dollar bills in Dewey's face.

Dewey snatched a handful of money from the table and threw it back at Kyle, hitting him in the chest, on his medals. Everyone around the table grabbed the money and began throwing it at each other, laughing, and yelling, "I don't want any filthy drug money!" Bundles of cash and loose bills were flying all over the room until there were none left on the table. Then, still laughing, everyone got down on his hands and knees to gather up the money and put it back on the table. When they were seated again and the laughter had died down, Dewey said, "Kyle, if you pull that shit again, I'm not going to throw it back." Everyone started laughing again, even me.

Dewey had one more tape for us. At first there were the usual irrelevant phone calls and conversations in the room. Dewey fast-forwarded to a call from Charlie Moon to Domenic Scarluci. The voice was distraught and crying, and then we heard, "They killed him. They shot my Bobby down like a dog. Twelve shots, his face, his chest. Who did this to my boy? Who could do this? Why? Who? I'll find them. I'll kill them myself. Help me, Domenic. Help me find them. Help me kill them...I have to go, his mother won't stop crying...she's sick...the doctor is here."

The next sounds were from the room; someone walked in to talk with Domenic. A steady voice said, "I know you've heard about Bobby Moon. They gunned him down, Domenic, but there's more, and it's worse. They've got Lisa Marie. She's working for them now. She gave them the drugs. She gave them Bobby Moon. Her name is all over the warrants. They did Charlie's house this morning. They have him on possession and conspiracy to sell eleven kilos. They have his whole operation. They know everything because Lisa Marie gave it to them."

"That's impossible! It can't be!" Domenic responded violently. "That's *impossible*! You should have known, why didn't you tell me?"

The voice answered, "It's true, she's a junkie. It's worse, everyone thinks you cut Charles's buy from Manchester and cheated him out of over two hundred thousand dollars. People are coming for you, Domenic. There's going to be war. It'll be a blood bath. You don't stand a chance."

"*That's not possible,*" Domenic replied. "*No one could do this to me. How could they do it and I not know? This is impossible. Who is doing this? The police? The FBI? They can't do this. I can beat this.*"

"It's over, Domenic. They've got everything. You can't fight them. It's not us. If it was NYPD I would have known about it. I review these types of investigations, and I would have told you. It's worse. It's not the FBI. It's 90 Church. You know what those people are like. They have Lisa Marie; they're fucking her, they have you, and both families are going to kill each other. I'm sorry for you and the Moon family. Only 90 Church could do something like this."

The tape stopped and everyone looked at Kyle. Kyle just stared at the table, shaking his head, then he said, "I know who this crooked cocksucker is, he's a lieutenant, his name is Sprague. Don't worry I'll get him."

As Silkey began to cue up the tape machine for the next round of calls, I began to think how perfectly the case had been executed. We had Lisa Marie, caught trying to sell me eleven kilos. Her father would try to save her and become our informant. We had Manchester for selling drugs and cheating on a drug deal to the Genovese family. He would live only as long as Michael needed him. We had started a Mafia war that would destroy two crime families and their whole drug operation. The impact on drug trafficking and organized crime was huge. Kyle would get the crooked cop named Sprague. Everything was legal and ready to go to court – although no one, not even me, would be telling the truth. How could I possibly explain why I tried to sell eleven kilos of stolen heroin to Lisa Marie or how we cheated the Mafia by cutting the heroin?

Pike and I were heroes, but the great irony in this case was that Michael's apprentice, Dewey, the boy agent who could not answer a single question on any case, was hardly even mentioned in any of the reports. It was outrageous to remember that on Dewey's last job performance Pike had written, *Agent Dwight Paris lacks initiative and needs a better understanding of investigation techniques.* And Michael – who taught, encouraged, and manipulated everyone – was never mentioned at all.

Silkey got the machine started again. The next sound we heard was Lisa Marie's voice. *"Papa, Papa."* And then Domenic said, *"The heroin, the eleven keys! You set that up, and now Bobby. Charlie called me. They murdered Bobby. They shot him in the street, over and over.*

Imagine his mother. It was you, Lisa Marie."

"No, Papa, no."

"Yes, it was you. Do you know who you are playing with, Lisa? 90 Church. 90 Church! Do you understand, 90 Church?" Then he screamed, "Your boyfriend was 90 Church, 90 Church!"

"No, Papa, I'll work it out. I'll straighten it out! I know what to do. It's not that bad. I'll fight back. I'll win, Papa. You'll see."

"No. Lisa, no! Everyone thinks I cheated my partners, my friends. I'm dead. They'll get me."

"Papa, you're not going to stop me! I'm fighting back. I'll get them. I don't need you."

All of a sudden there was a gunshot. Then a second. We all looked at each other. The silence continued, followed by uncontrollable sobbing, on and on, crying and sobbing. On and on the sobbing went, and then there was a long silence – and then a single gunshot.

CHAPTER FOUR

SETTLING IN

ILLUSIONS

The next weekend all my twisted stories and lies about 90 Church came apart. Daisy loved my version of the story of the Scarluci and Moon case. I told her how I had turned Lisa Marie into an informant, and how I developed information to get a wiretap that led to the arrest of Charlie Moon to end his drug organization. I showed Daisy copies of my official report to prove it was really me working as a secret undercover agent, and explained how I had sent Lisa Marie and her father into a witness protection program for their safety. It said they were part of the Genovese family and Bobby Moon worked with Joe Valachi. From the twisted story I told her, Daisy thought Pike and Blanker were heroes working side by side with me, and that Michael and Dewey should be fired.

The newspapers came out and reported the whole story exactly like I told her. It had pictures of Pike and Blanker holding up bags of heroin and referring to a "brilliant young undercover agent who developed the information to make the case on two Mafia families."

Daisy was proud of me. We went shopping and held hands with Mark. At last our relationship was coming back together. As we passed a carpet store I pulled Daisy inside. Our apartment had rough wood floors and was always cold. I chose the best carpet they had and arranged for installation the following Monday. I reached in my pocket and pulled out a couple hundred dollars and paid for it in full.

Daisy was quiet on the walk back home. We stopped to buy groceries and a newspaper. When we got back to the apartment, and I was pacing off where the rug would be, she said, "Tell me, where did you get all of the money? Sometimes there's thousands of dollars lying on the dresser in the morning, in bundles, or loose. I find hundred-dollar bills in your pants when I do the wash. Tell me what's going on."

"What do you mean? It's government money. Money they give me to work with, to buy drugs. That's what I do."

I could see the look in her eyes as she stared at me. "*They* give you the money? Who is *they*, and were you on a case today when you bought the rug?"

I was starting to get defensive. "The Bureau, and Michael and Dewey. It's traveling money."

"Dewey and Michael give you money? Why would *they* give you money?"

I felt trapped. "They give me money – for the cabs and drinks; it's expensive being undercover. And the Bureau gives me money too. Pike gave me seventy-five thousand dollars for the buy. There's money all over the office. Don't worry, I have to account for every dime, it all goes into the official government report."

Now Daisy was angry. "Michael and Dewey, who do nothing,

give you money? Money to get home. Money for you to drink with? They hand you money like you're a waiter or bellhop? They *tip* you?"

Daisy didn't say anything more. Mark took a nap and she began reading the newspaper. I was glad the whole money scene was over and relaxed on the couch. About twenty minutes later, Daisy started in again. "Where do you think Lisa Marie and her father are now? You said you put them in witness protection. Pennsylvania, Arizona, Utah? Where do you think they went for protection?"

It was a strange question. Her fingers were straight, holding the newspaper, and her eyes were blinking; she stared through me like I wasn't even there.

"My goodness," she said. "No wonder you need money for expenses." She handed me the paper and left the room.

It was folded to the local news section. The headline read, *Father, daughter, murder suicide*, with a picture of Lisa Marie and Domenic. The article said the deaths occurred three days earlier, but was withheld from the press pending a federal drug investigation. It described how the father became distraught when he learned that his daughter had been involved with a federal drug agent and was forced to turn on her own family.

Despite all my lies, Daisy tried desperately to hold us together – but week after week passed, with leftover dinners piled up in the refrigerator. Once I told her I would be home at five for dinner, but it was after midnight by the time I finally walked in the door. Daisy had fallen asleep on the living-room floor, waiting for me. As I tiptoed past her I saw her face had streaks of mascara and black circles around her eyes from crying. She woke up, looked at me, covered her face and lay back down on the floor and went to sleep instead of sharing the bed with me. I had lied to her, broken our bond of truth. I couldn't help her. We were now too distant. I realized how awful it was for her. Never again would I attempt to tell her about the cases, which had grown so strange and complicated that even I had trouble figuring out what I was doing. I knew that Michael and Dewey were wrong, very wrong and that someday I would have to turn them in.

THE TRIP

I soon got a reprieve from Daisy's anger and resentment when Pike sent me out of town for a few days to work undercover in upstate New York. The Federal Bureau of Narcotics was more than just an intelligence resource to other law-enforcement agencies; it often advanced money for drug buys and even lent undercover agents to work with local cops. Each group at 90 Church took turns handling these requests. My reputation had grown in the past two years, so I was asked to work with the police department in Millbrook, New York. Pike said they wanted an undercover agent to make a buy on a dealer selling dope to tourists in the mountains. The community was so small that the drug dealer knew all of the cops so an undercover buy was not possible unless done by someone from the outside. I looked forward to leaving the city and not worrying about coming home at night. The dealer, Eric, sold a variety of drugs – heroin, cocaine, and LSD – from a bar he owned. Pike decided that I should pose as a "biker" type since I rode motorcycles in college and we had a Harley-Davidson Sportster in the government car pool. The plan was for me to take the bike, drive to Millbrook, make contact with the local police, and set up the buy.

Early the next morning, I checked out the motorcycle from the motor pool and headed north on winding roads lined with trees and farms and lakes. It was fun, roaring down the highway through the cool, crisp, clean air. By mid-afternoon I found Eric's bar in a resort area by a lake surrounded by woods. I decided to stop for lunch at Eric's restaurant. It was small, but surprisingly upscale, with a well-stocked bar. I was hot and hungry from my ride.

My waitress, Sandy, was pretty with very little makeup, unlike the girls I was used to seeing in the city. The bar was empty so we talked a lot. I'd had a long hot ride and needed to cool off. I asked her if there was a place close by where I could swim. She told me to ride back down the highway for about a mile and I would see a small dirt road on the left that was chained off. She said the bike could easily drive around the barrier and that I should follow the road to the lakeshore where I would find a great place to swim in private.

I had no trouble maneuvering the motorcycle around the chain and found the lakeshore just as she described it. I took off my clothes and dove into the cool dark lake. In less than a half hour, I looked up at the bank and saw Sandy in a bathing suit, smiling. She seemed to enjoy catching me swimming naked. She dove in, giggling and laughing as she swam close to me. The attraction was instant. I told her I was looking for Eric to buy some drugs. She said I was stupid to be involved in such things but it didn't seem to matter to her. I wanted to see her later that evening and knew it was just a question of when and where. I had already cheated on Daisy once, so another time didn't seem to matter. Somehow it was just part of the job.

Later that afternoon I left my bike in a quiet street and headed to the Millbrook police station to meet the local police chief. He was fat, with red sores on his face, and his uniform was covered with all sorts of sewn-on patches for First Aid, Marksmanship, etc. He smiled as he told me about Eric's drug dealing and introduced me to a teenager named Jesse, who had been arrested for burglary. He was willing to rat on Eric for a reduced sentence. It bothered me that the fat police chief kept smiling as he talked about Eric. I could not forget Michael's warning about not trusting people who smile at the wrong time so I began to worry. Jesse would tell Eric that I was a drug dealer from New Jersey and a friend of his older brother who was in the Army. I needed a new drug source because my connection had been busted.

That night Jesse took me to a house party on the lake where I met Eric. The guests were mostly tourists and almost everyone was doing pot or coke. I told Eric that I wanted to make a score of heroin. He said he had no heroin, but he did have cocaine and LSD. I guessed that Eric's source was someone in New York City. So when he asked me about a lot of places where drug dealers hang out in the Bronx and lower Manhattan I was ready with the right answers. Then we snorted a line of coke together. After that he was absolutely convinced that I was a dealer.

I called Sandy and left the party early, riding my motorcycle through the dark to a house on the lake where she was house sitting. It was a beautiful house, with a big front porch that overlooked the lake. We necked on the porch then went inside to make love in the master bedroom. Later I called Daisy and told her I wouldn't be home for a couple of days. She was okay with it. Lying to her was easy, just like the lies I told every day on the job.

The next day, we went boating and sunbathing. I called Eric

and told him that I was ready to make a buy of cocaine. He said he would like to wait another day, which was fine with me. Sandy and I went for a ride on the motorcycle through the hills north of Millbrook and Poughkeepsie, and down the winding roads of Connecticut. I drove past Candlestick Lake, where Mark fell in and Daisy got muddy pulling him out of the water. That memory seemed to be about someone else, not me. We stopped for dinner and then went back to the house to make love again. Being with her felt so natural that I forgot about my past or what I was doing.

I dropped Sandy off at her apartment and met with the fat, swearing, smiling police chief to report my progress. They were delighted that I could make a buy so soon and pointed out that if it took place at Eric's house, they could go in, arrest him, and search and seize all of his drugs – so a second buy wouldn't be necessary.

I called Dewey and Ed Silkey and told them to bring three thousand dollars in government funds since I would be making the buy tomorrow night. Again I spent the next day with Sandy on the lake and told her that I wanted to continue seeing her. She hoped that I would stop buying drugs and "get a decent job." I wasn't ready to tell her that I was a federal agent, but planned to tell her everything when the time was right. That evening Dewey and Ed met me in town with the three thousand dollars. I told them that the plan was for me to go to Eric's house, buy the drugs, return, and give the drugs to the police chief. After the buy I would meet them at an intersection a mile from Eric's house, then they would raid his house, arrest him and I would get the government money back.

As planned, I went to Eric's house in the woods. We talked for a while and smoked a joint. Then Eric gave me two ounces of cocaine and I gave him the money. I told him I was going back to

Jersey that night. He thought I should stay over with him because it was beginning to thunder and cloud up. I said no and left to meet Dewey and Silkey with the local police. I showed them the drugs and they sped off down the road to raid Eric's house. Then I drove to Eric's bar and waited. About a half hour later I heard sirens. An ambulance roared up the dirt road toward Eric's house.

Soon it came back out, but without flashing lights or sirens. A few minutes later Dewey and Silkey came into the bar. Silkey said, "The crazy fucking police chief shot Eric. He opened the door, and he shot him. The kid never knew what hit him."

Dewey shook his head. "There was drug money all over the place and the police helped themselves. We were lucky to get our three thousand dollars back. Eric did have a gun, so the police will claim they shot in self-defense, but it was a botched amateur job. No one should have gotten hurt. These people didn't like Eric. It was a set-up. They were looking for a reason to kill him. They just shot him."

It had begun raining and by now everybody in the bar knew what had happened. One of the policemen joined us and tried to apologize. He said the whole town was talking about it. I asked the cop if he knew Sandy. The cop nodded, "Sure, Sandy is Eric's sister."

I was stunned, but I knew Sandy hated drugs and hoped that once I explained what had happened, maybe she wouldn't blame me. I called her at home. One of the local cops had already called her so she knew about Eric and the drug raid. She said sooner or later she knew this would happen. She also knew who I really was and understood everything. I felt relieved that I didn't have to tell her. I said I wanted to see her before I left. She told me to come back to the house on the lake.

Dewey and Ed had each taken a government car because Dewey refused to ride with Silkey. Although the rain had stopped, I took Ed's car, since I didn't want to risk riding a motorcycle if it started to rain again.

Sandy was waiting for me on the porch with a glass of wine in her hand. She had turned the house lights off and lit about a dozen candles all over the porch. I told her I was sorry and she just looked at me through her tears and said she understood. I hugged and kissed her, she poured me a glass of wine. I explained how I couldn't tell her I was an agent, but from now on I would never keep anything from her. She smiled sadly. I finished my glass of wine and told her I would spend the night with her. She answered strangely, "You don't have to. I know you were just doing your job." I hugged and kissed her again. "No," I whispered. "Can't you feel how I feel?" She smiled, holding me against her soft, long, blonde hair.

Just then, a bolt of lightning hit me. It came from the dark sky, lighting up the woods. I was knocked off the porch and onto the wet lawn. As I tried to get to my feet, I could see Sandy standing in the candlelight, smiling. Then she stopped smiling and her words pounded in my ears so loud it hurt. "He was my *brother*. He protected me. He was all I *had*. You came here to kill him, you son of a *bitch*." She mocked me, "Can't you feel how I feel?"

The lightning struck me again. I fell down holding my ears and pushing my face into the muddy grass. The thunder was deafening. I got to my knees and raised my hands for Sandy to help me. Something very terrifying was happening to me. She just stood there with the wine glass in her hand, laughing. Her laughter sounded as loud as the thunder and I staggered away, stumbling and falling, trying to get to the car. The laughter and the thunder came after me again. I fell onto the driveway, holding my ears. I crawled to the car and managed to open the door and climb inside.

I started the engine and began to drive away. Once again, the thunder shattered my ears. I tried to cover my head and steer at the same time down the winding dirt road. My right foot froze on the gas pedal. I could turn the steering wheel but I couldn't take my foot off the accelerator; my foot was frozen. I knew if I didn't find some way to remove my foot from the accelerator, I would crash. I used every ounce of energy in my body to move my foot while trying desperately to stay on the road, but it wouldn't budge. I started to scream and cry. I couldn't stop the car. I lost control. With horror, I watched the car slide into a tree.

After the crash I was on my back lying across the car seat. I could feel blood coming from my nose and a tingling all over my body, but I was still alive. I began to have a strange sensation in my foot – the one that had been frozen to the accelerator. I looked down and saw it was beginning to swell inside my boot. I ripped my boot and sock off to relieve the pressure but my foot continued to swell and tingle even more. Soon it became as large as a basketball and was still growing fast. I raised my foot, smashing it against the ceiling of the car. Now it was as big as a huge balloon, more than three feet across! It started to push me down into the seat. My own foot was crushing me between the seat and the car roof. I reached in my pocket and pulled out my knife. The only way I could save myself was to cut the huge balloon that used to be my foot. I slashed at my ankle. Blood spilled out on my hand and made the knife slippery.

I woke up in the hospital and remembered everything...Silkey and Dewey dragging me out of the car. I was screaming and fighting them, trying to cut my foot off. Now I laid in bed with my leg in a cast. Silkey just looked at me and said, "We've got the cunt. Don't worry."

"I don't want anything to happen to her, let her go. It wasn't her fault."

Dewey looked at me and said, "She gave you LSD. What do you mean, it wasn't her fault? Get real, she tried to *kill* you! I say we take her back to the City with us, give her to Michael. He'll find fun things for her to do, she's got a great body."

My eyes were getting warm and blurry. I pleaded, "No, please don't give her to Michael, please let her go." I turned away so they couldn't see my face.

RECOVERY

Dewey wrote the case report. It said that an unknown person slipped LSD in my drink and that I crashed the car while avoiding a deer crossing the road. I spent the next two weeks at home, playing with Mark and trying to salvage my relationship with Daisy. The doctors had tied the ligaments and muscle back together in my foot so well there was only one long scar along with a dozen small stab wounds that were stitched closed. Daisy couldn't understand how I got so many cuts on my foot from a car crash. I could never tell her the truth.

No one was really sure what the long-term effects of LSD might be, so, for a while, people at the office treated me with caution. Pike and Michael and the others downplayed it and said I would be all right, but I wouldn't be assigned any cases.

It was my four-year-old son who first noticed the change in me. Mark looked at me, blinked and pointed to my eyes, then he laughed. If you try hard enough you can force your eyelids open wider, giving your face a surprised or bewildered look. My eyes were open wider than usual. I stared into the mirror at least ten times a day to see if I looked better, wondering if there was really anything wrong with me at all.

Every day my anxiety grew over my wide-eyed condition. I began to think it was getting worse. I still had the cocaine from Eric so I began snorting it in secret to calm me down and cure my condition. Twice a day I would stare into my son's face to see if he would laugh at me. When he laughed I would snort more coke. Daisy was pleased that I was spending more time with Mark.

Despite my emotional problems that were growing worse every day, I began to come into the office a couple days a week to talk to other agents and do research. I got to know Del Ridley and Jerry Ramirez better. They began work at the Bureau the same day I did, but worked smaller cases. Ridley was religious and married to Sarah, a beautiful fashion model. He hated the way the Bureau operated, especially the case reports and money. Jerry Ramirez was Puerto Rican and had two children. He had been a Customs agent. Since he spoke Spanish, Jerry was needed undercover and was doing very well, although most of his cases involved small-time Puerto Rican dealers.

I also became friends with agent Tony Roma, "Tony Roma from Roma," who had transferred from the Rome office. He had worked undercover for years in Italy, supplying information on the Mafia and shipments of drugs coming in to the U.S. He was shy and very quiet. I learned from Michael that Tony's cover was blown in Italy and he had to come to the U.S. for protection. The Italian Mafia had tortured and killed his teenaged brother in Rome. He never really got over it so he just put in his time at the office and left at 5:00. Tony Roma had no future and could not face his past.

Agent Roma told me how heroin comes into the United States. Poppies are grown in Turkey and the "Golden Triangle" in Asia, then converted into morphine and shipped to Marseilles, where secret laboratories convert it into heroin. Then it is shipped to Italy, distributed to Mafia crime families, and smuggled into the United States through New York. The Bureau was the only agency that was brave enough to fight the Mafia. However, the Mafia would not retaliate against the agents as long as they made small cases. Roma said that Michael and Dewey didn't play their game and they were already dead. It was just a matter of time. I remember that Louis Turko had said revenge was coming when Dewey tweaked his nose, the night Charles Stuckey got shot. Roma told me that Turko had made bail and was back on the street. The federal judge who let him out was Carl Wineburg. Michael suspected Wineburg of having Mafia connections through the unions, who supported his political friends who got him the judgeship.

I liked to sit with Tony Roma while he ate his lunch and listen to his stories of adventurous cases. He ate the same thing every day, first carving slices from a dark purple sausage roll, then from a hard cheese block, and taking small sips of wine from a peanut-butter jar.

One day Pike saw him and said there was no drinking allowed on the job and made him stop. Since agents drank all the time while working undercover or on surveillance Dewey saw the whole scene as ridiculous and went around the office, telling the other agents, "Hey, Pike says no drinking on the job," getting a laugh everywhere he went.

As the days passed, coke and liquor seemed to help me recover, although I would still get a laugh from Mark when I stared at him with my wide bulging eyes. But oddly, no one else seemed to notice this physical change in me. Daisy thought I was drunk all the time, but she didn't say anything. She knew what I was going through and believed I would pull myself out of it. Michael was also concerned because he spent more time with me in the evenings than ever before. He didn't like to drive, so at the end of the evening I would drop him off at odd places, sometimes at a penthouse on Park Avenue, or a dark, deserted street in Harlem. One night, after we had about ten drinks, I was so drunk I could hardly drive. I had to snort cocaine to sober up. Michael told me to drop him off at an upscale apartment building by the United Nations. At first the doorman stopped him, but then backed away like he was afraid. Michael didn't carry a gun, yet I never worried about him. He was like a terrible monster loosed upon the city.

I drove downtown toward home. I took a short cut through the empty streets of the Bowery and stopped at a red light. There were no cars, no people, just a deserted street. All of a sudden, I heard loud strange noises: whistles, banging of steel upon steel, and escaping steam. Then a huge green garbage truck came lumbering down the cross street in front of me. It was enormous, with black greasy tires taller than my car. Its dark green side had hydraulic arms and compression levers that were almost two stories tall. The whistles and bells and clanging were deafening. I saw small garbage men in gray jumpsuits swarming all over the side like ants on a dead animal. They leaped and swung from handle to handle, platform to platform, carrying garbage cans or tools like wrenches or oilcans.

The huge truck belched steam as it rolled to a stop only a few feet from the front of my car. I could see the face of one of the scampering workers as he swung by one hand, carrying a garbage can with the other. It was Domenic Scarluci! Another female creature came down the side; face first, like a giant lizard crawling down a wall. Her hair pulled back, oil smeared on her face, it was Lisa Marie! I saw the faces of the others too. I saw Eric and Calvin dumping garbage and tending to the many moving parts as they leaped and jumped from the top to bottom and side to side like frenzied monkeys. I saw Charles Stuckey, just like the rest, too intent on his work to even give me a single glance, yet he was swinging by one arm just a few feet in front of me. I saw another creature with a pump oil can. At first I didn't recognize the face with the hair pulled back, under a dirty hat. She crawled up the side of the truck then stopped and stared back at me. It was Maureen from Scarsdale. They all had the same blank stare on their faces: the look of being dead.

The huge truck banged the overhanging traffic light as it lurched forward with a great calliope of noises and rolled out of sight.

I sat frozen, unable to think or move. Then I jammed the accelerator to the floor, screeching rubber. I turned into the intersection after the truck. In less than a block I pulled over and got out, pointing my gun back and forth. Shaking and crying, I stared at the empty, silent streets. Finally I wiped my eyes and drove home.

TASTY

The next morning I snorted a line of coke and looked in the mirror. My eyes didn't seem to bulge anymore, but I didn't want to test them out by staring into Mark's face. I knew from my training and street experience that coke, unlike heroin, was not physically addictive. It was, however, very dangerous because it was psychologically addictive. I was scared, very scared about what the LSD had done to me. I knew that my hallucinations were caused by anxiety, and the coke, for all its dangers, had calmed me down and restored my confidence. Everyone else could see how normal and self-confident I had become. Pike wanted me back on the street, making buys of heroin from broken-down junkies, but Michael argued it was too soon. I would get hurt. Pike insisted and introduced me to Tony Degaglia – my own Mafia informant – and we became friends. I even visited his mother's house, where she made us dinner. She was a sweet old lady, and an incredible cook. I had the best Italian food ever, better than any restaurant in the city. Every meal had three or four main dishes, pasta, meat, etc. She believed her son Tony could do no wrong and I was probably a bad influence. Tony was all that she had left in her life and it was more than enough. I told Michael about her and the wonderful meals.

Tony took me to a great party. He let everyone know I was a buyer. They didn't believe him. There was a line of coke laid out on the coffee table. I knew what they wanted to see.

I picked up a straw and sucked up a line. They smiled and followed me with their straws. I liked the taste of cocaine and I knew the difference between good and bad coke.

We partied most of the night. Girls came and went. By the party's end I had sucked up at least five lines of coke and was so drunk that I couldn't drive, so I spent the night at Tony's mother's house. The next morning I had no fear or desire to use cocaine at all. I understood addiction and knew that I could control it, but I didn't know why I believed this.

A few days later, Tony told me about a heroin dealer named Noodles. Noodles was Italian but not Mafia. He was at the party and had asked Tony if I was interested in buying pure heroin. Tony set up a buy for ten thousand dollars and told him I wanted three ounces. I didn't tell Michael because I knew he would pull me off the case. I went straight to Pike. The buy was to take place outside a dark tenement building in the Bronx. I met Noodles in the street and showed him the money. Dewey and Silkey were on foot, hiding about a half a block away. Pike remained in his car even further down the street.

Noodles said the drugs were hidden on the second floor of the abandoned building, so the two of us walked in and up to the first landing. As I got to the top of the dark stairs a man appeared out of the shadows with a pipe and hit me on the side of the face. The two of them began to beat me. When I fell to the floor, they started kicking and stomping me. I could feel Noodles reach into my pocket and take the ten thousand dollars, then continue to hit me. I screamed and cried for them to stop while they pushed my face into the filth on the floor. The more I cried and screamed, the more they kicked and beat me. I pushed my tongue on the filthy floor to keep from crying like a baby. Finally, they left.

I was gasping and crying so hard I couldn't yell for help. I crawled on my hands and knees down the stairs into the street. Dewey and Silkey dragged me over to the side of the building and sat me up;

Dewey looked in my eyes for a concussion. Blood, tears and snot covered my face. As I struggled to breathe, gulping air through my loose front teeth, I saw Pike drive up in his car. He parked and charged up the sidewalk yelling, "What the *fuck* is going on here? What happened? Where is the government money? We've got *ten grand* on this case!"

Silkey tried to explain. "It was a set-up. They beat and robbed him."

Then Pike turned to Dewey. "It's your fault. It's all your fault. You're nothing but a killer faggot."

Dewey said nothing. He just stood there, well-dressed, a tailored schoolboy with a big smirk on his face and a big strand of red hair covering one eye.

"We didn't lose the money; he hung onto it until we got here," Silkey lied. Dewey just stared back at Pike with an even bigger grin.

"Aren't you going to ask about the car?" I blurted out. "To see if there's any damage to a government vehicle? That's all you fucking care about, nickel-bag cases from broken-down junkies and protecting government cars and government money. You don't have the balls to go up against the Mafia like Michael and Dewey." I was shouting through the tears. "You don't give a fuck what happens to us – " Silkey gently kicked my leg and I stopped yelling and stared back at Pike.

"You'd better have the junk – or ten grand – on my desk in the morning," Pike said, turning away toward his car. Dewey just stood there with his smirk, still not saying a word.

My face was swollen, one eye was closed, and there was a four-inch gash on my cheek. Dewey and Silkey took me to Lennox Hospital for stitches then drove me home.

I kept the light off so Daisy couldn't see my face as I crawled into bed, but the next morning as she came out of the shower she saw me. "My God, my God, now what?" She covered her mouth so hard she slipped and almost fell on the bathroom floor. I assured her, "It's alright. Looks worse than it is. Got mugged trying to make a buy last night, it's okay." Mark came into the bathroom and stared at my swollen face. At least this time he didn't laugh.

At the office it was as if nothing had ever happened. Silkey wrote a report that said that an unknown drug dealer tried to rob me last night, but I wouldn't give up the ten thousand dollars of government money.

I had been beaten and almost killed, but it wasn't even mentioned in a report. Dewey took the ten thousand dollars out of his gambling stash and put it on Pike's desk to save my job.

Later, Tony Degaglia called. He said Dewey had told him what had happened. Tony said he didn't know Noodles and had no way to find him to get the money back. We agreed to meet for a drink later that afternoon at a bar on Beacon Street on the edge of Chinatown. I told Dewey that I was going to meet him.

I got to the bar early and sat at a table. My face was swollen so bad I could hardly drink and the vodka stung my cracked lips. My front teeth were loose and my gums kept bleeding. As I waited, someone came up from behind and gently placed his hand on my face, so softly I could hardly feel it. After a few seconds Michael removed his hand from my swollen face and gave me a half smile. Then he reached in his pocket and took something out and placed it on the table in front of me. Without saying a word he turned and walked out. It was an old egg timer, in the shape of a chicken with a white dial. It could have been an antique. I was in so much pain that the object had no meaning to me. I was on my second drink when Degaglia came in. He was shocked and sorry to see my face.

He began right away. "I swear I don't know Noodles, I can't help you. It's just the cost of doing business. I'll keep my eyes open, and sooner or later he'll turn up. Dewey said there was another guy. Did you see him?"

I didn't say anything. There was nothing to say. Tony ordered a drink and tried to change the conversation. Then he saw the egg timer on the table. He stared at it, blinking, then a strange look came over his face and he pleaded, "No, please God, no." He got to his feet and ran out of the bar as if something terrible was chasing him.

It was after midnight before I could track Dewey down. "What's with the egg timer?" I asked.

Dewey reached in his pocket and showed me two mug shots from the New York City police files. One was Noodles, and the other one was the guy hiding at the top of the stairs who hit me with the pipe.

I just shook my head in disbelief. "How?"

"Michael likes you, no one knows why. Tell me – why *does* Michael like you?"

I would never tell anyone why Michael protected me. I got back to Noodles. "How, Dewey? How did you find these guys so fast? What's with the egg timer?"

"You know how Michael gets when he wants answers right away. The timer belongs to Tony Degaglia's mother. You shouldn't have told Michael you had dinner over there."

I remembered the expression on Tony's face. I gasped in fear. "My God, what did Michael do to her?"

Dewey laughed. "Michael would never hurt anybody. He and

Greenway visited the old lady, told her they were from the Health Department and had to test her apartment for a contagious virus and that she had to leave right away or she might get sick and die. They put her up in a nice hotel for a few days. When Tony saw the egg timer he panicked. You know what Michael always says, 'If you're guilty you assume the worst.' When Tony rushed back to his mother's apartment, Silkey was waiting for him outside. The asshole was dumb enough to call Noodles from his mother's apartment. It was easy, we had the phone number, address, and he led us right to them."

Again Michael was ahead of everyone. "Dewey, Michael is dangerous, I don't care if he didn't hurt the mother, Michael is dangerous."

"You have no idea. If we don't get the money back right away, I'm betting even money that Michael's going to give the old lady a swimming lesson in the East River. If that happens, I've got three-to-one odds she'll make it. She only has to do about six feet to the dock, the water is a little cold and dirty, but she looks tough. How much can I put you down for? Silkey's in for thirty. The old lady is going to get wet. Michael is pissed. Noodles is Tony Degaglia's best friend, they grew up together. It's all up to Degaglia now – Mama or his best friend."

At about noon the next day Michael invited me to lunch. The last time he invited me to lunch he bought me a hot dog and told me to quit. Now he wanted to go on a picnic. Michael said he knew of a quiet place by the river on the Upper West Side under the highway. It was a little pocket park between the Hudson River and the elevated West Side Drive, very secluded, only two picnic tables. Michael brought a wicker basket of Italian sandwiches made with hard bread, ham, salami, cheese and fried peppers and a green bottle of wine. I knew Michael had something important to say. He sat down first, facing the river. I sat opposite, looking at the steel girders supporting the highway overhead.

Michael started, "How's your wife, your son...?" I knew he couldn't care less about my family and waited for the real purpose of our lunch. I saw a black car drive up and park about thirty yards away under the overpass of the West Side Drive. As Michael pulled a fried pepper from his sandwich, and I began nibbling through the hard roll with my swollen lips, two men got out of the car and opened the trunk. One of them was Tony Degaglia; the other was agent Ed Silkey. They dragged two men out of the trunk – Noodles and the guy who had hit me with the pipe. Their hands were cuffed behind their backs.

I tried to chew on my sandwich as Michael sipped his wine with his cold gray eyes staring at my cut and battered face. All the while, his back was to the car. He showed no emotion or acknowledgement of what was about to happen.

Ed Silkey threw the men on the ground. Degaglia knelt down and beat Noodles in the face with his fists. Then he beat the other guy with a belt and he kicked both of them while they lay on the ground. Degaglia got a baseball bat from the car and whacked their knees and elbows. At times Michael would stop his meaningless chatter for a moment because the screams and pleas for mercy were too loud to talk over.

Even though my teeth were still loose and bleeding, I couldn't stop gnawing at my sandwich as I watched one of the most horrible sights I had ever seen. Blood ran down my teeth onto the hard bread crust.

Still completely ignoring what was going on behind him, Michael said, "I'm glad you liked the sandwich; would you like mine? I've only eaten the peppers. The wine is excellent." He reached across the table with his napkin and dabbed away some blood on my lip.

TRUTH OR CONSEQUENCES

It took about six weeks for the stitches in my face to heal and begin to fade. During that time I sat in the office doing nothing – growing more restless with each day. Even more than the cocaine, I found I was addicted to the street – the excitement, the swagger, the danger. "Truth, Justice and the American Way" was slowly being replaced by "let's fuck up some bad guys today." I wanted back on the street. When Pike had a small case for me in the Bronx – just a couple hundred dollars, an easy buy – I jumped at it.

As Pike and I were talking to the informant, Michael came in and looked at me in a strange way. Then I heard him in Pike's office; "I don't give a fuck if it is an easy buy, he's not going back on the street, not till I say so; he does surveillance and drives me around." Then Michael came out of the office, looked at me and said, "Haven't you learned anything from the beating and LSD? You've got to take it easy for a while. Get the Benz; pick me up at Lorenzo's in thirty minutes."

I was humiliated. I deserved more respect, but no one ever went against Michael. The terrible truth was that Michael was right. I saw things differently. I wanted to get the Mafia more than ever, but now I was afraid of the street. I didn't want to get beat up again. I worried about what else was happening to me even though there were no more hallucinations and my eyes appeared normal.

That evening Michael took me to a club in Greenwich Village called the Showboat where I met Sally, a fat, effeminate, foppish homosexual. He either owned the club or had so much influence that he ran it. He was not on file as an informant for the Bureau but he traded information. If you wanted to know something you couldn't find in the library, you went to Sally. He would either know it or find out, but in return you had to give him something. Michael stopped by the Showboat to talk to Sally at least twice a week. I asked Michael how Sally knew so much. At first Michael answered, "Sally made a business of buying and selling information, that's all." But I wasn't convinced. Then Michael told me the truth: "Sally was once a spook for us, CIA agent overseas, a real party boy. He gave people drugs and whores, and once he got them hooked on coke then he gave them heroin. Then he controlled them; generals, politicians, their wives, their kids, Sally turned them all into spies – no information, no dope. He turned them all into his rats. The government paid him well and even helped him get the drugs and the women. But Sally partied too much...and after a while he *became* the party."

Michael smiled. "The ultimate undercover agent, he never came out, he partied – sex, booze, the whole trip – all to find Cold War secrets for his country. The government sold him out, gave him up, to get a Russian agent. It was just business. We were getting hurt somewhere else so we ratted him out. Everyone tried to kill him – us, the Russians, the Germans...Finally they gave up and he opened up a bar, but old habits die hard. He just keeps on going, one big party after another." Michael was on a roll. "Besides owning the nightclub, Sally is also a small-time drug dealer. He never touches drugs or sells them; he trades bags of heroin for information. If you're a heroin addict and strung out and don't have the money for a fix, you come to Sally. If you can give him information about your heroin connection or dealers in the neighborhood, Sally will give you a free bag of heroin. Or if you don't know anything, but need a fix, Sally will tell you what you must find out, just like the old days in Europe."

I looked at Michael and said, "I don't believe it. Junkies lie all the time, and they would certainly lie to get a free fix of heroin."

Now Michael was really enjoying the conversation. "You don't lie to Sally. You don't *ever* want to lie to Sally. Sally's still a spook in his own twisted mind. You see, here's the way it works. If you need a fix, you go to Sally. If he likes what you tell him, or if you find out things for him, he will give you a number."

"A number? What do you mean? Give you a number for what?"

"Washington Square Park is less than a block away from here. It's framed on all four sides by a black wrought-iron fence. When no one is looking, Sally's people tape little bags to the top of the steel bars. When addicts make deals with Sally, Sally gives them a number and they count the bars until they find their reward. For example, if Sally gives you the number thirty-five, you count thirty-five bars from the entrance and you find your reward. This way Sally doesn't take any risk in giving people drugs."

I shook my head. "I still don't get it. The addicts can lie to Sally, pick up their bag of heroin and off they go?"

Michael laughed. "No. No. It's not that easy. You see, not all the little bags hanging on the bars contain heroin. Some of them are bags of strychnine. If Sally believes you are telling the truth he will give you a number that has a bag of heroin taped to the bar.

If he thinks you're lying to him he will give you another number. You won't know the difference until you're shooting up, and then it's too late. If you lie to Sally you're dead. If you give him good information, you have a sweet reward until the next time."

Only Michael could think this was a good idea. I stared in silence, knowing it was all true. Everything had a price. It was business with Sally, like it always had been. Everyone was a welcomed customer. Death meant nothing.

PIRATES

Daisy was glad I was spending more time at home, beaten up or not. Of all the dragons that stalked me every day, loneliness was not one of them, but I knew it haunted her. Playing her clarinet in the park and raising Mark was not challenging enough for someone as smart as Daisy, but she was too loving and too loyal to give up on me. Eventually Daisy and I were able to joke about my first day on the job and she would still threaten to send me a fruit basket again if I didn't come home on time. She never stopped supporting me and pretended to believe the lies I told her about work. Seeing me hurt brought out great kindness and support. Her love and intelligence were the only beacon of light in my life, but I could feel them fading as I thought about going back to the street. My ambitious fight for truth, justice and the American way still burned inside of me, but I wondered if it wasn't just revenge against people like Mars La Pont.

One morning Dewey asked me to pick him up for a ride to work. Dewey had a family and lived in a brownstone in Far Rockaway, Queens. I beeped the horn a few times, and finally the front door opened and a woman waved me inside. She introduced herself as Maggie, Dewey's wife. I should have expected that she would be beautiful, wholesome, friendly, and intelligent. She had a deep voice, and a touch of arrogance like she was well-educated. I thought she would know who I was, but she didn't. When I told her that I was Dewey's partner, she seemed surprised. She was fixing breakfast for her sons; Maurice, six, and Dwight Junior, twelve. They both looked exactly like Dewey – or, perhaps even stranger, it was Dewey who looked exactly like the children.

As I waited with a cup of coffee, I saw some things on the living-room wall. One was a gold-embossed diploma from Annapolis, which noted that Dwight Paris was third in his class. I had heard that Dewey had come to the Bureau from Naval Intelligence and spoke several languages. I was still surprised to see a framed photograph of the deck of a ship. There were many rows of sailors in white uniforms, standing at attention, saluting, and at the center of the picture was the captain with short white hair, and burning blue eyes, standing at attention. Everyone was saluting one sailor, who was standing alone. His arm was halfway raised to answer the salute of the captain and his shipmates. The lone sailor was Dewey Paris. The caption read – "Dwight Paris and Captain Maurice Castlemann."

Dewey came into the room, tying his tie, and kissed his two sons and wife good-bye. The older son, Dwight Junior, followed us to the door and smiled bravely at his father, who messed up his hair as we left. I wondered why Dewey never mentioned that he graduated from Annapolis, or that he had a son named Dwight Junior, who looked just like him. But most curious of all was the picture of him on the ship deck, being honored by everybody.

When no one needed a ride, I would sleep late and just show up at the office in the afternoon and then bounce from bar to bar in Manhattan until after midnight. I usually drank alone because I looked so bad. I had let my hair grow long and had scars and bruises on my face. One night at about midnight at the El Hambra, the same bar where I had made my first case, someone called my name. I looked over to see a short man in a sport shirt. I didn't recognize him and couldn't believe anyone would recognize me in my condition. It was Elliott Goldstein, my first case, talking to me now. He had changed. He even appeared shorter. Elliott told me that he had been forced to make cases, that he had been beaten by the dealers, and that Pike sent him into impossible situations to find information and try to set people up, while constantly threatening him with prison. He had lost his family and his job, and now he was forced to peddle drugs just to stay alive and get closer to more dealers. He laughed at how bad I looked. He said he'd seen many faces just like mine. Incredibly, Elliott did not blame me for his troubles; he should not have been using cocaine. Elliott said I was like a pirate ship, strong and crashing through the waves, not knowing where to land next, or caring. I would always be okay. He said I was a true pirate, who would survive no matter what – or who got killed. Because I had no rules to stop me or even slow me down. I didn't really love or care about anyone. So nothing could ever get in the way of whatever I did. I would always survive. He looked at me with sadness and finished his drink and said, "I feel sorry for you," and walked out. I thought about Daisy and Mark. I began to realize that my lies to them held us together as a family. Michael had once said, "Your lies will become your reality. Lie all the time, it's good practice."

Michael thought I should relax for a few more days, so he introduced me to Charles DeWitt. DeWitt was an old black man with big hands and a wide grin. He seemed to be the kindest person I'd ever met – humble, polite, and sincere. DeWitt was a heroin addict but a great musician nonetheless. I went to see him at Count Basie's in Harlem. When I got to the club, there was a complimentary pass waiting for me. When it was Charlie's turn to perform, he stood up with his trumpet and played the most beautiful, soulful music I had ever heard. The crowd was stunned and gave him a big hand. DeWitt just sat down as if he was alone in the room. Afterwards, I saw him backstage and gave him a bundle of heroin bags that I'd taken from the evidence locker in the office. I could see the gratitude on his face. I knew I would become a regular at his gigs. Snorting cocaine had restored my self-confidence and then some, but I was still making stupid heroin buys for other people's cases. I wanted to make my own cases, not just get credit for them in Dewey's falsified reports.

CHAPTER FIVE

DANGEROUS LIAISONS

MANASSO

Edmond Manchester's life changed drastically after Domenic Scarluci and Lisa Marie were found in a pool of blood. His apparent double-dealing with Port Authority lockers, eleven keys of dope and mob money had placed him firmly within the clutches of 90 Church. The case against him remained open since he was now Dewey's informant. Dewey and I would hang out in his penthouse watching ball games on his TV. He became a nervous wreck anticipating what we would ask him to do next.

As usual, Dewey's use of Manchester's information was brilliant. His plans were never straight lines – always in circles. When Manchester told him that one of his drug couriers was Joe Angeleci, son of Aggi Angeleci – the Mafia Don who masterminded corruption of the Longshoreman's Union – Dewey began to spin his web.

It started as a "freak" minor traffic accident on the West Side Highway. Somebody rear-ended young Joe Angeleci and it turned into a fist fight. The cops came, searched both cars and – lo and behold – found a kilo of Manchester's heroin in Joe's car. Fortunately, Agent Silkey was just driving by and stopped to help. It was, of course, Dewey driving Pike's government car that rear-ended poor Joe. Pike tried to claim it was a major investigation. No one except Pike thought that all of this was all just a coincidence. Joe, only eighteen years old, was facing serious jail time.

Preying on the children of Mafia leaders never bothered Michael. Even the tragic deaths of Lisa Marie and her father were just, as Dewey said, "road kill." A couple days later I drove Dewey and Michael to a small restaurant in Long Island. Aggi Angeleci was sitting alone at a table in the corner. Dewey and Michael sat down at the table while I picked a stool at the bar nearby so I could listen. There were no greetings, Michael got to the point, "Too bad about Joe. Did I hear he was going to college?"

Aggi was a little overweight, but not the typical Mafia thug. He was intelligent and dressed like a banker. He didn't say anything; he just looked at Dewey's big grin with disgust.

A waiter came out of the kitchen, carrying a bottle of wine and a glass. He set the table for one, then he brought a plate of meat and cheese and placed it in front of Aggi. Dewey grabbed the only glass on the table and poured himself a glass of wine.

The mobster turned red and glared at Michael. "Let's get this over with."

A plate of rolls came out. Dewey grabbed them away from Aggi and started to make a sandwich. Michael smiled. I couldn't believe Dewey was eating the Mafia Don's lunch.

Finally Michael said, "Agent Silkey is very sloppy. His reports tend to be incomplete. I think he drinks too much. I've been meaning to talk to him. It could affect his testimony."

Aggi sat stone-faced and stared down at his lunch being devoured by what would have looked to him like a crazy smiling teenager who was already halfway through the bottle of wine.

Michael continued, "Joe needs to go to Syracuse University, not Attica. He'd make a good teacher, don't you think?"

Michael wrote a name on a napkin and pushed it across the table. Then he got up and said, "Thank you for seeing us. I know you're busy." Dewey wiped his chin and said, "Good wine, good cheese, but the rolls need less garlic." Dewey took the bottle of wine with him.

As we left I heard Aggi say, "You people go too far, you go too far. We have people who can reach you."

A few days later Michael received an "anonymous letter" with detailed information on a drug smuggler named Henri Manasso. It was the name Michael wrote on the napkin, the one originally provided by Edmond Manchester. The unsigned letter was sent, of course, by Aggi Angelici as part of his deal with Michael to save his son. It said Henri Manasso would be coming into the United States and that Customs should search him.

A week later Henri Manasso was arrested with ten kilos of uncut heroin when he entered the United States on a flight from Paris to Atlanta. Silkey received a letter of reprimand for reporting the wrong date in his arrest report and an improper search and seizure. Joe Angelici's case was dropped and he was off to college.

Michael and I interviewed Henri Manasso with George Blanker. Half French and half Cuban, Manasso looked like a weightlifter dressed in a silk business suit. He had cold staring eyes, manicured nails, and a gold bracelet around his wrist that was too tight to be removed. Manasso's file showed that he had military training by the U.S. government and at one time was a CIA operative. He smiled at us like we were children.

Michael explained the deal. If he worked with us and made cases in the United States and Europe we would forget about the smuggling and he would go free.

Manasso grinned at Michael, and said, "You expect me to trust that? I never break my word, although I know you'll break yours. Nevertheless, I propose that I walk out of here and come back in two weeks to make a deal. Or I'll stand trial."

Michael said, "Okay. Good-bye, see you in two weeks."

Manasso got up, put his hand on my shoulder and squeezed gently, then walked out the door.

Blanker was so angry his face turned redder than normal and he banged his fists on the table. "How can you trust him? You can't *do* this! How do you know he'll come back?"

"Because," Michael said, "he has something we don't have: integrity."

During the meeting Dewey had gone through Manasso's luggage and made photocopies of all his cards and papers. Michael looked at a business card and said, "He has a connection in Atlanta; it's probably his lawyer, named Caldwell. Let's hold on to this and find out."

RACHEL

Only Michael and Dewey expected Manasso to return. Everyone else, including me, thought he was long gone to South America. I tailored my suits, bought fancy boots and slicked back my hair.

With four lines of coke each day my confidence grew. I wanted my own case, this case. Everyone could see that Manasso liked me.

About a week and a half after interviewing Manasso I went to Greenwich Village to meet Agents Louie Gomez and Jerry Ramirez at the Showboat. Sally, Michael's ex-CIA snitch, was behind the bar and greeted me. Jerry was waiting for me. He had just finished a heroin buy with Louie in Spanish Harlem. Louie was farther down the bar trying to make it with a hot-looking Puerto Rican girl. While Jerry was not part of the Heidelberg meetings, he was a good undercover agent. However, because he didn't have the help of agents like Dewey and Michael, Jerry's cases were small nickel-bag buys – but still very dangerous because of the likelihood of being robbed.

After a couple of drinks Jerry told me he was unhappy and thinking about resigning. "My wife can't stand the job and I'm going nowhere. All I get are small cases. That's all Pike and Blanker want, numbers! And you, you're everyone's hero. After pissing your pants and freezing on your first buy, we thought you'd be gone, everyone laughed at you. *Now* look at you, a big-shot agent – making big cases, going undercover all the time against the big guys."

"Who laughed at me?"

"Pike, Louie, me, Blanker, everyone; it was funny when you pissed your pants."

"What about Dewey and Michael? Did they laugh, too?"

"Michael didn't laugh; he saved your job. Dewey didn't laugh either; strange, he laughs at everything, but he didn't laugh at you. Michael protects you – no one knows why. We know why Michael likes Dewey. Dewey is a homicidal maniac and the best shot in the

Bureau. Michael uses Dewey for protection."

Jerry stared down into his drink as he continued. "No, Michael and Dewey didn't laugh at you pissing your pants, and I shouldn't have either. You were right to not sign the reports about the shooting. They were just trying to get Dewey. In the end, you stood up and told the truth, you wouldn't lie on a government report. Everybody respects you for that. You're an example of what a federal agent should be. I think Michael takes care of you because you stand up for the truth. I try to be like you. Look at this." Jerry pulled back his suit jacket to show his gun tucked into his pants. It was exactly like mine, a blue-chrome Walther PPK with pearl grips. "I'm sorry I haven't been a better friend...and I hope we work some cases together."

Before I could answer, Louie caused a scene at the bar. His girlfriend tried to hit him. He twisted her arm behind her back and dragged her out the door. I'd seen this before; he was going to fuck her in the back of the government car and in a half hour they'd be back – laughing, dancing, and all over each other like young lovers.

Jerry looked at me with disgust, shook his head. "That's it, I'm out of here. I meant what I said. I trust you, I'd like to work with you, just give me a chance."

I watched him walk out the door as I sat alone at the bar. Daisy had taken Mark to Chicago to visit her parents. She had called last night to say she was going to stay another week. I could still hear her voice in my ears, asking how I was, genuinely concerned. "I'm fine," I had said. "How's Mark?"

"He's fine," she said. "He asks about you."

For a split second I imagined just leaving, going to meet her in Chicago and starting over, leaving the job like Jerry. Then I heard a woman's voice say to me, "Everyone knows who you are." She had come up from behind me and sat on the stool next to me. "Agent or not, I wouldn't let anyone treat me like that. Who do you people think you are?"

"Do you know what they're doing right now?" I asked.

"Yes," she answered coldly. She was thin and tall with straight, shiny black hair. She wore black high-heeled boots that reached her knees, a black miniskirt and jacket with a white silk shirt open halfway down her chest, and red manicured nails. She was brazen, no-holds-barred, street sexy, but her eyes captured me – deep, dark, like the shiny black bandit look of a raccoon.

She held her head high and spoke in a low raspy voice. "Everyone knows you. You and your agents come in here to drink and brag about your cases, and I know how undercover agent Louie the G treats his girls. You're from 90 Church, aren't you? Come here to play and show off and fuck the hot Spanish girls." Despite her words, her tone was friendly and inviting.

"You're right, we're 90 Church and there aren't too many bars in this town where we can relax."

She smiled with perfect white teeth. "I'm sure you're right. Do you want to dance?"

The moment we touched, we both knew. We didn't talk much. We just stared into each other's eyes, my scarred face and her dark pools of hidden light. Her name was Rachel. She was a legal secretary and a translator with an international law firm on Park Avenue. Besides perfect English, she spoke French and Spanish. She had come with her boss, who left with another girl, so she was alone. We danced and drank for about an hour. Then she asked me to drive her home.

She lived in Riverdale, on the Yonkers border. I parked the car and she invited me up. Her apartment was lavish, with red leather couches and bright paintings and mirrors. The bedroom was all white with dark blue wall trim. There was a big bed with fluffy pillows. A pair of long black stockings was laid out on the top of the bed. It was the only item that was out of place in the entire apartment. As her outstretched arms presented the last room, she said, "Well, do you like it? And yes, I always keep it this neat. What would you like to drink?"

"You and only you," I answered as I took my jacket off. She looked at the bright blue automatic in the black leather holster under my armpit and said, "Would you mind? I think you'll be safe here. Why don't you put it with your jacket?"

I took the holster off and rolled it in my jacket on a kitchen chair as she fixed herself a vodka tonic. "I don't bring people here. I can't believe I brought you. You're a stranger and this is my private place."

I gently held the back of her neck and drew her to me and we kissed. She blushed, but I made her kiss me again, longer and harder. She hugged me and with our arms around each other we walked into the bedroom. At the side of the bed we stopped and kissed even harder, our tongues inside each other. Then she reached inside my pants, inside my underwear and grabbed my balls. She whispered in my ear, "All off, all off, everything. I have control of you now." I began to undress as she held on, squeezing even harder if I slowed down. In just a few minutes I was naked and she was still squeezing; now it hurt, and I was starting to double over.

"So what do you think comes next?" Her tone was different,

harder. "You think I'm like the others, like Louie's girls? Buy her a few drinks and fuck her, then good-bye till next time? Is that it?"

She pushed me. I lost my balance and fell on the floor. I lay there on the floor naked and embarrassed. She laughed. "You'll never have me. Look at you, naked at my feet. I would *never* let you fuck me, *never!*"

As I started to get up, she pushed her boot on my neck, forcing me back to the floor. "Stop," I said. "I thought – "

"Stay on the floor where you belong. You *thought*? You thought *what*? That I *wanted* to fuck you? I'd have to be tied and helpless! You're not man enough for me! Now get your clothes on and get *out*, go find yourself a weak whore you can slap around." Then she pushed her foot harder on my neck.

When she took her boot off my neck I exploded. Leaping up, I shoved her down on the bed and got on top of her. She fought back but I managed to tie her wrists to the bed rails with the black stockings. Then I began tearing off her clothes. She screamed and fought, twisting and kicking, but I unbuttoned her blouse and pulled her jacket and blouse up her arms to her wrists. Then I wrestled her kicking legs, trying to undo her skirt. She was crying and biting me, pleading for me to stop, but I kept on. I found the snaps for her skirt and yanked it with her panties down over her knees and boots and flung them across the room, then I stepped back, shocked by my own behavior.

She was flat on her stomach, trying to hide her breasts, wearing only her black suede high-heeled boots. She lifted her head just enough to talk through her long hair, which covered most of her tear-streaked face and eyes. "Please don't do this. I'm sorry for what I said. I don't want this. Neither do you, not like this. Please don't hurt me, let me go." She buried her face, crying.

I couldn't believe things had gotten so far out of hand. Now I was ashamed. "Okay," I whispered, "I'm sorry too." As I moved toward her, reaching for the stockings around her wrists, she reared up on her knees and back-kicked me with her boot as hard as she could. Her high heel dug into my naked thigh, ripping through the skin and drawing blood. I lost my balance and fell down on one knee, holding the wound. Groaning in pain, I looked up at her tear-streaked face and her smile of satisfaction as she yanked on the black stockings, trying to get free.

Raging out of control, I leaped on top of her, pushed her kicking legs aside and twisted her half over. I dug my face between her thighs, held on as hard as I could, and began licking. She fought back with all the strength and energy she had, bucking, kicking, twisting, crying. I held on with everything I had, licking harder and deeper. We rolled and bounced, fighting each other until she was so exhausted that she struggled to breathe. I could hardly hold on but then she finally stopped and lay motionless. We were both covered in sweat, and my tongue was aching.

I slid my face up her stomach to find her mouth. I untied the stockings, as she raised herself and guided me into her. Stronger than any heroin, I was hooked on her and she knew it.

SENIOR AGENT

I took a vacation day and came back to Rachel's apartment the next morning. Despite our truly bizarre first encounter we were in love. Our sex was passionate, not the constant stream of jokes and gags that I was used to with Daisy. Her sophistication and deep understanding was something I had never encountered before. She knew the complex dilemma I faced every day when I betrayed people while working undercover. I told her about Michael and Dewey and how I was losing all sense of what was right or wrong.

We walked at night in Central Park through the cold dark footpaths. She had what Daisy could not give me: complete acceptance for what I was. It was okay that Dewey and Michael used me and that I was not quite strong enough to stand up to the corruption at 90 Church. But as she said, my day was coming, I needed to be ready.

Two weeks from the day that we first met Manasso, and four days after meeting Rachael, I heard arguing in the office. George Blanker had just left the discussion and passed me as I came in to Group Two. Michael was yelling, "You're going to get him killed! This is wrong. Can't you see it?"

They stopped when they saw me. I sensed they were talking about me. I asked what was going on. Pike said, "It's Manasso. True to his word, he came in to see us this morning. He wants to make a deal. He'll give us five major cases, and twenty kilos, but no overseas connections and, above all, no independent cases on any of his associates. And he will not testify. We have to make the court cases without him."

"That's great," I said. "That's incredible. He can do all that."

Then Michael said, "Listen carefully, there's one condition. He wants to work with you and only you, exclusively."

"Me? I only met him once."

"Don't you *see?*" Michael yelled at Pike. "He's picked the most inexperienced, weakest agent out of our first meeting so he can control everything."

Insulted, I said, "I can handle him."

"You don't know what you're talking about," Michael shot back. "Look at the man's record. He eats assholes like you for lunch. Dewey says he's totally independent. He's smart, he's savvy, he's connected, he's trained, and he's an international killer. He will find a way to beat us."

"What did Blanker say?" I asked.

"Blanker doesn't even *know* you," Michael said. "Blanker just wants nickel bags off the street with his meatball cases. He doesn't give a fuck about you."

"Michael, give me a chance," I pleaded. "I'll work with you every step, not like the Noodles case. I won't be alone. We can win here; let him and everyone else think I'm running the show. It'll give us an advantage."

Michael stared down at the floor and said, "You don't understand. When he came in this morning I studied him through the mirror for about fifteen minutes. He's the most dangerous man I've ever seen. He's going to kill us all."

"No, he won't. He's just another bad guy. We can handle him. If you don't let me do it I'll go to Blanker."

Michael shook his head, and handed me a telephone number. "Call him, but remember his deal."

I met Manasso alone at a French restaurant in midtown that same day. He didn't pat me down for a body wire or look around to see if we were being watched. He shook my hand and ordered lunch for both of us, speaking in French to the waiter. Finally I asked why he chose me to work with.

"It's very simple." He smiled. "Your agent, Pike, is a sadistic buffoon. Your senior agent, Blanker, is a hopeless alcoholic.

Michael Giovanni is very dangerous, very dangerous indeed. He's used to betraying people. He does it every day. He can't be trusted; his craft is deception. You are young, intelligent – but above all, you are honorable. You'll keep your word and our deal. I trust you. You're always searching for what is right." I felt proud of myself. I couldn't wait to tell Rachel.

The next day the whole office knew that Manasso had chosen me. Blanker called me into his office and said I could work with anyone I wanted, and have any resource – money, surveillance, taps, hotel suites – I needed. This was a big opportunity for the Bureau: at least twenty kilos of heroin. Blanker said he had confidence in me although I knew he couldn't remember my name until yesterday. I told Blanker I wanted Dewey Paris, Jerry Ramirez, Ed Silkey, and Michael to help me. I knew he hated Michael and Dewey, but he reluctantly agreed. Everything they were working on would be put on hold, to await my orders. They were all working for me now. Dewey, Michael and I met privately in a small conference room to plan our strategy. Michael asked Dewey. "What have your file toads dug up on our man?"

Dewey thumbed through a thin file. "Not much, only at this point that he sells heroin to a lawyer named Caldwell in Atlanta. Manasso was carrying his business card, for Christ's sake! Caldwell doesn't have a record, but he's all over the local wiretap chatter. I think he's harmless, but he hires some nasty hillbillies to do his dirty work and take all the risks. I don't think Atlanta is worth our time."

Michael agreed. "You're probably right, and we made a deal with Manasso: no cases on his associates. Let's stick to the deal. No Atlanta."

I argued. "Why not send Jerry Ramirez down to Atlanta to try to make a case on Caldwell?" I was hoping I could get Jerry in on a big case. "It's all we've got going and we need something."

Michael looked at Dewey, who just shrugged, then he said, "Okay, but you're already breaking the deal with Manasso, and Jerry Ramirez is small-time." Michael looked at me. "This is on you. Ramirez is over his head. This is two wrongs in a row."

That night, Rachel and I celebrated. She was proud of me. I told her about Manasso's lunch, how sophisticated and strong he was, and that I knew we were going to make major cases because he trusted me. I told her that for the first time Dewey and Michael were listening to me, actually doing what I asked, like giving Jerry Ramirez a chance to make a case on Caldwell, Manasso's lawyer in Atlanta.

The next morning Rachel took me shopping. First I bought bright silk shirts and several tailored suits, then a pair of burgundy red boots. Most outrageous of all, she bought me a black cape with leather trim. Now she said, "You look the part of a senior agent, an undercover agent and most importantly, you out-dress Manasso."

As we walked along Fifth Avenue with the winter wind blowing in our faces she pushed me against a building and kissed me; her nose was cold. Then she said, "I know you're a coke addict. If you want my love you must stop. I will help you, but you must trust me. Every day you will do one taste less."

THE DIPLOMAT

Three days later Manasso called and asked that I meet him at the Plaza Hotel for lunch, and would I please wear a shirt and tie, since he didn't like the open casual look of my appearance. We both arrived on time. He wore a grey pin-striped suit, blue shirt and gold tie. Dewey would have been jealous. I wore my new burgundy boots, blue suit and red shirt, but no tie. Manasso was impressed and got down to business. He knew of a diplomat who was carrying five kilos of heroin coming in from South America. I said it was unusual that he would be carrying heroin and not cocaine. He answered, "Money is money. Detours are safe. He's being paid to courier it."

"Who's the customer?"

He looked down at his plate and then looked up and said, "John Belonconi."

Belonconi was one of the biggest drug lords in New York City. He was all over our files. No one had been able to touch him, although everyone had tried. No one understood how he got his shipments from Italy. Now I did.

"How do you know this?" I asked.

"That's not the deal. Your job is to take the information and make a case."

"What information? You haven't given me anything yet."

He then took a slip of paper from his pocket. There was a Spanish name on it with an airline flight number and date and time of arrival. "Fernando, the courier, will be staying across the street at the Sherry Netherlands. He'll be in town for only a week. You've got to make the case right away. He comes in day after tomorrow."

It didn't take Michael and Dewey long to figure out a strategy. The Bureau had a taxicab in the carpool for surveillance purposes.

Fernando would be arriving through airport customs at 3:30 in the afternoon. Pike and the other agents stacked and controlled the cab line so Silkey, driving the Bureau's cab, was sure to pick him up at the airport and take him to his hotel. The plan was simple: Dewey would be dressed as the bellman at the hotel. When the cab pulled up, Silkey would open the trunk and take out Fernando's luggage. He would not place it on the sidewalk, but on the other side of the cab, in the street. Another cab, driven by agent Greenway, would pull up and run over the luggage. Greenway and Silkey would then have a big argument and attract a policeman – Michael in a cop's uniform – and then Dewey, dressed as a bellman, would try to straighten out the argument and pick up the crushed suitcase and, as its contents spilled out, find the drugs.

According to plan, Silkey picked up Fernando from the airport, driving the first cab. Greenway followed in his cab all the way to where Silkey parked in front of the hotel. Fernando had only one suitcase. The moment Dewey, dressed liked a bellman, put it in the street, Greenway pulled out and hit the suitcase, driving over it with both front and back wheels, cracking it wide open. Greenway and Silkey started yelling at each other, creating a scene, blaming each other for the crushed – and now wide-open – suitcase. Michael and Dewey rushed over to pick up the broken suitcase. Dewey found the five bags of heroin. The sting went down perfectly.

The whole scene seemed too easy. Dewey found the kilos of heroin in the suitcase immediately and showed them to Michael, bragging how this was now his case. But Pike moved in and pushed Dewey aside, almost knocking him down and grabbing the evidence. Pike did not trust Dewey or Michael, and after what I had seen Dewey do with the heroin in the Scarluci case, neither did

I. Pike told Dewey to take the broken suitcase and scattered clothes back to the Bureau while he took charge and initialed the bags of white powder. Pike put the five bags in his briefcase.

Pike and I interviewed Fernando. He honestly believed that the whole thing was a freak accident. We had five kilos of higher-grade heroin. Fernando sat there shaking with fright. Pike said politely, "Don't worry about a thing. Take your suitcase and clothes and go back to the hotel. We don't want any embarrassments here. If you cooperate with us, no one will know anything and you'll be back home in a short time. We just want your customer. We'll come and visit you tomorrow." But then Fernando's lawyer walked in the room, claimed diplomatic immunity and demanded his release.

The case against Fernando was coming apart fast. I didn't know what to do. Pike called Blanker into the room to help. He apologized for the arrest and said Fernando could leave.

Then he screamed at us, "Who had possession of the junk?"

Pike replied proudly, "I took immediate possession of it when Dewey and Michael found it in the suitcase in the street. I saw the whole thing go down, I had sole possession."

Blanker turned red with anger. "You imbecile! There *is* no *heroin*. All five kilos are talcum powder. It was a set-up. Get Michael in here *now*."

Michael came in, calmly smoking a cigarette, and Blanker told him what happened. Then Michael said, "Who thought we could make a case on a diplomat in the first place? Obviously the heroin has *already* been delivered to Belonconi; the talcum powder was a decoy. Manasso is playing us."

"Now what?" I asked, realizing that once again my case was out of control and that I needed Michael's help.

"Who *gives* a fuck about a meatball diplomat named Fernando?" Michael said, losing his patience with me. "You want Belonconi? Take Silkey and go to Fernando's hotel and listen in on his phone conversations." He turned to Blanker. "You have enough to get a warrant for the hotel phone tap, you have an informant, Belonconi's phone number in Fernando's address book, and now the decoy phony kilos. Fernando's your informant. Diplomats don't go to jail, but make good rats. They're supposed to tell the truth. From the wiretap we'll get a search warrant for Belonconi's restaurant and make a case."

There was stunned silence. Once again Michael's lightning-quick genius was going to save a very damaged case. His emergency plan was brilliant. Ed Silkey and I went back to the hotel while Blanker filed for the wiretap on Fernando's phone.

As Silkey and I were leaving the office to tap Fernando's hotel phone, Michael called me aside. "Blanker wants me to stay here and help write up the search warrant. If you get lucky with the taps, we won't have much time. I have a date tonight and she's waiting for me at the bar at the Blue Angel, just two blocks over from the Sherry Netherland. Would you give her this from me?" Michael handed me an elegant shopping bag with three gift-wrapped boxes in it. The bag and gifts all had Saks Fifth Avenue logos and blue ribbons. Never, until now, did I have a chance to learn anything personal about Michael. I was curious to meet his girlfriend, even if it just was to apologize for him.

Silkey waited in the car outside the Blue Angel as I carried the Saks gift bag in to meet Michael's date. I had no trouble spotting her. She was middle-aged, hard-looking, blonde, wearing a tight, white sequined dress. I walked up to her and said, "Here, I think these gifts are for you," and handed her the Saks bag.

She looked at me through her cigarette smoke and smiled, "Oh thank you, they're beautiful. You're so sweet. Are you Michael?"

Silkey and I sat at the hotel operator's desk all night to intercept any phone calls in or out of Fernando's room. Pike also set up surveillance around the hotel to make sure that Fernando didn't leave. The next morning Fernando called Belonconi and told him he was leaving town, things were too hot. That was all we needed for a search warrant for Belonconi's restaurant.

We waited until we saw John Belonconi enter his restaurant in the Bronx and then went in, Pike and Silkey crashing through the front door. We caught Belonconi with the five kilos of heroin and three other Mafia figures. It was the biggest case in years. The papers would refer to it as the "Diplomat Case."

The next day I returned Fernando's passport and made arrangements for him to leave the country. I told Silkey to pick him up at the Sherry Netherland and drive him to the airport. Outside the hotel someone walked up behind the car and shot Fernando in the head, blowing his brains all over the inside of the car. Silkey was covered with Fernando's blood but never saw a thing.

Despite Fernando's death, everyone was pleased with the case. We had caught a high-level Mafia leader and once again neither Michael nor Dewey were mentioned in the report. But I had questions: How did Manasso know about Fernando unless it was Manasso's drugs? How did Fernando get the heroin to Belonconi? And how did the killer know when Fernando was leaving for the airport? Why did Michael's date ask me if I was Michael?

Rachel said there was no way that Manasso could learn on his own when Fernando was leaving town. Someone in the Bureau told him that I asked Silkey to drive him the next day. We both knew Michael and Dewey were behind everything. I'd seen this all before and was angry about the whole case – yet John Belonconi, a major crime boss, was facing twenty years in prison, and five kilos of heroin were off the street. But, at last, I was a senior agent and the other agents respected me.

CIRCLES

Now I was a hero at the Bureau, and I couldn't wait for the next case Manasso would bring to me. I was staying over at Rachel's apartment at least three times a week and telling Daisy that I was bunking in the office because I was working after-hours clubs. Rachel and I always had dinner together every night, no matter what I was working on. A couple of times a week we would go to disco clubs and dance all night. We would talk for hours about Michael, Dewey, Manasso and the Bureau. I told her about the time I tried to cut my foot off. Her step-by-step method of getting me off cocaine was working. I was down to two snorts a day. She was also dedicated to her job, and often I would hear her talking on the phone to different lawyers, speaking in French or Spanish. She was so beautiful and smart that I knew her influence at work was far more than a legal secretary. Her family was in France and we made plans to visit them in the summer.

Oddly, my home life improved because of Rachel. I had stopped making love to Daisy months ago but we always had pleasant weekends with Mark. Daisy never stopped loving me; it was just that we had become lost to each other. She waited for me to quit, and bravely fought her loneliness. She never asked about my drinking, or bad moods, or troubles at the office. She just didn't want to know because she couldn't help me.

I waited for weeks for Manasso to surface. Then I came into the office one afternoon. Everyone had already gone except Pike and his secretary. I could see she'd been crying; her eyes were red. On the desk was an eight-by-ten glossy black-and-white photograph. It had been taken from a helicopter or someplace high up. It was a picture of a wheat field or tall grass. The grass was trampled down in a circular footpath that went around and around, growing smaller and smaller, curling in on itself until it stopped in the center. Something lay in the center of the circles. I could see a leg sticking out of the grass, but that was all. I asked the secretary what was wrong, but she was too upset to talk. Pike told her to go home. He said it was pretty rough on her, she'd been crying all morning.

Again, I asked what was wrong. I was holding the photo in my hand when Pike said, "I guess you haven't heard. Jerry Ramirez went down. That's him in the photograph. They shot him in the back of the head with a 22-caliber. It fucked him up so bad he couldn't stand up. All he could do was crawl. I guess he tried to crawl away. He ended up crawling through the grass all night, but he was crawling in circles...then he died."

I stared at the circles in the photograph, trying not to imagine what it was like and how long it took Jerry to die. Pike said it was Agent Jack Connors's case in Atlanta. There was a shoot-out and the drug dealer, who had killed Jerry, was already dead. Jack Connors was a good street agent, tough and smart. All of his cases were well-organized and professional. Jerry Ramirez was following up on the Manasso case and trying to get close to Caldwell. If Connors said the killer was dead, Jerry's killer was dead.

It was not easy to say good-bye to Jerry Ramirez. I kept remembering Michael's words to me: "It's on you. Ramirez is in over his head."

The funeral was held in Brooklyn and the whole Bureau showed up. Blanker gave a wonderful eulogy about service to God, country, family, and everlasting memories. Everyone was in tears except Jerry's widow and his two children. She was so medicated she just stared into space and his two children were so young that during the service they rolled a ball between the rows of chairs and chased after it.

There were so many people that Jerry's parents held a private wake for just the immediate family. Daisy and I went home and took Mark for a walk in the park for the rest of the afternoon. It was a very sad day and I made it worse. Instead of saying that I was glad to see them, I said, "I want a divorce."

Daisy was zipping up Mark's jacket and pretended not to hear. She held his hand as he walked alongside her. Then she said, "I'm sorry, I don't know you, you seem familiar. Have we met before?" Then tears rolled down her cheeks.

We walked on through the park, stopping every few yards to let Mark play or look at the ducks in the pond. Then she said, "You don't realize what you've become. You don't trust anyone, certainly not me. You think everyone is against you. I used to be afraid you'd get hurt or killed, like Agent Ramirez...but now it's something worse. You're hollow, there's nothing inside you...I'm so lonely I can't stand it." She walked over to a tree and tried to hold it for support, but her face slid down the rough bark as she sobbed, falling to her knees, touching the scratches on her face.

I grabbed Mark and walked ahead a few yards to give her privacy, then waited. After a few minutes she caught up with us, wiping her eyes, and said, "I think it's a good thing. I can't stand waiting for you every night, and when you come home you're dead inside." I moved in with Rachel that night.

WINTER'S NIGHT

Rachel welcomed me into her life. In three months she knew more about me than Daisy knew after five years of marriage. It wasn't Daisy's fault. In fact, she was right about me coming home dead inside. But I felt alive with Rachel. She understood me – understood what was important to me. She knew what the Manasso case meant to me now, and she encouraged me to come out of it a winner.

Manasso called and we had lunch at the Plaza again. He told me about an electronics store on Canal Street, only five blocks from our office. They would be receiving a shipment of television sets whose cathode tubes contained heroin. He gave me the name of a longshoreman who would be picking up the TV sets once they cleared Customs. During lunch Manasso seemed to be less friendly than usual and he took more thought in choosing his words. He never mentioned the Diplomat Case until we were through eating. "Chabrier did not have to die," he said flatly.

"Who's Chabrier?"

"You plant bags of talcum powder on a man and allow him to get his brains blown out and you neglect to ask his name?" he replied. "I chose you because I thought you were principled, but you're proving to be a disappointment. Our deal was very simple;

twenty kilos of heroin and no independent cases on my associates. I thought I was very clear on these two things. Be very careful, my young friend. Life is a balance sheet; mark well your accounts payable."

He handed me a piece of paper with all the information I would need for the next case, then paid the lunch bill and walked out.

We put the electronics store under surveillance. I worked on the docks as a longshoreman for three days before the shipment arrived. From the docks to the store, we used Dewey's favorite stunt; we arranged a street accident and grabbed the shipment. The problem was that we had nothing on the electronics dealer. He had simply ordered a shipment of TV sets. We had the drugs, but the dockworker claimed to be innocent and we couldn't prosecute him because Manasso wouldn't testify. Five kilos of heroin were off the street but we had no defendant, and no case.

Nevertheless, Blanker and Pike were pleased and I remained the office hero with my kilo-size cases. Michael again complained that somehow Manasso was manipulating the shipments and setting people up. He argued that the retailer truly didn't know what was in the TV sets and that someone knew we were going to intercept them at the dock – and set the dockworker up for the bust. Worse than all of that, Michael said Manasso was buying his way out of jail with his own heroin. I knew he was right.

My withdrawal from cocaine, thanks to Rachel's help, was progressing very well. I was down to only a line every other day. I knew the addiction was mental so my cure depended on Rachel's love and encouragement. She was my coach to being a senior agent. Rachel reminded me that it was more important to follow the law than catch criminals. Someday I would clean up 90 Church, not as an informer but as a leader. I looked into her dark eyes and became more determined every day.

Manasso's third case was a straight buy: ten kilos of pure high-grade heroin. The Bureau gave me $50,000 for the buy. This time Manasso called a New Jersey drug dealer named Carlos and made arrangements, telling him that I was Mafia, trying to make a deal direct without sharing with my boss. The buy was to take place in a bar in Greenwich Village. I met Carlos at a bar on Houston Street in lower Manhattan. I easily convinced him of my Mafia cover story. The arrangement was that I go to his car to inspect the heroin, and then Carlos would go to my car and look at the money. Then we would swap car keys, so no one would see the exchange. My car, with the money, had a radio device so we could follow it. We all knew from my previous phone conversations with Carlos that he was coming from uptown Manhattan and we assumed he would be returning in the same direction. We had surveillance cars in a four-block radius ready to follow him up the West Side.

Two things went seriously wrong. Carlos didn't like my car, and didn't care who saw us. He wanted to keep his own car, so he gave me the suitcase of heroin in the street and I gave him the money, knowing we could still follow him as he drove back to his drug source, but he drove in the opposite direction and headed for the Holland Tunnel. Two of the surveillance cars moved in on the pursuit, with Silkey in the lead car. But by the time they got to the Tunnel, Silkey was two cars behind Carlos. In the middle of the Tunnel, Carlos jammed on his brakes and slid his car sideways, blocking both lanes. He then jumped out, carrying the money, got into another car in front of him that had stopped and was waiting for him. Then he continued on – leaving the tunnel completely blocked with his abandoned car. We had the drugs, ten kilos of heroin, but Carlos had escaped into New Jersey with the money – and we had no leads on how to find him since the car he was driving was stolen. The case was a complete disaster. Once again Manasso had outsmarted us, giving us exactly what he promised – kilos of heroin, now up to the agreed twenty kilos. The only good case was against Belonconi and that was only because of Michael's quick thinking.

When I told Rachel what had happened, she couldn't believe it. We'd planned this operation for a week. Now I began to think that someone besides Michael was controlling things from the inside. At first I thought it was Silkey. Silkey was in the car with Fernando and could have set up the killing outside the hotel. He might also have deliberately lost Carlos in the tunnel. Silkey knew everything and had been in the right place when things went wrong. The problem was that Silkey wasn't smart enough, and would never betray Michael. Then I thought about Pike, but he wasn't any smarter than Silkey. Blanker could have done it, but would need help from the other agents. As I thought about it, it seemed to me that only Michael would be smart enough to cast doubt on Manasso, while working from the inside. It all came down to Michael making a deal with Manasso. Only Michael would have the guts to arrange for Fernando to get murdered; he had done it before with Stuckey. Rachel warned me to be careful and trust no one. She said I had to find out who was corrupting the cases and expose them. It was my duty as a senior agent and it would be a defining moment in my career. She said I had to be brave and keep investigating, but I could see the fear in her beautiful dark eyes.

Blanker and Pike, who had been so proud of my work, now

openly criticized me, calling me a "novice" and "out of control". They said Manasso had not acted in good faith even though the kilo count was what Manasso had promised; they believed that the cases had been set up to protect the drug source, which was Manasso. I reminded them that I had made a case on John Belonconi, one of the biggest Mafia kingpins in New York. I argued that shortcomings in the cases were not Manasso's fault but ours, and maybe we would find Carlos. They didn't care. They said Manasso was a dope dealer and that deals with criminals didn't count. He would either come clean with all of his sources in Europe and the United States or he would go to jail and the Bureau would tell everyone, including Belonconi, that Manasso was the informant in all three cases. I insisted that this was wrong; we were breaking our agreement, but they wouldn't listen. They gave me five days to bring Manasso in. I wondered what Michael would do next.

Rachel shared my outrage and disappointment. I would have to betray Manasso. It was wrong, but I had no choice. We knew Michael was behind everything, but there was nothing I could do. Michael was too smart.

Rachel laid her head on my chest. "You can't do everything yourself; the Bureau should have helped you control the cases better. They're weak, they let an evil drunk like Michael manipulate things and steal money. You must be strong and do what's right. In the end good always wins."

Rachel was right and I knew it. She was right about Manasso and my whole life. I was too weak to stand up against Michael and the Bureau. From my first day as an agent I knew things were wrong. I should have stood up then; now too much had happened.

"I can't," I confessed. "I can't go against everybody, I can't do it.

Please understand. There is no one to turn to, no one can help me."

"I understand. I love you. Do what you must do to survive. We'll work it out. To survive you must pick the best time to stand up for what's right. You will know when."

The next day Manasso called me. He asked that I meet him alone in the Bronx. He named a good Italian restaurant in a bad area. I said I'd meet him there at 9:30 p.m. Dewey had loaned his car to Silkey, so I said he could take mine after I met Manasso. After the meeting I would take a cab to Rachel's apartment in Riverdale. We had planned Christmas dinner.

It was a cold bitter December night when Dewey and I drove to the Bronx. The snow was beginning to cover the sidewalks and street. As we pulled up in front of the restaurant, the windshield shattered from gunfire. We ducked below and huddled on the floor. Dewey pulled out his forty-five and smashed the dome light. More shots came crashing in at us from a vacant lot next to the restaurant. "Stay in the car until I tell you to get out!" Dewey screamed. "Then go forward, to the front." He opened the driver's side door; the car remained dark. He crawled out onto the cold street on his hands and knees. The bullets kept smashing into the car, ripping open the dash. Dewey scrambled past a parked car to the edge of the building next to the lot. I saw him wave me forward. I got out and crawled to the front of the car. With my head down I stuck my gun over the fender and took wild shots into the vacant lot. More bullets rained down on the car. It was all Dewey needed; he stepped from the side of the building and got off two quick shots. Everything was still. He looked at me and laughed. "Got him."

Slowly I raised my head and looked over the vacant lot at a body lying in the dirt, being quickly covered by the falling snow. I walked closer, pointing my gun. It was Manasso. I could see the blood pouring through the outside of his jacket. He was fighting back tears, but he looked up at me with a forced smile. "I thought I told you to come alone."

I leaned down and held his head and asked, "Why? *Why?*"

"Because you were going to betray me."

I didn't say anything at first. "How did you know?"

"Twigs." His face turned gray; he coughed up a little blood and his eyes went vacant.

Dewey stood over the body, chanting, "Son of a *bitch*, son of a *bitch*! A Christmas killing. Merry, merry, fucking Christmas!"

I ran back to the car. "Dewey," I yelled, "I have to take the car." The car had bullet holes all over it and the windshield was completely smashed out. I shoved it in gear and floored the accelerator, ignoring Dewey's shouts.

I drove as fast as I could; the wind rushing through the broken windshield numbed my face and hands. I kept repeating the name, "Twigs, Twigs." I was so cold by the time I got to the office that I could hardly open the door with my keys. Finally, I got in, rushed into the Library, turned on the fluorescent lights, and stared at the rows of files and index cards. Someone had helped Manasso. "Twigs" had to be a code name. Someone here in the Bureau was a double agent, and it could only be Michael. I had him now. I would stand up, expose the whole rotten mess. Now was the time. I had to do what was right. I thought about the strange turn in all three cases. Blanker? Dewey? Silkey? Then I almost screamed, *The money! The money!* Michael always played for the money; nobody else could set things up so completely. I had had enough of being set up, double-crossed, and falsely written into the reports. It was going to end here with Michael. I was going to prove his treachery. It was my time to stand up for what was right. It was now or never.

I went to the file cards to look up "Twigs". Incredibly, I found it right away, a three-by-five index card that simply read, *Twigs. Reference file Manasso*. There was something else, something very strange. As I stared at the card, I felt a deep chill. The words were *"smuggler,"* then *"photo."*

I rushed to the file cabinet to find the Manasso file and leafed through it. My hands were shaking. I found it halfway through the file. It was a large color photograph of people sitting at a table, a picture you pay a photographer to take at upscale clubs. Manasso was standing with his back to the camera – there was no mistaking his muscular profile. The caption said *"Twigs second from the left"*. Second from the left was a girl seated at the table. She was overweight, plain-looking, next to a guy in a bad suit with lots of jewelry. I kept staring at her. I didn't recognize the girl. It made no sense. Then I felt colder than the wind rushing through the broken windshield on my way down to the office. I had seen something that my mind could not accept. I looked at the caption again: *Twigs second from the left*...I was missing someone in the photo. I looked over Manasso's shoulder. There was only part of a face, almost completely hidden under a flat-brimmed black matador hat with silver buckles. There was a hand on Manasso's shoulder with long fingers and red nails. Under the hat I saw the eyes of Twigs, the unmistakable, dark, deep, raccoon eyes.

CHAPTER SIX

A TANGLED WEB

"MR. HEYMAN"

"Life is a balance sheet; mark well your accounts payable." That's what Manasso had said and warned me: "No independent cases on any of my associates."

I had killed agent Jerry Ramirez when I told Rachel that Jerry was going after Caldwell in Atlanta.

Rachel's apartment had been leased to an overseas corporation in Spain. My clothes were still there but nothing else, no sign that she ever existed. I called her work number. It rang to an answering machine in her bedroom closet. Someday I would find her, but I didn't know how. I had nowhere to go; I couldn't stand the thought of going home, after what I had done to Daisy. I was too stupid and ashamed to beg for her understanding. I went to "Heyman's" whorehouse, the place that Michael had taken me to several months earlier while looking for an informant. It was the only place that seemed appropriate for me now. I didn't even know Heyman's real name. He was Jamaican with a heavy accent, always saying, "Hey

Man," which is how he got his nickname.

For two days I lay in bed, drinking vodka and snorting coke until Heyman got tired of me bothering his paying customers. Before I left, there was a commotion. Heyman started to argue with a white man. It was the father of Gabriel: the main attraction, a white teenager junkie whore. She was getting her daily fix from Heyman by sucking everyone off. Her father was a dentist from Long Island. He and his wife had tried many times to get Gabriel into drug rehabilitation, but she would never go. Now he had come to take his daughter home. I didn't think Heyman would give her up easily. At first the father was brave; "I've come to get my daughter." Then he pleaded, "Please, may I see my daughter?"

Two of Heyman's bouncers grabbed Gabriel's father and threw him on the floor, leaned his arm up against the radiator, and snapped it at the elbow. He lay on the floor screaming and crying. Then they stood him up and threw him down two flights of steps. Gabriel watched the whole thing, standing there in her blue silk robe with her wide cold eyes staring out into space. I just stood there too and never said a word. In fact, it was kind of amusing, seeing him somersault down the stairs, screaming and crying. Heyman watched this horror take place and laughed with great satisfaction. There is a limit to how bad you can feel and I had reached it. I could not feel any worse.

Finally, I dragged myself home to an empty apartment. Daisy and Mark had gone to Chicago to her parents for Christmas. I was glad; I didn't want them to see me. I took a shower, changed my clothes, shaved. I hated being home more than being at Heyman's whorehouse. I tried to hold back the tears, surrounded by Daisy's clothes, pictures, and Mark's toys. The apartment was still decorated for Christmas, which made me feel even worse. Over and over I kept remembering how I bragged to Rachel that I was sending Jerry Ramirez to Atlanta to make a case on Manasso's lawyer, and how I ordered Silkey to pick up Fernando from the hotel, giving Manasso an opportunity to shoot him. I had killed them both and I would live with it the rest of my life.

Dewey's file clerks filed a report on Manasso's death. The autopsy said he died from two gunshot wounds to the chest. There was a footnote: they had to cut the gold bracelet off his wrist and on it was engraved just one word – *Rachel*. Guilt grew inside me like a horrible tapeworm. I went back to work, and months passed. I took any case, no matter how badly put together or how small. I bought heroin in Harlem, or cocaine on the East Side, anywhere there was an opportunity. I lived, ate, and slept with drug dealers to become their best friend – then looked forward to the day when I would betray them. I had evolved into a predatory creature of the night. There were no more bothersome thoughts about right and wrong. I was comfortable with my addiction to cocaine. It had helped me get through the guilt and madness of Rachel, and of Jerry's death. Perhaps it even saved my life.

Now the person who I respected more than anyone else, and wanted to become, was Michael Giovanni.

CHAPTER SEVEN

HONOR AMONG THIEVES

HOUND FROM HELL

Winter turned to an early spring, without any major cases. Then one day Pike came back from a meeting with George Blanker, and said to Michael, "The FBI wants us to do a joint investigation with them on some Colombian cokers. They want me to meet with them tomorrow morning, and I'd like you to come with me."

Michael was reading a newspaper and lowered it to look at Pike. "I'd love to join you, but I've got a busy day tomorrow. Why don't you ask Dewey? He's always well-dressed."

Pike was irritated. "Michael, I want *you* to come."

Michael kept reading his paper. "Sorry, Ted, I can't make it. I'm sure you'll do just fine. Dewey looks the part. He'll go with you. He never has anything useful to do. No way am I going."

"You have to go, Michael. It's an opportunity for us to work with the FBI. They specifically asked for you. Blanker told me to tell you to go."

Without lowering his newspaper, he looked at me. "Okay, Ted, we'll be there. What time?"

The next morning Michael and I met Pike at the FBI headquarters on 69th Street in Manhattan. Their offices were nothing like 90 Church. There was a big illuminated FBI emblem on the wall, wood furniture, carpeted floors, and a receptionist with an English accent.

Pike was dressed in a navy blue suit, white shirt and a red-striped tie. He was fat; every button pulled on his shirt and his pants pulled so tight it exposed the zipper on his fly, but at least his tie didn't have food stains on it. Michael was dressed in the same wrinkly clothes that he had on the day before, and the day before that, and he hadn't shaved in days. My hair was almost shoulder-length and I wore my usual coal-black shiny mohair suit with a bright green silk shirt open at the throat, and a pair of burgundy-red deerskin boots. I'd snorted a line of coke for breakfast so I was feeling just fine.

The receptionist ushered us into a conference room where there were four FBI agents, all looking the same – dark suits, white shirts, red ties, clean-shaven – and every one of them had a crew cut. They stared at us like we were three clowns from a circus. As we made introductions, Michael said nothing, and no one said anything to him; he just sat at the end of the table without looking at anyone, like a pouting schoolboy. An older, balding agent walked in and introduced himself as Special Agent John McDermott, from Washington, D.C. He was definitely in charge. He greeted Pike, calling him "Agent Pikerman," ignored me and glanced at Michael without saying a word. He sat with the other agents at the opposite end of the table. One of them, Campbell, rose to his feet, started a slideshow presentation and pointed to the first slide, a map of

South America. He began, "South America, the world's number-one source of illicit cocaine..."

Michael glanced at me with a big stupid grin. I knew we weren't going to be here very long. Then he took out a pack of cigarettes and began to light up. Agent Campbell stopped. "I'm sorry, there's no smoking here in our conference room." Michael lit the cigarette, blew out the match and threw it on the middle of the wooden table. After a moment of awkward silence, McDermott said to one of the younger agents, "Would you please get Agent *Michael Giovanni* an ashtray?"

Campbell resumed his silly presentation with a map of North America and the main points of entry of smuggled cocaine: El Paso, Miami, New York. The next slide was a series of mug shots. He said this was the Hermes "Medal-*lee*" family, pointing to picture after picture: Juan, Orlando, Horenda, Isabella, and its leader, Hermes.

As he continued to name them, Michael interrupted, "Like a small street."

Campbell ignored him. "Isabella Medal-*lee* is – "

"Like a small street," Michael interrupted him again.

Irritated, Campbell said, "What are you talking about? *What's* a small street?"

"It's pronounced *Medalley*, Med *alley*, like a small street."

Pike got pink.

McDermott said calmly, "Agent Campbell, please continue with your presentation of the *Medalley* family." The next slides were pictures of streets in downtown Bogotá, and Campbell continued, "The FBI, in concert with the Colombian government, has conducted investigations of the Medalley family, but has been unable to penetrate their tight-knit inner circle. It would be unusual, but we think possibly they are also working with the Carlo Gambino family. These investigations continue but have had limited progress. Six months ago, one of our agents assigned to our embassy was killed by this cartel. The Medalley family is headquartered here in New York City and as the next eight slides will show – "

Michael cut him off, "What was his name?"

"What was whose name?"

"The agent that was killed in Bogotá."

Campbell was irritated. "We're all professionals. It doesn't *matter* what his name was. We're here to investigate the Medalley family."

Michael pulled on his cigarette. "What was the agent's name that died in Bogotá?"

There was an uneasy silence. Pike started to apologize, "I'm sorry, we're all professionals, the name doesn't – "

McDermott interrupted, glaring at Michael. "He was my son. He was an advisor to their civilian government law enforcement. He was a teacher. They tried to ransom him. They tortured him. He was killed."

A long awkward silence, Campbell continued the presentation. Michael grabbed his cigarettes, stood up and nudged me to follow. As we walked toward the door, Michael stopped and looked at each of the FBI agents, then pointed his crooked, dirty finger at the smallest agent, wearing glasses, who had not said a word. As he pointed, Michael looked at McDermott and said, "Him."

McDermott bowed his head and said quietly, "Thank you."

Michael and I walked out, leaving Pike and the agents staring at each other. I knew we were going after the Medalley family. McDermott had just unleashed the hound from hell to get revenge for his son. On our way out we passed another conference room being prepared for a meeting; Michael grabbed some donuts off a tray and stuffed them in his pocket.

LIAISON

That afternoon our receptionist announced that I had a visitor, "Special Agent Tyler Springfield, from the FBI." My unknown and unexpected guest was the agent that Michael had pointed to at the meeting earlier in the morning. I tried to be nice. "Hi. What can I do for you?"

He was a little surprised. "I asked to see Michael Giovanni."

I chuckled. "No one sees Michael Giovanni. Anyone asking for Michael, they call me. What can I do for you?"

"I have some information that I can only discuss with Agent Giovanni."

"You're in luck. I think Michael is here. Come on, I'll take you to him."

I walked him down the vinyl-floored corridors of 90 Church, past our old gray steel desks until we heard Michael's voice. He was arguing with Dewey. "I don't *give* a shit if you get him killed! One more case and then you can bury him."

Dewey looked at me, then my guest, who was shocked by what he had just heard. "Who is this geek, a Jehovah's witness?"

Michael grinned. "Don't talk to him like that, Dewey. This is my new partner."

Michael took Tyler by the elbow and the three of us went into a small conference room. Agent Springfield, trying to hide his irritation, said, "I'm here to discuss the case *only with you, Agent Giovanni.*"

"Yes, of course you are. It's just you and me. Look around; do you see anyone else in this room?" I sat there with a straight face and then Michael said, "Good, we've settled that. Now, what do you have in your little bag?"

Springfield opened up his briefcase and placed the files on the table, and began his presentation to Michael. "The Medalley family are vicious killers and – "

Michael cut him off. "Who killed McDermott's kid?"

Springfield started again, "Preliminary investigations and based upon surveillance – "

Michael cut him off again. "Who killed McDermott's son?"

"Based upon our – "

"Tyler, what I *want* is *one name*! A name! Just a name! Give me the *name*!"

He glared at Michael. "Pepe Lamaros."

Michael nodded. "See how easy that was? So it was Pepe Click-Click Lamaros...Tyler, do you know how Click-Click got his name?"

Agent Springfield shook his head no.

"They call Pepe Click-Click because when he kills people he clicks back the hammer of his revolver, then imitates the noise. The last thing you hear is click, click, and you're dead. Now...what are these files?"

"McDermott said these files are for your eyes only, they are not inter-departmental, and I have to return them right away."

"Yes, of course they are, I can respect that," Michael said.

"These are top-secret, FBI files," Tyler added. "As you know, we don't share information with other agencies."

Michael turned to me. "Give these files to Dewey's toads, tell them to cross-reference them with the library. If there's anything we don't already have, tell them to copy and file it. Cross-reference people, buys, killings, phone numbers and addresses with our informants, and narrow the list down to twenty and give it to Dewey. Have him pick out the five informants who can help us. Now take Special Agent Tyler out and buy him some working clothes and then take him down to the Nassau. Maybe he'll get lucky. Get him laid."

He then looked at Springfield. "I picked you to work with us because you are harmless. That can be useful." Michael lit a cigarette and left the room.

Tyler Springfield sat in silence.

Finally I said, "Tyler, we work different here, but I guarantee these people are going down. Come on, I want to drop these files off at the Library, and then we'll have to do some clothes shopping along Canal Street, if you want to work with us."

I dropped the files off to Janet, our head researcher in the Library, and gave her Michael's instructions.

Afterwards I bought Tyler Springfield some new clothes: black sneakers, cheap khaki pants, short-sleeved Banlon shirts, and a stingy-brim black hat. On our way to the Nassau Bar I told Agent Springfield if ever he was to come to 90 Church again, or to meet Michael, or conduct surveillances, these were the clothes he had to wear.

I left him at the bar, talking to two young prostitutes.

Pike presented the FBI version of the case to everyone at our next Monday morning meeting. He had sat through the entire FBI briefing after Michael and I walked out, but now, in re-presenting it, only the new agents bothered to stay and hear the complete case.

Nevertheless, it was a priority for the Bureau and an opportunity to improve relations with the FBI. Pike told everyone how Michael had insulted the FBI, and assigned Del Ridley to head up the case and work with FBI Agent John McDermott. Later the same day, McDermott told Pike that Giovanni "must be in charge of the investigation" and that all Bureau liaisons would be through Agent Springfield.

Everyone except Pike knew why FBI Special Agent John McDermott wanted Michael. When most other agents were in charge, people went to jail. The agents knew how to investigate and apply the law. Michael thought search warrants, arrests, and trials were a waste of time. When Michael made a case there would be no one *left* to go to jail. We all knew what kind of case this was going to be, and so did McDermott.

Dewey reviewed the files on the Medalley family, and Michael called a meeting at the Heidelberg. Lately we had been eating mostly Italian so it was a relief to be catered by a South American restaurant, the Café Del Sol, but the rice was mushy and tasteless, so everyone was anxious to end the meeting and go someplace else to eat.

Michael began. He held up an organizational chart of the Medalley.

The Medalleys were headed by two brothers and operated a simple but very efficient drug operation. Hermes, the eldest, controlled the product and financing, with Orlando handling sales. Hermes lived on Staten Island at the mansion while Orlando lived a life of endless parties in Manhattan, selling coke. Pepe "Click-Click" was the enforcer, and worked for both brothers. There were about fifteen dealers, or "account executives," who worked for

Orlando. They handled everything and Pepe stepped in if anything went wrong.

The Bureau had made drug buys from the Medalley dealers before, but the cases never led to any cooperation. The two brothers held their organization together with Pepe, the enforcer, and a strong fraternal code: cheating on drug deals meant death, there was loyalty, no exception, they were all "brothers." However, none of this bothered Michael, and everyone knew that one way or the other he would find a way to get inside.

Michael held up a map of the various family houses and apartments in Staten Island, Brooklyn, and Manhattan. "All of these locations have been under surveillance by us and the FBI periodically, and have not resulted in any useful information. Their operation is family-controlled and very tight. There are no second chances, no skimming of profits, no informants, no way to corrupt it. We know that coke is being shipped to the cartel from Bogotá to either Port Newark or New York City. Our intelligence in Bogotá is even able to give the departure date and name the ship that carries the drugs, but Customs here, in the United States, has never been able to intercept anything at port when the ship docks. Nor has anyone ever been able to connect any of the ship's personnel to any member of the Medalley family here in New York. We must begin the hard way, and get someone into the brotherhood."

Dewey threw his pencil down in disgust. "That's bullshit. We're as dumb as the FBI. That's how they get their people killed. These people are just a bunch of dumb spics with cheap jewelry. Not once have they been caught smuggling the shit through Customs, not once. That's how dumb they are!"

Silkey showed his ignorance. "What's so dumb about not being caught?"

There was a consensus in the room that this might be a good question, but Michael answered, "What Dewey is saying, is that because they are beating the system and they know everyone is looking at the port of entry, if they allowed themselves to get caught once in a while, everyone would continue looking for them in the same wrong place." He looked at Dewey and said, "You're right, Dewey, but so what? We still don't know anything. Where's their stash and how are they getting it in?"

Dewey stood up. "Everything, the whole smuggling operation, is in the mansion at South Beach on the Staten Island shore."

"How do you know that?" Michael asked. "There's no information in the files. How can you say that?"

Dewey shook his head. "Michael, we've got to stop thinking like the FBI." He held up an aerial photograph. "Look at this picture of their compound in Staten Island. What do you see?"

The photo was passed around and then Michael said, "We all see a big house on the beach with some nice boats. So what?"

"No," Dewey answered. "That's just it. They are *not* 'nice boats.' With all of their millions of dollars there's only one small yacht; the other two boats are for fishing – not recreational fishing, *industrial* fishing. Look at the booms on the decks and the nets hanging on the port side. Do you think that these spics, with all their money and fancy jewelry, are in the fishing business? The drugs never come in through Customs. They're delivered direct from South America to their doorstep. Ships on their way in to Port Newark and New York pass right in front of the Medalley beachfront property."

"They can't offload a commercial freighter in the middle of

a busy harbor channel," Michael said. "The Coast Guard and Customs aren't that dumb."

"Yes, they are, Michael," Dewey answered, "and so are we. Look, first of all, the ship never stops. The drugs are thrown over the side, probably at night, just as they pass between Brooklyn and Staten Island, getting ready to dock, either in Newark or New York. Look at this open water." He held up a geographical map of the harbor.

"How do they get the coke out of the water and how do they find it?" Michael asked.

"I think I know," Dewey answered. "There's a Coast Guard open frequency ten miles offshore, so any homing device would be detected immediately, as would any light or bright color. This channel has heavy traffic: Coast Guard, police, and other ships. Almost anything put in the water would be detected. Besides that, they would have to know when or where to throw the drugs overboard; there's a river current. This is how I think they do it. Look at the map. Here is the Medalley's mansion on South Beach and here – directly across the channel – is their apartment in Brooklyn. Does anyone see it?"

There was silence around the room, no one did. Dewey continued, "Jesus *Christ*, you guys are dumb! All the property they own is upscale, luxury, but the apartment on the Brooklyn shore is a *tenement* and it's *directly* across the channel from the Medalley mansion on the Staten Island shore. As the ship passes between the two points, they throw the drugs over the side. It would be easy to have a light in the apartment and a matching light in the Medalley mansion as an intersecting point of reference. And the reason the Coast Guard can't find the drugs is that there's no homing device, no signal light, no bright buoys, nothing. They're probably using a salt drop, or something similar."

Silkey asked, "What's a salt drop?"

Dewey drew a deep impatient breath. "It's very simple. The drugs are strapped to a buoy, probably made of cork or Styrofoam, and then tied to a bag of salt to weigh it down. When it's thrown into the ocean, the package is heavy and sinks directly to the bottom. The salt begins to dissolve and twelve hours later, or whenever everybody is gone, the package is freed from the salt and rises to the surface. Along come their fishing boats with their nets to pick it up, and no one knows anything."

Michael looked at Dewey and shook his head. "How would they think of something like this, and would it work?"

"Michael," Dewey answered, "*yes*, it works. And *yes*, they would know about it. Smugglers have been using salt drops since the Revolutionary War. They're probably using something better than a salt weight, something that dissolves at a measurable rate. You can get cable connectors, used in marine construction for underwater cement forms, with a spring-lock release, that are very accurate, so they know exactly when the drugs will surface. Then they measure the current so they can predict exactly where to pick it up in their fishing nets."

Everyone was stunned. It looked as if we had made a major breakthrough in the case and we hadn't even gotten started.

Dewey's experience with Navy Intelligence had certainly paid off; although it was still a theory, it was a very good theory. This was going to be easy. Everyone knew this was the place to start – everyone except, of course, Michael. Instead of congratulating Dewey, Michael said, "How do you know these spics are wearing cheap jewelry?" There were a few forced laughs. "I don't care how they get the dope, we're going in, someone is going inside."

I wanted to be that "someone." This was going to be a big case. Undercover agents rarely controlled cases. I certainly never did. We were sent in to make a drug buy with little or no background. Most of the time, I didn't even know who the informant was. I was simply told what to say and who to meet. But this case would be very different, and I felt sure that I would be chosen to lead the undercover operation. This case was major and – everyone knew – very dangerous. I had earned it and I had been loyal to Michael for a long time, keeping the dark secret of his awful rape – which I knew had bonded us and protected me. I carried the chrome-blue automatic, a gift from Michael, as proof of our secret. But now Michael stood up, cutting Dewey off before he could continue his theory, "Our first step in this case will be an undercover buy of eighty thousand dollars for three kilos of pure cocaine. One of our informants knows Chevy de Falla, who sells for the Medalleys in Queens, and I have chosen Louie the G to be the undercover agent on this case."

I was shocked. Louie was a good undercover agent, but I had earned the right to lead this case. Michael owed it to me, yet he acted like I wasn't even there. Everyone gave a little round of applause for Louie, who pretended he'd just gotten some type of award.

THE SHOOTING

I was completely shut out of the Medalley case. For the next week I continued to work on other cases and even came home early in the afternoon several times a week.

Then one afternoon Michael asked me if I would like to come

with him on surveillance. I knew they were getting ready for Louie to make a cocaine buy from Chevy de Falla, one of the Medalley dealers. I hadn't told Michael about my disappointment; it wouldn't have mattered. He cared only about the case, which was what made him the most dangerous agent in the office.

That night I drove Michael to a quiet residential neighborhood in Forest Park, Queens. He told me that Agent Louie Gomez had already given Chevy eighty thousand dollars and was now going to pick up the cocaine here at Chevy's house. Ordinarily, an agent would never front drug money and pick up the drugs someplace else; you could never trust anyone and easily lose the money. But with the Medalleys, I assumed things were different. They had a code of honesty.

After about a half hour, two cars pulled into Chevy's driveway. A muscular male about my age, who I assumed was Chevy, drove the first car. A girl with long black hair, probably his girlfriend, rode with him. Both were well-dressed. Louie followed alone in the second car and pulled in behind them. All three went into the house. When they turned the lights on we watched them through the front window. Michael handed me a pair of binoculars.

Within minutes, another car pulled in the driveway: a white Cadillac with chrome wheels and gold trim. I recognized the car immediately, it belonged to Mars La Pont. Two black men got out wearing nylon stockings over their faces, walked up to the front door, opened it, and went inside. I watched them through the binoculars as I told Michael. He just stared at the house, unconcerned.

Through the window I could see there was trouble. Louie and the girl had their hands up and Chevy was agitated, walking back and forth. Then I saw one of the black men hold a gun to the face of the girl, and Chevy handed him a gym bag. Then both of the masked men turned on Louie, their guns pointed at his face. Chevy bolted out the front door, down the steps and around the side of the house. Michael saw the whole thing and laughed. One black man tried to follow Chevy, but gave up and returned to the front porch. Louie, the girl, and the other black guy carrying the bag came out of the front door. Then Louie started to walk away, toward his car, but stopped and began arguing again with both of the men. The black guy who had first followed Chevy raised his gun and shot Louie. Louie grabbed his stomach and fell in the grass. The girl began yelling and waving her hands.

"My God, they shot Louie." I dropped the binoculars and pulled my gun and started forward. Michael stopped me and put his finger to his lips, motioning me to be silent. The masked black man on the porch grabbed the girl to quiet her, then ripped her blouse open and tried to grab her breasts. She kept screaming and fighting until he pushed her down. Then the two men walked to their white Cadillac and drove off.

Louie struggled to his feet, holding his stomach, looked at the girl and staggered toward his car, falling down one more time before he managed to get behind the wheel and drive off.

Through all of this Michael just stared, then he had a strange smile when he saw Chevy return from the back of the house, hug the girl and kiss her. They both went inside. Incredibly, Michael was not the least bit concerned about Louie. Louie was an undercover agent on his own; it was up to him to try to make it to the hospital. That's just the way things worked. Those were the rules of the game and, if anything, Michael seemed amused.

We drove back to Manhattan in silence. Michael's disregard for an agent's life nauseated me. Instead of going back to the office Michael told me to stop at the Nassau Bar near Wall Street. We had still not said a word to each other.

There at the bar, surrounded by girls, was Louie – laughing and drinking. His shirt was gone. He was wearing his suit jacket over his bare chest. Cleo Brown and Sam Holmes, two black agents, sat next to him at the bar. When Louie saw us he threw Michael his shirt. "Well, Michael, what do you think?" Then Agent Brown handed Michael the gym bag that I had seen at the house in Queens.

Michael opened it up, showing me three kilos of cocaine, then ordered drinks for everyone. "You were all great. You were so good you even fooled him." He pointed to me. "I wanted an outside opinion," he said, pointing to me again. "You scared the shit out of him. He almost shot Cleo!" Everyone laughed and raised their drinks in a silent toast. After a while Dewey came into the bar. "The car is back, he never even knew it was gone. We didn't use much gas. No problem at all."

As usual, everyone knew what was going on except me. I called Dewey aside. He laughed. "You know Michael, he never tells anybody anything. I think he wanted to test the whole scene with someone not in on it, to see if it really worked, and it did. If you were convinced, so were they."

"Convinced about *what*? What happened?"

Dewey grinned. "It's easy. I had one of my informants borrow Mars La Pont's Cadillac without him knowing about it and gave it to Brown and Holmes."

My obsession to get Mars La Pont, who had whored Maureen and froze Calvin to death, had never weakened. "But why?" I asked.

Dewey laughed. "You got me. I don't know. You know Michael. No one ever knows what he's doing. Only he knows why and everybody had better do what they're told. He even told me to put up the eighty grand in drug money. Michael doesn't want Pike involved and worrying about the government money." Dewey added, "Michael is a genius, he does things no one understands until the end. Besides, didn't you ask Michael to get Mars? Well, trust me, when you ask Michael to help you, look out."

Michael spread Louie's dress shirt out on the top of the bar. He then took a hard drag off his cigarette and burned a round hole in front of the shirt in the stomach area. He handed me the shirt. "Take this home. Tomorrow morning go to a butcher and get a cup of blood, pour it on the front of the shirt, but not on the sleeves or the back, dry it out in a dryer and bring it to the office." Then, looking at Dewey, he said, "You and Silkey meet us at the office tomorrow afternoon and take him" – pointing to me – "over to the Medalley mansion in Staten Island and drop him off." Then Michael looked back at me. "Louie's out. He's dead. You're going in tomorrow. You're going to give them this shirt. Tell them they've got your eighty thousand dollars and they got one of your guys killed by two coke-stealing niggers. Tell them you'll be back the next day to settle up with Hermes himself. I want you inside the family."

Michael left me holding the shirt, and Brown and Holmes talking and laughing. Dewey smiled at me and said, "Well, only Michael can think of doing shit like this, only Michael. You can't keep up with him. He's the best. He's insane. Oh, and guess what? I've got their coke in my car."

THE STING

Two days later Dewey, Ed Silkey, and I drove to Staten Island. The mansion sat at the end of a long dead-end road with a spectacular view overlooking the channel water across from Brooklyn. A large wooden gate with a surveillance camera protected the house and the garden.

Ed pulled up to the front, got out, opened up the car trunk, and walked back to the gate, carrying his pump shotgun; with one blast the camera completely disappeared. He then began blasting away at the lock on the gate, with empty shell cartridges flying in the air. Frustrated, he stopped to reload; Dewey walked up to the gate, turned the handle, and opened it. We were still laughing as we drove up the driveway and stopped in front of the house. Four huge, muscular bodyguards filed out the front door and stood in a straight line, all of them carrying guns. Ed got out of the car, shotgun at his side; Dewey followed, holding his black .45 and smiling. I was in the back seat and got out last, carrying the bloody shirt with the cigarette-burn hole. I walked up to the biggest of the four bodyguards standing on the porch and threw the shirt in his face. He didn't move; just let it fall to the ground. I looked straight into his eyes and said, "You've got eighty thousand dollars that belongs to me, and one of my guys is dead. I'm coming back tomorrow at this same time to settle up with Hermes. Be sure he's here to meet me."

They said nothing. We got in the car and left. On the way back, Ed and Dewey laughed about the disintegrated surveillance camera and how Ed had blasted away at the unlocked gate.

Michael's plan was brilliant. I was going straight to the top – no prolonged surveillance, no informants to worry about, no middle men to climb over – just straight to the top with a big complaint on how the Medalley family did business. Pure genius, but typical Michael. Dewey got a phone call in the afternoon from the informant who had helped him "borrow" La Pont's white Cadillac. The police had found La Pont's body. He had been strapped to a chair and shot in the head. One of his hands had been dipped in batter and boiled in oil, so his hand looked like fried chicken. The Medalley family wanted their coke back, but Mars La Pont was no help. It was a proper ending for Mars. I would never forget what he did to Calvin, and Maureen's scream still haunted me.

The next day Michael picked me up at about two in the afternoon and we drove toward Staten Island. I hadn't slept; I kept rehearsing in my mind what to say about my cover, knowing that one mistake would get me killed. I had been undercover many times before, but the dealers were always stupid, and I always had plenty of back-up waiting if things went wrong. I usually made up my own cover story as I went along. They always believed me because they were greedy. Just like Michael told me to do, I would show them all the money I was carrying. It made them stupid. This was different, very different. I knew it and so did everyone else.

As much time as I had spent with Michael, I still felt awkward being with him; he seldom spoke, and never listened to anyone. He was either deep in thought or spaced out. I was never really sure which, but I knew Michael cared about me.

Just before we got to the Medalley mansion, Michael pulled over at a small roadside park with picnic tables. "Take everything out of your pockets and lay it on the dashboard, everything."

I unloaded my pockets: credentials, wallet, money clip with

about two hundred dollars, a receipt from paying my apartment rent, and a handkerchief.

"You're not dealing with some dumb junkies here," Michael said, "and any one of these things will get you killed, even your handkerchief. You're supposed to be from Europe. Carry paper Kleenex if you want to blow your nose. Your handkerchief goes in the breast pocket of your suit. Your name is Nico. Nico Prestovo, you're half-Swiss and half-Italian."

Michael reached into his coat pocket and threw me an old wallet, which was coming apart at the seams. Inside were an International Driver's License and two receipts from Patsy's and Jokers Wild—two mob hangouts. From another pocket Michael pulled out a wad of cash, more than a thousand dollars. Then he said, "McDermott helped me with this; the ID is an alias."

"What happens if they check up?" I asked.

Michael shrugged. "That's just it, they will. Your alias is Peter Bruno, an assassin, smuggler, and playboy, wanted by Interpol, and your picture is now in his file. When his file pops up I want to know who's asking for it. The Medalley family can't operate on a scale this large without police or federal support. When they check you out, they'll expose themselves. We have to watch our back."

Michael stared out the window. "You must understand a few things. The Medalleys operate on honor and strict discipline. They have rules that can never be broken: no cheating, no lying, no forgiveness – only total loyalty. There is no lesson to be learned, no form of punishment – only death. If you or anyone else fucks up, no matter how small, you die. But they care about each other, that is their greatest strength. Honor and loyalty, that's why we've never gotten anyone close to them. You must attack them at their greatest strength. If you try to find their weakness they will see you and will track you down and they *will kill you.*"

I tried to make sense out of what Michael had just said, but I couldn't. It was no help, and my hand was shaking.

"One other thing, give me your gun. It will only aggravate them."

I took off my shoulder holster and put the gun on the dash with everything else.

We then drove down to the gate of the Medalley mansion. I saw that the surveillance camera had been replaced and the gate was open. It was a hot day. Never had I felt such fear. These people were not afraid of us. They wanted to find us. They liked killing and torturing people, and I was going in alone with a silly cover story. I couldn't even pronounce my new name!

Michael looked at me and asked, "Are you ready?"

I nodded, but my eyes were blinking, and Michael knew I was afraid. I could see it in his face. I opened the door, walked through the gate, and started up the driveway. As I walked and stared at the huge mansion with its gardens and sprawling green lawns, I thought how pitiful all this really was. These people, like the Mafia, had millions of dollars and an army willing to kill anyone who interfered. 90 Church had only thirty-five drunks and psychos like Michael, who didn't care about anything. It was odd that I didn't see that before. The agents weren't afraid because they simply *didn't care* – not about money, not about promotions, not about their health, not about their future. They were all like Michael, suffering from some deadly illness in their souls that had made everything meaningless.

As I walked up the driveway I had an unexpected memory of a conversation with one of my college football coaches who was dying of cancer. We were in a bar when he told me what it was like. He said he was always afraid of getting cancer and then when he got it, he wasn't afraid anymore. When he found out he was going to die from it, he didn't fear that anymore either. His whole life changed. He didn't care about anything or anyone because there was no future. He just cared about two things: living with the pain and fighting back – nothing else, absolutely nothing else.

I looked up at the mansion. Then I knew. The agents were not going to win the war against drugs. There was no retreat, no caring for the wounded. We were alone and we were going to lose. There was nothing to worry about except living with the pain and fighting back as hard as you could. I reached the stairs leading to the huge front door. I was calm, my fear gone. At the top of the stairs, in front of the door, I turned around and looked down the long driveway to where Michael was standing alone by the gate, watching me. I gave him the finger and he returned a big grin.

I didn't have to knock; they were waiting for me.

The front door swung open and two of the muscle-bound goons that we'd seen the day before dragged me inside. A third, the largest of the three, started to pat me down for a wire or a gun but first he gave me a slap across my face. He kept grabbing and pushing me while the other two held my arms tight. He felt up and down my arms and legs, then grabbed me by the balls, and started laughing. He was at least six inches taller than I was, and he kept calling me pussy. "You are just a big pussy." When he stopped, the other two released my arms and he stood smiling and puckering his lips like he was going to kiss me.

I lost it. With both hands I pushed him as hard as I could, sending him toppling onto a glass table. It exploded, slicing his arm and leg with slivers of glass. He didn't go all the way to the floor, instead he held himself up with his arms and his legs, trying to raise his stomach up as high as he could to escape the shards that were already piercing his back, arms, and leg, splashing everything with blood.

The other two didn't know whether to kill me or save their friend from being impaled by the glass, so they just stood there and waved their hands in frustration, watching him scream in agony, pleading for help. Finally they reached over and pulled him up and started to pick fragments of glass from his arms and legs, while he continued to bleed all over the white marble floor.

I stood there, waiting for someone to get around to killing me, then I heard a calm voice, "I am Hermes Medalley." I turned around and saw a man in his fifties with gray hair, wearing a white suit and pink shirt. He smiled, ignoring the screaming and the carnage on the foyer floor, and said, "I understand that you have some business with me. Come this way, we will talk."

He was completely oblivious to everything that had just happened as he led me toward the back of the house. We passed a small room and looked inside. There was a row of TV screens on the wall from the outside security cameras. In one we could see the front entrance, and Michael standing next to the car. He had a box of shells on the hood and was firing his revolver at the camera. After emptying his gun, he reloaded and then fired again; as if on cue, the camera went dark. Again Hermes just ignored the whole thing.

We continued to go deeper into the mansion. I had never seen a restaurant, a home, a museum, or any building as beautiful as the inside of the Medalley house. Everything was orange, yellow, pink, white, and soft purple with flowered wallpaper of country vistas and jungle scenes with pools of water. Flowers were everywhere: table vases, wall hangings, draped over lamps, and strewn on tables and chairs, even lying on the floor. The furniture was big and comfortable in pastel leathers with soft pillows. Paintings, sculptures, and water fountains demonstrated a great appreciation of art. It had a peaceful effect on me. Strangely enough, I felt welcome, despite my anxiety. Finally, Hermes led me into his lavish study. Business papers, notebooks, and correspondence covered his desk. We sat – him behind his desk and me in front. It felt like a job interview. Hermes put on his glasses and stared at me more closely, and said, "You've lost one of your men. I'm sorry about that, and I understand that you've entrusted us with some funds, and we were unable to deliver product. Is that right? Tell me your side of it."

He acted like we were talking about crates of cabbage, and that somehow the delivery boy got lost in traffic. His calm, controlled manner, fixed eyes and wide smile forced me to try to answer in the same polite fashion. Before I could answer, something caught my eye at the side of the room. There were French doors leading into a smaller room full of hanging plants with bookshelves on the back wall. I could see a shadow on the floor; someone was hiding there, listening to us.

I looked back at Hermes and said, "He was not my 'man,' he was my *friend*, and he died in the hospital of a gunshot wound to the stomach. I also lost eighty thousand dollars. Your people assured me that things would be under control, and I trusted you and the amateurs that work for you. I fronted the money in complete trust and then when we went to pick up the coke it was a set-up. They knew the coke was in the house; they just walked right in, killed my friend and took your dope."

Hermes studied me for a while and then said, "What is your name?"

I pronounced my last name as best I could. Hermes continued, "We've never heard of you, Nico. What did you intend to do with our coke?"

"I don't normally deal," I replied. "I'm a wholesaler. I have friends, restaurant people, upscale, both Italian and French. They want good-grade cocaine for their better customers. I used to be in the import business, gourmet foods, that's how I made connections with many of the restaurants in New York." I could see that he was impressed with my story and it even surprised me, because I had just made it up. As I was speaking I could see that he was taking notes on a yellow pad.

Then he looked up at me and said, "Do you know anything about selling cocaine, heroin, or hashish?"

"No. Only through my friends. They said there was a profit to be made. That's how I made the mistake of dealing with your people."

That irritated Hermes. He picked up the phone, touched a button, and began a short conversation in Spanish. He hung up and continued our discussion. "No one makes a mistake when they deal with the Medalleys," he said coldly. "Only if they choose to misuse our trust. It is unfortunate that you had a bad experience. Things can happen in any type of business. You seem honorable and intelligent and capable. You injured one of my boys and broke some furniture. I don't like that. I'm not sure if that was about courage or stupidity, but I am impressed that after all of that fuss you are still calm and reasonable. My people could have killed you on the spot and thrown you in the water, but perhaps they were rude. I don't like your gun-happy friend hanging outside our gate, shooting at my home, either. You should be dead, but you have a legitimate grievance and the Medalley family honors all business relationships."

As he talked I glanced back at the shadow in the smaller room off the study. It seemed to be swaying back and forth, listening very carefully. Then I said, "Mr. Medalley, please understand. I gave you eighty thousand dollars for three kilos of high-grade cocaine. My friend is dead. I don't take this situation lightly, and I am not alone. I have friends who have a shared interest. I'm here to make things right, or this situation will get worse, much worse."

Hermes smiled at my threat, but before he could speak, he was interrupted by a knock at the door. He said something in Spanish and the door opened; it was one of the goons that had grabbed me at the front door. He was carrying a red velvet box that he placed on Hermes' desk. Without saying a word or looking at me, the goon walked out of the room and closed the door.

Hermes said, "Here, this is for you. You were wronged and I am going to make it right." He motioned for me to take the box.

I opened it. Inside were six kilos of cocaine, wrapped in silver paper, sealed with the red Medalley wax stamp, with large numbers. They looked like gold bullion bars, neatly packaged, equal size.

I was stunned. Hermes Medalley had just walked into my trap. We had given him eighty thousand dollars and he had now given us six kilos of cocaine. All I had to do was to walk out the door carrying the box and Hermes Medalley would go to jail for the rest of his life. I kept thinking how proud Michael would be and how easy this whole thing was. I would be a hero, getting Hermes on the first visit – then I had an uneasy feeling. I glanced at the room with the shadow, it was very still; someone was listening closely. All this was too easy.

Then I did something so impulsive that it surprised both Hermes and me. I rocked back on my chair and looked at him across the desk and said, "You're very generous, I see that you are willing to solve this problem. I came here for the drugs but now I don't want them. Even though they are more than twice what I bought. The return of my money will be sufficient, along with your handshake."

Hermes was shocked. He sat in silence, staring at me. I understood why I was not going to make a case on Hermes. I worked for Michael Giovanni and Michael was not interested in drugs, not even six kilos of the best-grade cocaine in the world. Michael was certainly not interested in Hermes Medalley. To Michael, it was like finding a cockroach in his kitchen. You could kill it, even if it was a big cockroach, and you'd have some satisfaction. The problem was that there was a *nest* of cockroaches, and killing one, even the biggest one, would not solve the problem. You had to kill *all* the cockroaches.

Then he said, "Very well." And he got up, pulled at the side of a wall picture frame. It was a small door with concealed hinges. Behind was a wall safe. Within minutes he removed a large manila envelope and emptied the contents on the desk. Out tumbled bundles of brand-new hundred-dollar bills. He counted out eight bundles and pushed them in front of me. He opened his desk drawer and put the money in a manila envelope without saying a word. He put the rest of the money back into the safe as I kept glancing at the shadow on the floor in the back room.

Hermes came back to his desk and picked up his pencil again. "I would like to be able to contact you, and perhaps we might do business. I like you. We always have need for new customers and people who will respect our organization."

I gave Hermes the phone number for an undercover phone at the Bureau. It was connected to an answering machine; if they talked long enough we could trace the source of the call.

I reached in the envelope and pulled out one bundle of hundred-dollar bills and put the rest of the money back in front of him. "I would like that. I'd like to be your friend. This is money on account. Please call me. I would be proud to work for you and your organization."

Hermes stared at the remaining seventy thousand dollars. I could see that he was impressed, and then he said, "Have a good day...my friend."

I walked out of the room, back through the magnificent house to the front-door foyer. I had not been in the Medalley mansion for more than twenty minutes, yet the foyer was completely clean and the furniture rearranged as if nothing had happened. Outside I looked down the driveway and there was Michael, sitting on the hood of the white Mercedes.

On our way back to Manhattan I told Michael every detail: the bloody bodyguard, the decorations, what Hermes looked like, even the shadow of someone listening in the next room, which seemed to interest Michael. He asked me if I had any idea who it was, and I said I thought it was probably a bodyguard or perhaps even his brother.

Michael shook his head. "Hermes would not trust a bodyguard to listen in on his conversations. Besides, you were already frisked and unarmed, and if it was his brother, he wouldn't have to hide, he would be part of the conversation." He then cautioned me, "Whoever the shadow was, I would fear him the most."

I told Michael that Hermes had offered me six kilos of cocaine, but before I could explain my reasons for not taking the drugs, he said, "You were wise not to take the six keys. It was a trap. No one as smart as Hermes Medalley would ever give you even an ounce of cocaine and let you walk out of his house alive. If you had taken the cocaine you'd be dead by now. He wanted to see if you were setting him up. Only a dumb cop, or a dead agent would be dumb enough to think they could make a buy on Hermes Medalley so easily in his own house...You're smarter than I thought. You might even become a good agent someday."

THE PARTY

Several days passed and nothing happened, but Michael didn't seem concerned. The Medalleys still had seventy thousand dollars of our money, but they were honest business people and would eventually call to complete the deal. Then there was a strange message on my undercover phone at the office – from a woman. When I returned the call, it was from a law firm in Manhattan. The caller was a secretary who put me on hold several times to answer other calls. Finally she explained why she had called. She was extending an invitation to a pool party at the Medalley mansion on Saturday. Of course I accepted.

Dewey ran the name of the law firm through our files and found nothing. The Bar Association records said they handled primarily international law, import taxes with corporate clients, small companies in South America, Mexico, and Europe. I looked forward to the party. I picked out a shiny, light, powder-blue suit and black silk shirt. I bought a new pair of gray deerskin boots for the occasion. I certainly looked the part, and I liked the look.

On Saturday I drove the white Mercedes to the Medalley mansion. It was very hot. The gates were open, and the same bodyguards that had roughed me up the last time waved me through. After parking, I saw the one I had pushed on the table staring at me, his arm in a sling. Another bodyguard showed me to the pool. Although I was a half hour late, the caterers were still setting up and I was the only one there. For the next hour I just stood around trying to look interested and trying to talk to the waiters, most of whom did not speak English. As I waited by the pool I looked up at the house to the second-floor corner window that overlooked the water. There was an opening in the window curtain and I could see a dark silhouette watching me.

An hour later I was sweaty from the sun and nervous from having to stand around and do nothing except watch the waiter prepare huge trays of seafood, canapés, fruits, candies, and tubs of ice with champagne and every kind of liquor imaginable. The party was centered around the huge tiled pool. A cantilevered stage of glass hung over the pool deck. The other end was set up for a small orchestra. There were Roman columns around the pool and patio. At least a hundred red banners, of all sizes, fluttered in the breeze. Red was the Medalley family color.

At around six-thirty about fifty people arrived all at the same time. Everyone knew everyone else, and the party began like someone had flipped a switch. The music, the dancing, the bars, the food, and the guests were stunning. The men had slicked-back hair, bright silk shirts, expensive pants, alligator loafers, and gold jewelry. The women wore plunging necklines and short skirts with high heels that showed off their long, tanned legs. The overall impression was a gathering of the most attractive, well-dressed, well-mannered people I had ever seen. I tried to mingle and overhear the conversations. There were only two topics: the women talked about making love, and the men talked about killing people. I began to feel very uneasy among these incredibly glamorous people whose interests focused only on sex and death.

Finally I found someone as badly dressed as I was to talk to. I knew that he was a cop by the way he carried himself, and his girlfriend was a typical low-life, a gum-popping blonde with a heavy Queens accent. He said his name was Larry Sprague; I remembered him from the Scarluci case. He was Domenic's secret advisor.

When it got dark the music began. It was very erotic – jungle drums with a beautiful girl singing in Spanish, in a very sexy, deep voice. It wasn't long before everyone was dancing, and some of the girls were swimming topless in the pool. The glass stage and part of the dance floor overhanging the pool were lit underneath. The excitement began to build. It became the most magical party that I had ever seen or could ever imagine.

Among all the pretty people, one person stood out. He was the ugliest, meanest-looking person I had ever seen. His long black hair, pulled tight in a ponytail, framed a scarred, acne-pocked face with burning black eyes. There was a terrible wide scar on the side of his face that looked as if it had healed without the benefit of stitches or any medical help. Little peaks of flesh puckered up along both sides of the gash. He was short and wide, practically square.

I had no doubt that this creature was Pepe "Click-Click" Lamaros.

Hermes came out of the house with a handsome younger man who wore a bright yellow-and-purple shirt, expensive gold rings, and a chain around his neck. I assumed it was his brother Orlando. He was with two girls who looked like they were from a Las Vegas chorus line.

Police Lieutenant Sprague and I clearly didn't fit in, so we stuck together, trying to make the best of things, ogling the women and wishing we could have as much fun as everyone else.

A young couple climbed up on the glass stage and began to dance. The girl had a perfect athletic body, long black hair, and a tight see-through miniskirt with an open-to-the-waist shirt. She had big eyes with high cheek bones and looked wild and independent. The light from beneath the stage revealed everything as she danced with her handsome partner. I had seen great floor shows at the Blue Angel, at Basin Street, and at some of the nightclubs in Harlem, and this impromptu amateur performance was as good as any of them.

Watching her dance, I suddenly realized that I knew her. When I looked at her partner, I realized they were the couple at the staged robbery when Louie got "shot." Her boyfriend was Chevy de Falla, the drug dealer. I remembered him running away and her on the porch screaming, as the two black agents pretended to shoot Louie, and groped her breasts. Sprague told me she was Hermes' stepdaughter. Her name was Leah. Unlike Rachel, who was cool and deep, Leah seemed fiery and defiant. I couldn't take my eyes off of her.

Hermes and an elegant woman in her fifties then took the stage. They danced slower than Chevy and Leah, but were just as beautiful. At the end, Hermes "presented" her with open arms to the crowd, as Latin men like to do to show off their women.

Hermes recognized me and brought her over to meet me. Her name was Regina, his wife. With great charm, she engaged me in a conversation about my background, how I met Hermes and how I happened to come to the party. I sidestepped every question with an innocent response, never admitting to anything brutal, illegal, or connected with drugs. She seemed amused with my clumsy deceptions. Her piercing eyes saw and understood everything. Wherever she went, people paid attention to her; even Orlando, who had turned into a loud-mouthed drunk, became a gentleman in her presence. She had a quiet manner, often extending her hand to be gently kissed or carefully shaken.

Hermes ordered her around like a servant: "Darling, get our guest a drink," or "Darling, I don't like the line at the bar, please see to it, don't let it happen again." She tolerated the humiliating treatment and after several rounds of greeting the guests, she continued her conversation with me. She remembered my name and took me by the arm to the shrimp bowl, pointing out the types of sauces and side dishes that she felt were special. Nursing a glass of champagne, she tested my knowledge of art, law, politics, food, and wine. We were the only two people at the entire party conducting a normal conversation. When we talked about travel she asked me how I liked Switzerland. This surprised me. I made up a story about my uncle living there and said that all of my visits were just to his house, hoping she would not ask me about restaurants and hotels, and then find out that I knew nothing about the country.

Eventually Regina introduced me to her two daughters, Leah and Mercedes. Mercedes was not as pretty, nor as wild, as Leah. She dressed moderately and stayed close to her husband. He was shy and wore a cheap suit. He didn't seem to be a drug dealer.

Hermes seemed to ignore his stepdaughters and was busy laughing with the other guests. Often he would grab and hug some of the females. This didn't seem to bother Regina, at least not as much as I thought it should have. I also noticed that no one ever discussed drugs, sex, or any illegal activity in her presence.

Finally around midnight, after Regina made the rounds with everyone again, I said goodnight. I was surprised to see the many inconspicuous types of cars in the parking lot: Chevrolets, Fords, Chryslers, even rentals – not one BMW or Cadillac, or any luxury car. This was smart. The cartel did not want to draw attention to themselves.

The next day I told Michael about the party and the people. He was irritated that I didn't get closer to Hermes and Orlando, since, after all, they were my targets, and worse, I had only met Pepe Click-Click once, just in a brief introduction. When I had nothing more to say, Michael opened up his briefcase and pulled out a file, opened it, and placed some photographs on the table. They were surveillance shots taken by FBI Agent Springfield. He pointed to one, of a man crossing the street, and asked, "Do you recognize him?"

"Yes. That's the cop I told you about. That's Sprague."

"His name is Lieutenant Larry Sprague of the hundred-and-fifteenth precinct. Do you remember the name from the Scarluci case? He was the guy on the tape talking to Domenic."

I looked at Michael, "How did you find out about these people?"

"Sprague pulled your file from BCI the day after you met Hermes. We know he's dirty, but we don't know how deep. He may only be providing information, or maybe he's running things for them, giving them protection. We have to know. He could be as dangerous to you as the Medalley killers."

I remembered Regina and her conversations with me, especially her question about Switzerland. "Michael, does the file ever say that I was in Switzerland?"

"It says you spent four years in a Swiss prison for assault and battery. It would be nice if you read the file. Your life depends on it."

THE CAR

It didn't take long for things to start happening. A few days after the party there was another message from the law-office secretary, inviting me to lunch in Manhattan with Regina at the Quo Vadis, an expensive society restaurant in midtown.

I found Regina waiting in a booth, sipping a glass of white wine and talking to a well-dressed elderly man with gray hair that reminded me of Domenic Scarluci. Regina motioned me to sit down, but did not introduce me.

The stranger was less rude. "How do you do; I'm Carl Wineburg. I must go, just wanted to say hello and thanks to the wonderful lady here." I remembered the name Wineburg. It was Judge Wineburg who was handling Louis Turko's case.

Regina got right to the point. "Hermes couldn't be here, but he likes you very much. My husband would like to know if he could employ your services. He wants you to be close to the family, come to the house to protect us."

I wondered why Hermes would want to hire me as a special bodyguard. There were more killers at that party than in Sing Sing.

Regina spoke with such wisdom that I was instantly convinced that everything she said had to be absolutely true. Regina was the most impressive person I had ever met in my life. I also knew that Hermes could never respect me. He'd sent Regina to hire me, like the rest of the domestic help around the house, like a butler or gardener. I suspected that my job would be to hang around like those goons I met the first day, but at least I would get inside the organization. I accepted.

I went to the Medalley mansion almost every day at about noon to look after Regina. Sometimes I'd accompany her to Manhattan in her limousine. After about a week I was able to report back to Michael what I thought was important, but in fact most of my information was useless. I told Michael about meeting Carl Wineburg with Regina. He knew the name. "He's a newly appointed federal judge. Seems to be honest, but his political friends get a lot of money from the union, Longshore Teamsters. He could be dirty also. I know he let Turko out on bail. I'll tell Dewey."

Again Michael told me that the cartel was ruled by a brotherhood code and had great influence. The Medalleys gave drugs to dealers on consignment! Of all the people in the world, drug dealers are the least trustworthy – yet the Medalleys trusted everyone. Apparently they had so much coke they consigned it to any willing dealer, and the dealer took the risk of being caught or getting killed by the Medalley family if he broke the trust. Pepe Lamaros made people think twice about crossing the family. Each day their operation grew larger and more powerful.

I knew that the partygoers at the Medalley mansion were "account executives." They were well-paid and knew that they would die if they ever betrayed the trust. The family recorded and carefully numbered all product – heroin and cocaine – with a red wax stamp. They took great pride in the quality of their cocaine. The numbers on all the packages of coke represented quality, as well as strict inventory control. When the Medalley dealers gave drugs on consignment the numbers were carefully recorded like inventory control in any other type of business. Michael was very interested in how they managed their inventory and their willingness to give drugs on consignment.

The primary job of the account executives, however, was not to sell drugs, but to collect the money. The Medalley organization was not a group of drug dealers. They were cold-blooded killers. Their trademark punishment was to cut off a hand of someone who owed them money before murdering him.

For several weeks I performed my duties as one of the house bodyguards while Regina met friends for lunch, visited the health spa, and shopped with her two daughters, Leah and Mercedes. My compensation was four ounces of cocaine a week, provided to me by Orlando, who I would call on Friday and set up a different drop each week. Meanwhile my cash remained in Hermes' safe until I proposed a bigger deal.

Michael didn't care in the least about me being paid with cocaine, so it just piled up in my locker. He was uncharacteristically patient while I spent my time hanging around the pool and sucking up some of the best cocaine in the world. I still met with him almost every day to pass on anything that I learned, but none of it seemed of much use. My family was gone and my apartment was empty. I had no home and I began to day-dream during my long hours at the pool that these people were my family and the beautiful house was mine. Leah had become an obsession as I waited for her to make her afternoon visits. The more she ignored me the more I fantasized about making love to her.

I still couldn't figure out how the cocaine entered the country, but some of the things I had seen confirmed Dewey's theory of the fishing boats pulling the drugs out of the channel. I never saw the fishing boats being used or overheard conversations about boat schedules or fishing.

After about a month into my poolside job Michael left word I should meet him that night at a bar off Bleecker Street in the East Village. Michael's drinking habits were getting worse, so I wasn't surprised he'd picked a bar to hear my report. That evening after parking the car, I walked down the sidewalk toward the bar when I saw a commotion. In front of the restaurant several men were struggling with somebody, then I saw Michael go flying across the sidewalk and bounce off the side of a parked car, lose his balance, and sprawl onto the pavement. I ran up to help him to his feet, and reached for my gun, but he held me back, "No, no!"

I stood there glaring at the bouncer. He was huge, dressed like a Mafia wise guy. "What are *you* looking at, faggot? Get this piece of shit off the sidewalk."

I held Michael in my arms and glared back at the man who had thrown *the* Michael Giovanni out of the bar and was now calling me a "faggot." I figured that his life could now be measured in minutes, or at most an hour. Michael staggered to his feet and asked me to take him uptown to an address in Riverside. I helped him to my car. He smelled of liquor, hadn't had a bath in days, and was bleary-eyed. We drove in silence until I pulled up in front of his building and he told me to park. His head weaved and bobbed, his eyes were red and teary. I tried to joke with him and said things were going well at the Medalley mansion, but I was really waiting for him to tell me what to do next. Michael kept rocking back and forth as if he didn't hear what I said, and then he leaned over close to my face and stared into my eyes. I could see he was trying desperately to tell me something. He would start and stop, and start over again. His breath was unbearable. It was as if what he had to say would take all of his energy just to say it – and finally he did, through quivering lips, "Say it was a green Chrysler."

Like half the things that Michael would say in his drunken stupor, it made no sense. I was stunned, relieved, and disappointed in what he'd finally muttered. I pretended this nonsense was important, and repeated it back, "Say it was a green Chrysler." He just nodded, grabbed for the door handle, and staggered out across the sidewalk and into the building. I felt sorry for him – brilliant, ruthless, and dedicated, but now just a pitiful drunk.

As I drove back downtown I began to think more about Michael's humiliation at that bar in the Village. My anger grew, focused on the bouncer who had thrown Michael in the street and called me a faggot. By the time I reached Midtown I had decided to return to the bar.

When I got there, it seemed normal – couples, people dancing – the kind of place that I would have chosen to have a drink. This surprised me because I always thought that Michael hung out in low-life places where no one would know him. I sat at the bar, watching for the bouncer. Finally he walked across the room and up a flight of stairs to the second floor. I followed him up to the top of the stairs, but he was gone, so I leaned against the wall and waited.

After a few minutes he came out of an office door and started to walk toward the steps to go back down. At first he didn't recognize me, but then he nodded. When he got closer, his expression changed as he looked at me. "Oh, it's you, how's your faggot friend?" As he walked past to begin the descent, I got behind him and stomped on the back of his calves, sending him tumbling down the stairs. Then I followed him down and as he tried to get up I pulled out my blue automatic and raked it across the top of his head as hard as I could. Most of the bar heard the commotion and I could see another bouncer on his way to get me. As he got closer he saw my arm down by my side, holding my blue automatic. He stepped back, and I turned and walked out the door.

LIFEGUARD

The next day I went directly to the Medalley mansion. Regina was at the pool with her daughter Mercedes and a child in a wheelchair. The young boy had cerebral palsy or muscular dystrophy and looked like he was starving to death. Regina told me he was Mercedes' son. After a few awkward moments I went for a swim.

I changed and began doing laps in the pool while Regina and Mercedes chatted under the sun umbrella, drinking tea. After about a half hour of laps I climbed out of the end of the pool and walked over to the wrought-iron fence that overlooked the channel between Staten Island and Brooklyn.

The pool deck stood about fifty yards from the shore, elevated, and separated by high thick brush. As I stood there looking through the wrought-iron bars at the passing ships I noticed the tall brush moving in front of me; something was coming through it. Then suddenly a man staggered out, wearing a yellow silk shirt and brown pants, which were wet on one side. His right arm crossed his chest and held his left forearm. He had a terrible twisted expression on his face. I remembered him from the party. He was a friend of Chevy de Falla. Tears were streaming down his cheeks, and as he staggered forward I could see that his left hand was gone and gushes of blood were spilling onto his pant leg. He looked at me with a blank stare as he held his wrist to stop the bleeding. Then two men broke out of the bushes behind him, grabbed him, and dragged him back into the brush out of sight.

I stood there in shock. I watched movement in the brush as they dragged him down toward two fishing boats, one of which was cranked up and puffing black smoke from its stack.

Like ignoring a child who had become a nuisance, or a dirty glass or a piece of broken furniture, I believed that Regina would have considered it impolite of me to say anything about what I had just seen. I felt a deep coldness as I turned toward Mercedes and Regina. They were still sitting around the table, laughing. In Regina's mind, the incident seemingly amounted to no more than a domestic embarrassment, all part of the daily routine at the Medalley house.

I went back into the boathouse to change and dry off. Still naked, I became so unnerved that I leaned against the wall, then slid down to the floor, unable to speak or move. After about ten minutes I got dressed and went out to the pool as if nothing had happened. Mercedes and Regina were in the water, throwing a ball with the little boy, who paddled around in a lifejacket. I walked over to the edge of the pool where I had seen the horror earlier, and looked down across the brush. One of the boats was gone. Without asking I went over to the pool bar and poured a glass of vodka.

Hermes came down to the poolside. Regina and Mercedes invited him into the water, but he was looking for me. I was already half drunk and still unhinged by what I had seen. We went into his study, where it was cooler, sat in comfortable chairs, and drank vodka tonics.

Hermes kept smiling and joking, and he finally said, "I like you and so does Regina. You've almost become part of our family and you are our trusted friend. Surely" – again he smiled – "you have a greater interest in our enterprises than just a career as a lifeguard." His voice was soft, almost lyrical.

"Yes, of course," I replied. "You forget. That's how we met. I've been patient and I still think I have money on account with you. I have sources that are new. I would like to do business at the right time." I surprised myself at how good I sounded, particularly half drunk and reeling from seeing a brutal murder.

Hermes sat back in his chair, giving me a brand-new smile. "Yes, I wanted to talk to you about that. Your friend that got killed, did he say anything to you?"

I was taken off guard by the change of subject. "Like what? He just said that he was robbed and shot. Then he died."

"Yes, I know, but did he say anything like, for example, did he tell you the kind of car that his killers drove, or who they were? It's important that you remember. What kind of car did he say they drove?"

All of a sudden I knew this was a set-up. My life depended upon the right answer. "Yes," I said. "He said they drove...a green Chrysler." I didn't know what else to say, but I felt that Michael knew more than I did, and this answer would somehow save my life.

Hermes seemed satisfied and changed the subject. He asked me how much cocaine I thought I could sell and if I understood how the Medalley family worked with their consignment program. I said I thought I could probably move a kilo a month. He was happy with that and told me Pepe would make arrangements for all the coke I needed; after all, I still had money on account.

We then returned to the pool. Regina and Mercedes were back on their lounge chairs, drying off and talking about a new restaurant in Manhattan. Regina suggested that I take the afternoon off. I accepted the offer and left.

DEATH WARRANT

Sitting in traffic on my way back to Manhattan, I kept thinking about the green-Chrysler conversation and the doomed man that I had seen in the bushes below the pool. The heat, the vodka, the blood, and the conversation were making me nauseous. I had to find Dewey or Michael as soon as possible.

I couldn't find Michael. He wasn't home or he didn't answer the phone, and no one in the office had heard from him all day, but I had a good idea where I could find Dewey. He had a mistress and usually hung out at Jimmy Ryan's bar on Park Avenue. At about 7:00 Dewey walked in with his girlfriend: a beautiful, high-powered advertising executive. The two of them looked very affluent as they sat at a table and greeted a half dozen well-dressed people as they came in.

The ride over from Staten Island had sobered me up, but I had gotten drunk again, waiting for Dewey. I wondered if his fancy friends, or even his girlfriend, knew what he did for a living. When Dewey saw me I knew he was embarrassed. I looked desperate and sweaty. My shiny suit and open shirt didn't fit in with the upscale crowd at Jimmy Ryan's. I didn't care how I looked, or how he felt about seeing me; I had to know what was going on.

Dewey left his friends and the two of us sat down at a quiet table in the corner. I came right to the point. "Dewey, who owns a fucking green Chrysler?"

Dewey looked down at the floor and shook his head. He could see the anger in my face. "Stay out of it. This is Michael's case. You know how he works; you're just carrying the luggage."

"Tell me what the *fuck* is going on."

He took a long pull from his drink and said, "Michael wanted to test that NYPD lieutenant, Larry Sprague. I had one of my boys put a kilo of the coke we stole in Chevy's car. The idea was to see if Sprague would make a case of possession against one of the Medalley's dealers. It was to test him, to see how deep he is with the organization. He's dangerous and he's supposed to be on our side. He could find out about you. We put the coke in Chevy's car and then Michael had another informant call Sprague to pop the car."

"Well, what happened?"

Dewey took another sip from his drink. "Nothing happened. Sprague and his boys tossed the car. Sprague did the search, he looked under the seat like he was supposed to, but he said he didn't find anything."

"Wait a minute," I said. "You had your informants plant the coke in Chevy's car, Sprague tosses it and he doesn't find it. That's it?"

"Not quite. Sprague found it; he just pretended he didn't, to protect Chevy. The coke was stolen. It was numbered. It was the coke from the sting. You know what happens when you steal coke from the Medalleys; no matter who you are, you die. So you see, Michael had it figured out. If Sprague popped Chevy for carrying a kilo of coke around, he was off the street, but if he covered for Chevy and pretended not to find it, Michael knew he would tell Hermes, and Chevy would be dead, so either way there was no way to lose. Chevy was going down one way or the other. See, that's how Michael thinks. Now if you don't mind, I want to get back to my friends, you must have something else to do."

"Wait a minute," I said to him. "There's something else. You're holding back. What is it?"

"Nothing," Dewey insisted. But I knew he was lying.

"Dewey...what was the make of the car that you and Michael planted the coke in?"

Now I could see he was nervous, but he answered, "It was a green Chrysler."

"Chevy was driving a green Chrysler?"

"Yes," Dewey said, "but it wasn't *his* car. He was just *driving* it. He borrowed it from Leah. We put the stolen coke in Leah's car. He was driving it that day." Dewey picked up his drink and returned to his friends.

I walked out into the night air and began to think. I remembered Michael's drunken teary eyes. The vodka had slowed my senses. Dewey and Michael knew something terrible that I should know... then suddenly it came to me. The stolen cocaine in Leah's car had condemned both her and Chevy to death. That's why Hermes asked me about the car. He wanted another source of information about Leah stealing the coke with Chevy and trying to blame it on Mars La Pont, and he got it from *me*!

I started to run as fast as I could. I had parked two blocks away and was sweating and out of breath by the time I reached my car. I began driving recklessly, like Ed Silkey, down Lexington Avenue toward the tunnel to Queens, but the traffic was at a standstill so I pulled over to look for a pay phone. I found one, but it was being used. Some guy in a business suit was having an intense conversation, probably with his girlfriend or his wife. I couldn't wait. I grabbed the phone, hung it up and pushed him. He fell to the sidewalk. He started to get up to fight back, but I pulled out my automatic and pointed it to his chest. I didn't say a word, just motioned, waving the gun side to side; he stood up and walked away. Frantically I dug in my pockets for change and my little notebook with Chevy's home phone number.

Leah was with Chevy that night we pulled the sting and stole the coke. When they french-fried Mars La Pont's hand, he couldn't tell them anything because he didn't *know* anything. When Sprague told them the coke was in Leah's car, they believed Chevy and Leah shot Louie, stole the coke, and lied, blaming Mars La Pont. Pepe and Hermes had to be convinced that she was in on it. The drugs in her car, and me telling Hermes it was a green Chrysler, now convinced everybody that she and Chevy had lied about what had happened the night Louie got shot. The trouble was, I told Hermes that the only car there was Leah's green Chrysler, blowing their whole story about a "white Cadillac and two black guys." Hermes and Pepe figured Chevy killed Louie to cover up the theft. The guy staggering out of the brush without his hand was someone who had been with Chevy at the party. They were torturing and killing people trying to find out about Leah and Chevy. All of this because of me. But now I had to save Leah.

After two rings Leah answered. I was so relieved I almost started to cry. I told her not to leave the house, not to go anywhere, that I was coming over and had to talk to her, and I pleaded with her to do exactly as I ordered. She said she was on her way to make a drop with Chevy.

"*No!*" I screamed "*No!* Send someone else, *please* send someone else."

It took me about forty-five minutes to get to the house where we had staged the robbery with Louie. There were no cars in the driveway, but there was a light on, so I banged on the door.

Leah appeared, wearing blue jeans and a T-shirt, in her bare feet. I hugged her, but she pushed me away. "What's the *matter* with you? What's wrong?"

I realized I couldn't explain anything to her. I fumbled for a story and finally blurted, "I heard something. I heard you might be in danger. Something about Chevy. That's all. I was just concerned."

"That's it? Well, I'm okay, as you can see." She seemed annoyed. "My mother may need your help, but I don't. What did you hear?"

The whole scene was strange. She had no interest in me, even though I was falling in love with her and had to protect her. "I just heard they were trying to rob Chevy and I didn't want you to be around if anything happened."

She laughed. "Rob Chevy? Rob him of *what*? You know how we work. We always use some kind of a drop, and I go along as a lookout."

I could see by the look on her face she wanted me to leave, and I didn't have an excuse to stay. I was beginning to feel silly, so I turned to go, not knowing what to do or where to go, and then she said, "Don't worry. I'll be fine, Chevy's coming back."

As she said this I looked for the green Chrysler, but it was gone. She said, "Chevy will be back soon. After you called I told him to take Mercedes. Someone's got to be the lookout."

Fear and panic flooded my mind again, and without saying another word I ran to my car. I just stared into space; I didn't know what to do, or where to go.

I drove towards Queens Boulevard. I would find Dewey and Michael and straighten the whole thing out. There had to be some way to get the suspicion off Leah. At an intersection, about ten blocks away from the house, I saw red and blue flashing lights, and traffic was stopped. I parked the car and began to walk up the street through the stalled traffic. I was less than half a block away from the intersection with the lights and ambulances when I saw the green Chrysler sitting in the middle of the street. There was a yellow plastic tarp over the top of one side. A man was walking toward me, away from the scene; he kept staring down at the ground, shaking his head, and waving his arms up and down. I asked, "What happened down there?"

"It was awful. Some guy and his girlfriend were stopped at the intersection and there were three guys in the car in front of them. They got out, one of them had a shotgun. They just opened fire on them. Shot the hell out of both of them. Then they got back in their car and drove off, just like that." He shook his head again and walked off.

There was no need for me to go back to protect Leah. There was no need for me to talk to Michael or Dewey. There was no need for me to do anything that night. I had been drunk and sober three times during the day and I was exhausted. I would be lucky to have enough strength to make it home for the evening – to have another drink, snort a little coke, and go to sleep.

CHAPTER EIGHT

ALL IN THE FAMILY

ASTRONOMY

I knew what to expect the next day at the Medalley mansion. Again I was waved through the gates. Everything seemed normal, except inside there were no fresh flowers; yesterday's had wilted. I moved through the mansion like I lived there, and got a glimpse of Hermes as he walked into his study and closed the door. Strangely, he didn't seem bothered. I asked the maid where Regina was and she pointed to her bedroom. I waited for a while and finally Leah came out of the bedroom, her eyes puffy and red. Dabbing at her nose, she said, "My mother is awake now. She would like to speak with you."

I knocked quietly on Regina's bedroom door and heard her soft voice say, "Come in." The room was almost dark, Regina was in her bed and I could barely see her through the dim light. Through the shadows she said, "You knew... Leah told me... You knew, and you tried to stop it. My daughters are innocent. You tried to protect them. You are independent; you learn things. You're loyal to me...

Thank you, thank you for trying to help."

Her calm control gave me a cold chill, and somehow I had this feeling again, that I didn't know everything. Something else was going on. My profound guilt prevented me from saying anything, except, "I will protect Leah. I will protect you. As God is my witness I will protect you both." At that moment I wasn't sure who I was going to protect her from; her own people or 90 Church – or perhaps from me.

She smiled at me like I was a child. I expected her to be straightening flowers around the house by noon.

I didn't see Michael or Dewey until the next evening when I knew everyone would be at the Heidelberg to discuss the case. I wasn't sure what to say at the meeting. No one knew why Mercedes was murdered – she had nothing to do with drug trafficking. Leah should have been in the car. I sat in silence, trying to contain my hatred for Michael. Michael knew they were going to kill both Leah and Chevy. That's why he had trouble talking to me the night he was drunk. I was just as guilty. It was my fault Mercedes was dead.

Then came my turn to speak. I simply reported that I was a trusted member of the household and was looking after Leah, and stayed mostly around the pool. There were smiles and smirks, and then Dewey and Michael started in with a barrage of questions: How many people were in the house during the day? Did I see any drug activity? Who did Hermes meet with? How often did Pepe come over? Did I overhear anything? What was the house like? It went on and on. When I was describing the Medalley mansion, I did remember something unusual: on the roof was a sundeck with a mounted telescope and it always seemed that there was someone looking through it – all day and all night.

Only Dewey seemed to be interested in this information. "Describe the telescope."

"It's a telescope, on a tripod, and there was always somebody in a chair staring through it, next to a phone. So what?"

"Where is the telescope aimed?"

"It seemed to be level," I said, "as if looking across the water at the ships."

Dewey pressed on. "What color is it and how big is it?"

I lost my patience. "What difference does it make? It's a fucking *telescope*! The guy sits there and watches the ships. It's about twelve inches in diameter and it has two little sights on it, and it's short. What difference does it make? Some dopey spic sits and stares at the ships all day long next to a phone. So what?"

Everybody around the table gave me a "You are really stupid" kind of look.

"Michael," Dewey said, "I think it's time we stopped screwing around with these dumb spics around the pool. Let's go after the drugs. We all know where they are."

Everyone around the table agreed, but I objected. "I haven't seen any drug activity at the Medalley mansion at all."

Dewey turned to me. "You're right. If you had read the surveillance reports that Springfield filed, it's just normal comings and goings. Even at the docks, no one comes and picks up drugs, drops off money, or anything. It's just a normal household...and do you know why?"

There was silence around the room while everyone waited for Dewey to answer his own question. "Because *you*, our young undercover agent, have discovered where the drugs are. You know where the stash is, don't you?"

I shook my head, feeling stupid. I was the undercover agent on the inside but Dewey knew more than I did.

"Why, they're in *Brooklyn*," Dewey said. "I can't believe how slow everybody is. They're at the tenement on the shore, the *Brooklyn* shore. That's where they keep their stash. The telescope on the roof at the Medalley house is manned twenty-four hours a day, but it's not a telescope for looking at ships; it's a high-powered reflector-mirror, used for astronomy. It's not the kind of instrument that someone would look at a ship with. It's too powerful. Do you think these spics are interested in looking at the stars? It sees across the bay to the building in Brooklyn and watches outside. It watches for cops, dope dealers, and thieves. If the guy sees something he picks up the phone and calls the apartment. It's perfect. They're able to guard the apartment without ever being seen. The last thing they want to do is to draw attention to themselves by having someone hanging around in the street, so they can *see* if they're under surveillance."

Michael didn't seem to care. "Dewey, I think you're right about them throwing the drugs overboard and fishing them out of the water with their boats, and I think you're right about the stash being in Brooklyn. Springfield's surveillance report indicates a lot of Medalley cars coming in to that neighborhood, but I don't care. We've got other things to do. I don't care about the dope."

Michael usually had the last word, but not this time. Dewey said, "Things are getting out of hand. Mercedes shouldn't have been killed. We fucked up when we put the dope in Leah's car. We should have known Chevy was using her car. They're killing each other off with their stupid code. I already count four dead, with Mercedes."

I didn't mention the guy that popped out of the weeds without his hand, and wondered if he was number five, or one of the four. It was the first time I had ever seen Michael challenged by another agent, and it was the first time anyone felt that another agent knew more about a case than Michael. My concern for Regina and Leah grew: knowing Michael, sooner or later they would end up dead.

Dewey stood up. "Well, you know, it just doesn't seem right. We have to draw the line someplace. We've got to stop this before someone else like Mercedes gets killed. The FBI says there's a ship coming in soon and they'll probably make a drop. It's time to shut them down. What do you say, Michael?"

Michael was on the defensive. "What about Pepe Click-Click? That's why we started out. He's still running around. McDermott doesn't want a bunch of low-level people rotting in jail. I want Pepe, Orlando, and Hermes."

There was silence, and then Michael broke the deadlock. "Okay, we let the case go another two weeks, or wrap it up when they start fishing the coke out of the water. Agreed?"

Dewey and Michael nodded at each other.

THE CHEATER'S BAR

I waited a couple of days, then I went out to the Medalley mansion, as usual, around noon. Regina was by the pool, but she looked different, quiet. There were fresh flowers throughout the house.

Leah showed up around two. She had someone with her, her own "bodyguard." I couldn't tell if he was South American or Puerto Rican. He had a gut and his buttons pulled on his shirt. He kept smiling and joking around, leering at Leah and acting like he was a real tough guy. Regina was trying to ignore him. He was so obnoxious that he took out his gun and played with it, laying it on the table to show it off. Leah liked him, teased him, tried to push him in the pool, as he kept trying to grab her. When Regina left, Leah sat on his lap, and he touched her ass. His name was Roland and I couldn't stand him. My feelings for Leah had turned into burning jealousy and disgust. Only three days had passed since her lover and sister had been killed, and her new slob of a boyfriend was feeling her up.

Finally Regina called Leah aside and told her that I was to guard her. Roland had to go, at least for a while. Leah seemed okay with this, at least temporarily. So I ended up driving Leah around and promising Regina that I would guard her twenty-four hours a day. I tried to hide my jealousy and created a ridiculous story that I felt she should be more socially active so that anyone trying to kill her would know she was well-protected. However, she shouldn't visit her old social haunts. I suggested I take her out that night to some of the more safe places in town, such as Basin Street, Count Basie's, or Small's Paradise, and other upscale clubs. All of these places were in Spanish Harlem, the most dangerous part of the city, but strangely enough that's where I felt most comfortable. She accepted this.

Leah looked absolutely beautiful in her tight miniskirt and high heels. When we walked into Basin Street to see DeWitt play his trumpet, she literally stopped the show as everybody turned to look at the beautiful white couple. After a few drinks and one of DeWitt's sets she disappeared into the bathroom for about fifteen minutes. When she returned I asked her what took so long, she said she had been arguing with Roland on the phone. All evening

I tried to impress her, but after a while I could see it was useless. I kept thinking how incredible it was that she went from being in love with Chevy to now, a few days later, with a new boyfriend, a real creep, as if nothing had ever happened. She thought Basin Street was dull, although she liked the "old black man playing the horn," and said it was too bad there weren't younger, white, "decent" people in the club like us. I drove her home to Staten Island. She gave me a peck on the cheek.

The next day as usual I sat around the pool with Regina and Leah. I kept thinking about my failure with her last night, and my jealousy grew. Throughout the afternoon I kept staring at two of the most beautiful women in the world, Leah and her mother. They were my family in a private, twisted way. By mid-afternoon I was drunk in the hot sun.

Hermes called me into his study. I thought he was going to give me my money back and get rid of me. But instead he said I could pick up my salary for the past two weeks from Roland today: eight ounces of cocaine. Every week Hermes would tell me a different way to pick up the cocaine. He never directly handled dope, he simply told me who to contact. I knew he was disappointed in me. He had hoped I would be a major dealer instead of a stupid lifeguard hanging around his wife and step-daughter. I called Roland and arranged to meet him at the White Horse bar in Queens at four o'clock to get my two weeks' pay.

I left the mansion and drove a few miles until I found a bar, hoping to get something to eat. It was a cheater's nest – very dark, cool, with private high-backed booths, and a big-chested blonde, with cleavage, behind the bar in her bare feet. Instead of eating, I sat alone at the bar, drinking vodka. After a few drinks I picked up the phone on the bar and called Michael.

"Michael, Roland is going to be at the White Horse bar at four o'clock this afternoon with eight ounces of coke. Do you want to pop him?"

Michael seemed surprised. "Why? Who gives a shit about eight ounces of coke, and a dumb low-level spic named Roland?"

"Michael, I know this guy really well," I lied. "You can turn him. He's the Brooklyn connection, maybe even part of the Gambino crew. He can get us into the stash, I know it, and he's carrying eight ounces. Take him down hard. You'd better take Dewey and Ed Silkey. He's a hothead, he won't go easily."

"Anything you want. What's he look like?" Michael asked. I could tell Michael was annoyed, but at least I was finally making a case.

I replied, "He's a pot-bellied spic with a ponytail." Michael hung up.

I had a couple more vodkas and thought *I was as bad as Michael* and started to feel guilty, all the way down into my soul. I was setting Roland up because I was jealous, I wanted him out of the way so I could make it with Leah. This was wrong, all wrong, and I knew it, and I had to stop it.

Finally, I grabbed the phone off the bar again and called Roland. I couldn't tell him I had set him up with the drug agents, but I had to stop it. When he answered, I said, "Roland, let's not do the deal this afternoon. Something very bad has come up."

"What's wrong? Why not, big fellow?"

"I've been dating this girl," I replied, making up a story, "and told her I would have some coke for her this afternoon. She's a good customer. She was going to come with me to pick it up, but then she called and said *her* customer is a *little too interested*. He wanted to go with her. Her customer works for the La Pont family. They're still mad over Mars. I think it's too hot. Let's just call it off; it's not worth the risk. They may be waiting for us, especially you. It could be a set-up."

"Okay," Roland replied. "Thanks. They can wait outside all they want. Call me tomorrow and let's reschedule, cause I've got it here for you, big boy." Then he hung up.

I drank some more. I thought of Michael and Ed and Dewey sitting outside the bar, waiting for Roland, who was not going to show up. For some reason I thought it was funny; I could imagine Michael swearing, mad as hell. I sat in the bar, flirting with the blonde bartender until she got busy. I left about six and went home to my empty, lonely apartment in Brooklyn to sleep it off. Like acid, my loneliness ate away my heart and mind until there was nothing left except desperation. I had betrayed Daisy, and lost my family, now someday soon I was going to betray Regina and Leah.

A MAJOR CASE

You know something big has happened at 90 Church Street if, before you walk into the building, you see cars lining the street with sun visors down to show their press badges. The office was buzzing with camera crews and reporters. I knew it was big when I saw Kyle, the Queens detective on the Organized Crime Task Force.

"What happened, Kyle?" I asked. "What's all the fuss?"

He looked at me with surprise. "You've got to be kidding. You don't know what happened last night with the Medalley family?"

"No," I replied, as fear swept over me.

"Well, four of the Medalley henchmen tried to ambush Michael, Dewey, and Ed outside a bar in Queens, the White Horse."

I realized instantly what happened. Why didn't I see it coming? Roland was a hothead, a loudmouth, a two-bit killer. He would never run from the La Pont gang. After all, the Medalleys were still not sure if Leah told the truth about being robbed by Mars La Pont. It was their chance to get the La Pont gang, who were still after them for french-frying Mars La Pont's hand; instead, Roland and his friends had met 90 Church.

I rushed into Group Two, afraid somebody had been killed, but there they were, Michael, Dewey, and Ed Silkey. Dewey had a bandage on his hand, but other than that, they were fine. I pulled Dewey aside; he'd cut his hand on the car door trying to dodge a bullet. He put his arm around me and we walked down the hall to an empty room.

When we sat down Dewey said, "It was a set-up. The moment we drove up to the bar, the assholes came out shooting. Funny, Michael said it might go like that. Why didn't you show up? It was really wild. We didn't know he would bring three others to the party. Why didn't you know it was set up? All four of them walked out when they saw Michael driving up in Pike's Cadillac. We had to drive away and shoot it out in a parking lot. Ed nailed two with his pump, I got one, and Michael got one. It was bad, a lot of gunshots. I even had to use a second clip. Pike is going to take credit for it, and his Cadillac got all shot up. They don't want us at the press conferences. Roland had eight ounces of coke on him. It was self-defense; they all began shooting – first at Michael. Speaking of Michael, he's pissed at you, you better straighten it out with Michael; he has a lot of questions...Oh, and one other thing –

one of the spics that Silkey hit with his pump was Pepe Lamaros's son. Ed tore him up pretty bad, and he died this morning."

As Dewey turned to leave he said, "There's something else; the boat's coming in. We're going to have to stop this shit. The way things are going there won't be anybody left alive to pick the dope out of the water."

I couldn't face Michael; I walked down the hall and out the side door to the elevators and into the street. I wasn't sure where to go, so I drove to Central Park and wandered around the paths, watching the school children eating lunch and the lovers strolling hand-in-hand. It was so calm and peaceful, but everything in my life was out of control.

I tried to convince myself that none of this was my fault. It was all kind of an accident. I might have been drunk, but even if I was sober I would have made the same decisions. I tried to tell myself I *wasn't* like Michael; Michael set people up as an art form, playing one against the other while they dealt drugs. Now I knew I was doing the same thing. There was a perverse logic to all of it but, logical or not, I was scared.

Eventually I drove to the Medalley mansion, not having any idea what I would find. Perhaps death, or perhaps they figured out that they just lost four more "account executives" in a hail of gunfire because of me – and by the end of the day I would be on a one-way trip in one of their little fishing boats.

As usual I was waved through the gate and entered the Medalley house without knocking. The pool area was empty, but I sensed something eerie about the house. Incredibly, there were fresh flowers, despite all the crisis and death. Regina had the presence of mind to make sure there were fresh flowers; always the perfect wife and supportive homemaker, the calm, sophisticated, cultured woman in the eye of an evil, violent storm.

Regina, Hermes, and Orlando were in the study, watching a special TV news bulletin: a delayed taping from the morning press conference. There was Pike with his shirt buttons pulling open and his hands waving in the air. Pike and Blanker explained how the Bureau – working with the NYPD Organized Crime Task Force – had been investigating the Medalley drug ring, and finally shut it down with a bloody shoot-out. They mistakenly identified Pepe Click-Click's son as Pepe himself. Mug shots of the dead drug dealers, including a bloody picture of Roland, were shown on the screen, next to "major crime figure" Pepe Lamaros. Pike was proud to announce that they seized eight ounces of cocaine in the shoot-out. Everything was so ridiculous that I just sat in shock with the rest of them. To think that these four low-level punks and my two weeks' payment of cocaine for being Regina's lifeguard added up to a major drug case, disgusted me.

Four people, including Pepe's son and Roland, were dead, shot down in the street, and here they were watching television just like business as usual, like nothing had happened. Orlando said good-bye to everyone and left. I looked out the window to the pool area where Leah lay on a lounge chair, topless, covered with shiny suntan lotion, talking on the phone.

"Nico," Hermes said, and pointed to me. "I have a special assignment for you. We're worried about this unfortunate incident with Pepe's son; perhaps it may cause him to act reckless or even irrational against us. We are losing control; I would like you to work with him. I worry about Regina and Leah. Work with Pepe, take orders from him, then come to me. I want to know how well he's doing. We will know what to do next, you just always be with Pepe. You see, Pepe somehow thinks that this thing with Leah has caused the death of his son. The La Ponts used to be good customers, now we just don't know. Pepe's such a hothead. He could be very dangerous." Hermes ended his little speech with a big smile.

I gave Pepe two days to get over the death of his son and then called and agreed to meet him at his house later that day at about four o'clock.

JUSTIFICATION

I had not spoken to Michael in days. I began to worry about my relationship with him. Michael was not the kind of person you'd want to have against you. Finally I called him and suggested we have lunch before I went to Pepe's house. I sounded like I was calling an old friend that I hadn't seen in a while. It was a silly invitation, since I'd never seen Michael eat any food for lunch. We both knew we had very serious issues to discuss.

Michael and I met at a seafood restaurant in Midtown. It had an impressive bar built around a huge aquarium with exotic fish. We both had a few drinks without saying much and then Michael got down to business. He started off in a strange way: "Do you see how smart Dewey is? I trained him…He's smarter than me now. Do you see how skillfully he makes cases? McDermott, the Bureau, they don't care. They just want us to stop them. They want them all dead. Stop the drugs. That's all anybody cares about. No one cares about the law, or us. They think people like Pike and Blanker are in charge. They take all the credit. We do the dirty work." After his rambling stopped, he leaned over close to me and said in a whisper, "You're too close. You're too close to these people. They're all going to die. Don't go down with them."

I thought of Leah, Regina, and the beautiful house. "Michael," I said, "you and Dewey and the others are just a bunch of killers. Look what you've done to these people." The strangeness of my own words startled me. Then I tried to make sense of it. "This is not what McDermott wanted. He *is* the Justice Department, the FBI – surely he can't be happy with what's going on. What ever happened to the justice system, due process?" As soon as I said this, I realized how wrong it sounded. Then I said something even worse: "You didn't fool me about Stuckey, you set him up, you set him up for Lollipop."

Michael ignored me and leaned down and picked up his briefcase and set it on the bar, angling it as he opened it, so no one else could see inside except me. I could see the usual bags of heroin – and a gun and a knife, both wrapped in plastic. He fingered through the file folders and pulled out one that I recognized as the FBI folder that Springfield had given to us the first day of the case. Michael went through it and pulled out a manila envelope and shuffled through a series of black-and-white photographs. He found two. The first was of a forearm that had been tied with a rope – it was a bloody stump, the hand was missing – and then he threw another picture on top of it. I could tell it was a face, but I couldn't recognize much else. I could see that an ear had been cut off, and there was a black jagged spot where the nose should have been. It looked like a huge photographic blemish. I stared at the photograph, but it didn't mean anything to me.

Michael got close to my face. "His name is Lucas."

I still didn't get it. I knew this was the work of the Medalley family, but who? I shrugged.

"Lucas McDermott...Now tell me what the FBI wants us to do," Michael said almost in a whisper. "Tell me about due process!"

For once it was Michael that was sober, and I was drunk. I just sat there shaking my head, and Michael stared back. "They're all going down – Pepe, Hermes, Regina, Leah – for what they're doing, for what they've done, and for what they will do."

I started to shake my head even harder. "No, Michael. Not like this. I'm going to stop you. It has to stop here. You're not going to kill the mother and daughter. You don't know them like I do. You have enough on Hermes and Orlando; you can turn Sprague. No more, Michael, no more. You're just a fucking killer."

Michael rocked back in his chair and sipped his drink, then started a strange list; "Ormonte, Galentine, Two Fingers, Jimmy Lorenzo, Pepatone, the crazy Gallos, inside on Columbo, and the asshole who got us into the Medalley's in the first place. It was all Lollipop. Lollipop gave me all that information, made all those cases. Stuckey was already dead, long before I sent him 'to meet you uptown.' There were probably six people trying to kill him, he just got it early. After all, his death meant something; it was probably the only good thing he did in his life. Stuckey was sacrificed to protect Lollipop. Every good combat commander knows he must sacrifice some of his troops to win battles. It's war, it's how wars are fought. It was either Stuckey or Lollipop and I chose Lollipop. It was a smart move. Just like I must choose to sacrifice someone to protect you!"

"You mean Leah, don't you? You son-of-a-bitch! The green Chrysler, that was to protect me, to keep me inside, undercover?

You couldn't tell everyone you put the dope in the wrong car, it would blow everything – including my cover."

Michael spoke with a cold calmness. "Including your *life*! What do you think the Medalleys would do to you if they found out about the sting with Louie the G, or found out you're from 90 Church? Don't you see these people are *different*? They're stone-cold *killers*. They don't play by anyone's rules except their own. They would hunt you down and kill you. The only way to save *you* is to take *them* all down so no one's left. Don't you see it was either her or you? I chose you! I chose you over them!"

"Nothing matters to you," I fired back, "or Dewey and the others, except to get these people no matter who or what gets in your way. Right? You don't really care who gets killed."

Michael just stared at me, and I knew his answer.

"I'm going to stop you," I said, "even if I have to kill you myself."

I threw a few dollars on the bar and walked out. For once, since starting at the Bureau, I knew what I was doing. I was right. Yet, the strange logic of it all kept eating at me. I was going to save one of the most ruthless, evil, drug cartels in the world from my friends at 90 Church who were trying to protect me. What an incredible, perverted crusade!

NIGHTMARE

On my drive to Pepe's house in Queens I made my plans to protect Leah. As long as she remained at the Medalley compound she would be safe. The real threat came from Pepe, who wanted revenge. I doubted that the Medalley code of honor and family would keep the balance and prevent a bloodbath. I knew Pepe would hate Hermes for corrupting the Medalley brotherhood code by trying to protect her. Leah would be the first target, and Pepe would probably cut her throat himself. If I stayed close to Pepe and kept Leah in Staten Island until Dewey and Michael intercepted the drugs and shut the whole operation down, I could save her life. Regina was safe because she was never involved in anything.

Pepe lived in an upscale neighborhood on Long Island. I had been there before and remembered how tacky it was, furnished with cheap spindle-legged furniture, plastic flowers, baseball glasses, and pictures of Jesus on the walls.

Pepe's wife greeted me, and I remembered her from the party – overweight and dumb. Black mascara was streaked on her wet, teary face. The house stank of cigarette smoke, dirty dishes, and half-filled glasses left over from the funeral reception.

Pepe was at the bar in the back of the house, sitting on a stool, hunched over a drink, smoking a cigarette. His long, greasy hair hung down over his face like a black curtain. He was so drunk and sad he could hardly talk. I tried to console him as he mumbled incoherently, and sipped his tequila. "My son, my son, my only son. They took him. They will pay. They will pay."

I didn't know if he was talking about 90 Church, Orlando, or Hermes, but it didn't make any difference. I sat down and started lying to him. "I'm sorry I didn't make the wake. Hermes has got me very busy. Hermes is concerned about you and the others that got shot." I didn't mention Leah because I knew it would set him off.

Pepe grinned with his yellow teeth and rubbed the horrible scars on the side of his face. I said, "Pepe, I want to help you. I want to work with you. I want to be by your side, one of your men. We will get through this together. I respect your bravery, your honor. I will take your orders."

He kept blinking his bloodshot eyes in disbelief. "Thank you," he whispered, slurring his words. "I need a good man like you. I've got to get that cunt before she gets us all killed." The black curtain of his hair fell down again, completely covering his face and the glass. I heard him slurp.

I felt my blood run cold for Leah. He then pulled me to the stool next to him so he could speak in a whisper, placing his arm around me and overwhelming me with his wretched breath. "Go back," he said. "Live with them. Be there. I will tell you when. I want to kill the cunt myself, with a knife. You can be there to see it, put your hands in her blood with me." His hatred for Leah inflamed and sobered him up.

"Okay," I whispered. "I'll do it. I'll be there for you." As I got up to leave, he smiled, took a few more swigs of tequila, and pointed to the door.

As I left Pepe, I was shaking with fear for Leah, and passed through a hallway with side windows that overlooked his swimming pool. It wasn't anything like the Medalleys' pool, but it was well-kept. Something caught my eye at the side of the pool patio. At a table under an umbrella was a tanned athletic woman talking on the phone, wearing sunglasses and a baseball cap, and a jeweled sandal half falling off her bobbing foot. I was thrown into a horrible dream and had to hold onto the wall for balance. I kept denying what I was seeing, waiting to wake up, because none of this could be possible. I stared again at what I knew was just an illusion, but it wasn't. How could she be in the house of the man who wanted her dead? Completely oblivious, chin almost resting on the table, totally absorbed in her phone conversation, was Leah. She glanced up, gave me a slight wave, and turned back to her phone.

I went to Harlem that night to Count Basie's to see DeWitt play his sweet trumpet. Now I was working for both Pepe *and* Hermes, who wanted to kill each other, and I had to protect Leah from Pepe – while she was staying at his house! Nothing could be more fucked up. I felt completely alone. I turned my back on Michael just like I had turned my back on Daisy and Mark. The feeling that everything I had thought and done was wrong overwhelmed me, and here I sat listening to some junkie play the trumpet, realizing, profoundly, that I didn't know what the hell I was doing, and I was endangering everybody.

By the next morning there was only one thing left for me to do: return to the Medalley family and play dumb, which would actually be the most sincere and truthful thing that I had done in a long time.

Regina was, as usual, by the pool, straightening vases of flowers and giving orders to the domestic help. I decided to be straightforward. "Regina, I was at Pepe's last night and I saw Leah. Why is she there?"

She smiled. "Oh, you needn't be concerned; it was her idea. She has friends in Queens and wanted to be close to them for a while. It was also Hermes' idea. You know, Pepe and Camello suffered a terrible loss, an accident with their young son. Leah will be there for just a few days and then she'll come back and live here."

Her explanation seemed logical, but I'd lost my self-confidence to question anything. I spent the rest of the day lying around the pool, drinking vodka and snorting coke like I had done so many days before, but this time I had no fear, no caution, no purpose, no ambition, no scheme, nothing. I was drifting and everything was swirling around me, and there was no one I could turn to, to help me understand. I was so out of control it never even occurred to me to be afraid of being discovered.

I went home early and, when I checked the office for messages at about eleven o'clock, there was one on my undercover phone line from Regina, asking me to come back to the mansion early the next morning.

Early to me was ten-thirty, and I was happy to have somewhere, anywhere, to go. It was unusual to see yesterday's flowers still in their vases; there was wilt on them, just like the time when Mercedes was killed. Regina was in her usual spot by the pool, but I could see from the look on her face there was something bothering her. She was happy to see me and stood up so she could look me in the eyes. "Pepe has Leah."

I was confused. "I know. You said — "

She cut me off with a desperate tone. "You *must* get her back for me. You *must* not fail. Do whatever it takes."

"What do you mean? I thought that she was *visiting* Pepe's."

"No." She shook her head with impatience. "Don't you *see*? She was there with Pepe and Orlando as a sign of good faith. A sign of trust. We had to do something to restore the code, the code of trust of the family." Her voice changed slightly, more soft. "It was Hermes' idea. We have a large inventory now. She was meant as security, to ensure that everyone will work together in peace at this crucial period. But Pepe is crazy, crazy with grief. Orlando and Hermes worked it all out, but now Pepe has her. He has, I think, an evil ambition, although Hermes tells me not to worry. I want you to find her. Go and *find* her. You're close to Pepe...Make sure she's safe, bring her back here to Hermes."

I left with the dreadful feeling of helplessness after this strange conversation. How could Regina allow her daughter to be used as "security"? I went to the office to call Pepe on my undercover phone. Pepe acted dumb. He hadn't seen her. She had left his house. He didn't know anything.

I didn't believe him, but I pretended I did. I was convinced that Pepe was holding her captive, or had already killed her. Somehow I had to force him to tell me. I just prayed it wasn't too late. As I sat at my desk with a dull stare, Ed Silkey came in – and my plan of action came together.

Later that afternoon I called Pepe and asked to meet him that night at Pargo's – a bar on the edge of Queens, not far from his house. It was a busy place, and safe. I knew he'd feel secure. We agreed to meet at nine-thirty. I told him I had learned something interesting at the Medalley mansion that he should know.

At about ten o'clock I called the bar at Pargo's and paged Pepe. I told him that I'd driven into a ditch, asked him to come pick me up. Less than twenty minutes later his car pulled up behind mine on a deserted back road in Rockaway, Queens. Pepe got out and walked around the side of my car where I was standing, pretending to look down at the right front wheel. He looked around at the deserted roadside and I saw him pull his gun from his waist and hold it down by his side as he approached. His eyes scanned the dark woods along the road.

"So. What is wrong with your car? Why do you bring me here?"

"I want to know where Leah is," I answered. "You've got her."

He started to laugh. "Is that what this is about? That little tramp.

Fuck *her*, fuck *you*. I don't have time for this."

As he turned to walk back to his car, he confronted Silkey. Ed Silkey loved this kind of thing. He took a natural comfort in beating and shooting people. He even carried special tools. Although Silkey was best known for his pump shotgun, his favorite weapon was a blackjack of two steel balls, each about two inches in diameter, separated by a ten-inch spring – all sewn together with black leather. It looked like a small, floppy dumbbell. Silkey never said a word; he just whipped out the blackjack and shattered Pepe's collarbone. Pepe's gun dropped to the ground.

Pepe turned to me and stared. "I will kill you and that tramp. I will kill that little tramp."

It was the wrong thing to say. Silkey never showed any compassion or any emotion at all. He began to work Pepe over with his little dumbbell. He swung it again, cracking Pepe's rib. Pepe was tough; he fell to his knees, but there was never any of that "please stop" kind of language. Compared to what he had done to his victims, this was probably nothing. He only groaned when Silkey whacked his kneecap. When he bent down to grab his leg Silkey kneed him in the face. Blood spurted from his nose and mouth. He hugged the ground for safety. I pulled him up by his shirt and said, "Tell me where Leah is, or you will die right here."

Through his yellow teeth, his bad breath and bloody mouth, he glared back at me and said, "I don't know where the fucking tramp is. She left. I will kill you and the old cunt."

I threw him against the side of the car. He collapsed and lay motionless. Ed kicked him in his broken ribs. Pepe was silent.

Silkey shook his head and said dryly, " You're not making any new friends here. Now what do we do?"

I looked down at the limp heap and then said, "I really don't know what to do. I don't even know why I'm doing this. Let's get out of here."

Before I dropped Silkey off at his car, he gave me some advice. "I don't know what we just did here but you need to get straight with Dewey and Michael. Vigilante bullshit over some broad can cause a lot of trouble. That guy's not dead, he'll want to come after you. It's like Dewey always says, we gotta think and get organized. Maybe you should find another girlfriend."

Now I was scared, frustrated, and desperate.

ANSWERS

The next morning, rather than go to the Medalley mansion, I went to the office around noon. Dewey was in one of the small conference rooms and had told everyone that he should not be disturbed. I didn't care. I walked in to find Dewey with an old man kneeling in front of him. There were swatches of fabric strewn all over the table, and the man was measuring the pants for a new suit. He looked at me. "What do you think? It's a soft plaid. It's a little different. Great fabric. I also got a new navy blue suit, because someday I may even get a chance to meet with the FBI like you get to do."

I looked in disbelief and wondered what Blanker and Pike would think of an agent being attended to by his tailor in government offices, but in view of everything else that I had seen, it all seemed normal.

"I gotta talk to you, Dewey. I'm in trouble. I need your help."

"Go ahead. What do you need? Don't worry about Bruce here, he's almost done."

"Leah is gone," I blurted. "I have to find her. I think they're going to kill her."

Ignoring me, Dewey said, "No, Bruce, just a little longer. I want a break here. Have you tried Pepe? I never did trust him. Did you notice how he dresses? Not like Hermes or Orlando, those guys have class. Why don't you talk to Pepe? I'll bet he knows. If anybody is going to kill her it will be him, he likes that sort of thing...That's it, Bruce, right there. Pin it."

I tried to hold back my anxiety while Dewey fooled around with his tailor.

"Dewey, I've already tried that. We're not getting anywhere. I have to find her. Please help me."

Dewey saw how serious I was. "Okay, this must be true love." Then he turned back to the tailor. "That's all, Bruce. Get all of this shit out of here. You know what I need." And then back to me he said, "A pretty girl like that can't stay lost very long unless she's already dead. Let me think about it. Let's get together after lunch."

"Please, Dewey, it's important. We have to move *now*."

"All right," he said. "All right, but I need a little time. I have a lunch date in Midtown. I'll see you back here at two."

At two-fifteen I returned from lunch. Dewey, Michael, and Pike were laughing at a dirty joke when I walked in. Michael turned away when he saw me. Dewey knew I was worried and we walked into a conference room for privacy. He looked at me and said, "This is getting out of hand. You've got to work with us. You're not alone. Michael told me that you're coming apart. This is not good. We're your friends, and we're all you have. Don't you see that? 90 Church is your home, it's your life."

I tried to hold my temper. "Dewey, I *don't* want a fucking *lecture*.

I've got to find Leah. Are you going to help me or not?"

Dewey looked back at me. "Silkey told me that you 'tuned up' a spic last night. It was Pepe, wasn't it? What was that all about? We just don't go around beating up people. I would expect that from Silkey, he likes that kind of thing, but you're a lot smarter. You don't see Michael hurting people, do you? We here at 90 Church don't go around beating up people; we have *style*! You've just got to get organized."

I was out of patience; I bowed my head, shaking it back and forth, and started to leave the room. Then Dewey reached in his pocket and pulled out a piece of paper. "Here." He handed it to me. "I think you'll find her here."

The address was in the East Village, at Avenue C, the same area where Pepper lived. I was surprised. "Where did you get this address? How do you know she's there? Tell me, how do you know?"

Dewey smiled. "You're not thinking. I told you we have to get organized. Look at you! Michael's right, you're coming apart."

"*What* is this *address*?" I almost screamed. "How did you find this? What *is* this? This is a *slum*. Why would she be *there*? Where did you *get* this?"

Dewey looked at me and shook his head. "We've been pulling the phone records on the Medalley house for weeks. Someone has been calling this address and talking for a long time, sometimes as long as an hour, almost every day. Who at the Medalley mansion would talk for hours?"

He shook his head again and walked out of the room. I sat there staring at the little scrap of paper, feeling stupid.

A BETTER PLACE

At about four o'clock I drove down to the East Village to find Leah.

The neighborhood was just as I remembered it when I was living with Pepper: trash on the sidewalks, junkies. It was a strange pocket of poverty in lower Manhattan, not far from Washington Park, with the upscale East Village only a block away. The address led me to the second floor of a typical four-story walk-up. The hallway stank of marijuana and garbage. In my shiny suit, deerskin boots, and silk shirt, I looked as out of place as a nun in a whorehouse. I walked down the hallway, scanning the door numbers, and wondering how I would get inside. Then I saw a hippie come out of the apartment and walk down the hallway toward me. He seemed harmless. As he walked past I turned around and grabbed his long hair and yanked him back toward me. I pulled my automatic and reached around in front of him, shoving the barrel under his chin. He froze. I whispered to him, "Do you have a key to that apartment that you just came out of?" He nodded. "Good." Still holding his hair and the gun under his chin, I pushed him back toward the door and he unlocked it.

As the door opened, I shoved him sprawling face down on the floor, and walked in to find Leah. I couldn't believe the filth. The furniture was so dirty and badly broken that I couldn't make out if the shapes were a chair, a couch, or a bed. There were food wrappers and garbage strewn everywhere. The smell of marijuana almost choked me. I scanned the room with my blue automatic, and found two people huddled together, sitting on the floor, both of them dressed in what should have been colorful rags: bandanas around their heads, sandals, wildly-colored torn T-shirts. And there on the floor, hugging the dirtiest and ugliest hippie of them all, sat Leah. I almost didn't recognize her. The beauty, the elegance, the culture, the sophistication, the money, her future – everything was gone. She was just a hippie child holding onto another wild-eyed, misguided teenager hiding from the world. They held each other and shuddered with fright as they turned their eyes away from me and my blue automatic.

Then Leah's eyes, almost unrecognizable, glared at me with burning hatred. "I'm not going back. You can't make me. I would rather die here than go back."

I tried reason. "But your mother loves you. You're all she has."

"My *mother*?" She tried to laugh. "I would rather *die* and go to *hell* than be with my mother! I can't live with her and her vampires. I would rather die right here. You're not going to take me back. I belong here. This is my life. I hate you."

Before I could answer, the hippie that I'd grabbed in the hallway started to reach for a fireplace poker. I kicked him in the ribs. He just groaned and lay there in silence, pretending to be dead.

"You're one of them," Leah said. "You're a vampire, just like my mother. You're a vampire, a *vampire*!" she screamed as she held her hippie boyfriend even tighter.

There was nothing I could say. I'd lost all credibility I had with her.

I don't remember leaving the apartment, or even walking down the flight of stairs to the lobby. I had lost Leah, lost her to a way of life that I could not even imagine – yet, compared to mine, it seemed peaceful and inviting.

REGINA

The next afternoon I sat by the Medalley pool all afternoon, drinking frozen margaritas. I told Regina that her daughter was safe, but wasn't coming home. She disappeared into the house and I just sat there, working on my third frozen pitcher of green slush and wondering what to do next. At least Leah was safe from Pepe. I remembered the hatred in his face as he had called her an "old cunt" and said how he planned to kill her. I knew I had to renew my relationship with 90 Church, and bring this case to a close. Then Regina and Leah would be safe.

Finally, when it was almost dark, I went to the bathhouse across the pool from the mansion to get dressed to leave. From the window I saw Regina strolling by the pool with Orlando and Hermes. What beautiful people they were, so sophisticated, yet it was widely known that both brothers were illiterate. I deeply respected Regina's style and culture and how she imparted her grace to those around her, and how she turned a blind eye on the family business, in exchange for her art, lifestyle, family and dignity. All three of them disappeared into the house.

There was no need for me to say good-bye, but as I left, I chose a route around the pool close to the house, rather than through the backyard gate, which I normally used. The door was partly open to the study and as I walked past I could hear the conversation. They were screaming and angry. I heard Orlando say, "She was to be your symbol of *trust*. We don't *know* exactly what happened, it doesn't matter, but she was a symbol of trust and look how it's turned out! Pepe was beaten to a pulp. He was on *crutches*. After they broke his ribs, his knee, and he was on crutches! Then they shot him down in the street while he was on crutches, like a dog they shot him four times. You did this, Hermes. How could you do this to your own people? How could you violate the trust? You're my brother, why do you listen to her?"

After a brief silence I heard a voice I didn't at first recognize. "You're both fools. I didn't trust Pepe with Leah, I sent her there as security, but he was going to abuse her. He drove her away; she left for her own safety. What kind of trust is *that*? The issue was not who beat Pepe, but who killed him. I didn't kill him. I may have had him beaten, but I didn't *kill* him. If you two clowns continue to fight, the entire operation is going down. We're flush. Now's the time to be cautious and wait. I can't *work* with you two idiots."

I was stunned to hear a woman's voice, calling the two most vicious and powerful drug lords in New York "idiots and clowns," berating them and telling them what to do. The voice belonged to Regina – the doting mother, the obsessive housekeeper, the sweet, innocent, and devoted wife! Of course *she* was the "cunt" that Pepe hated, not Leah. Regina was in charge. She was behind it all. She was the one who sent me against Pepe; she knew I would beat him up. She was the one who had watched me in the shadows the first day when I met Hermes, and she was behind the curtains at the party. I was her "ace in the hole" against her husband, or anyone else, and she baited me with her beautiful daughter. But of course it was Regina! She gave these illiterate thugs style, culture, manners, and, above all, a fraternal macho "honor code" for them to do business without cheating and killing each other. Shell-shocked, I just stood there, unable to move.

After more shouting, Orlando left. Hermes and Regina were alone, and I heard her again. "You must act. You must act now.

He's weak, he's a party boy, and you've always known it. Don't you see, everything hangs in the balance? You must go tonight, go after him, kill him. When we were younger, you wouldn't hesitate. You were a man then, you had nerve, you were brave, you were smart. You built this organization by yourself, with your own courage; you never failed to act; now you must do it. You know it. I sacrificed my child to keep the honor, but Orlando and Pepe killed Mercedes, an innocent child. Those fools. You can't take two children for one crime."

Then I heard Hermes' soft voice, "He's my brother."

Regina exploded. "Mercedes was my *daughter*! He's in the way. He's broken the *code!* He's not going to kill Leah too; he cannot live. Enough I tell you...Go now."

Now I began to worry about being discovered. I could get killed for overhearing what I had just heard, so I quietly walked out the back gate. I drove away from the mansion and pulled over to the wooded picnic area, the same place that Michael and I had stopped to talk on my first day of the case. I sat in the darkness, staring into space. How wrong I had been about Regina. I had been unknowingly protecting the ringleader! No wonder Pepe hated her. No wonder Leah wanted to escape. Regina controlled everything in secret through their macho honor code. When everyone thought Leah stole the coke, Regina was willing to sacrifice her "because anyone who steals dies," but when the wrong daughter was killed she had had enough. It tore the whole organization apart. What could they do? The horrible irony was that Leah was really innocent and I knew it but couldn't tell them because they'd kill me. This terrible dilemma exposed Regina and the organization couldn't handle that either. Now Regina didn't care about the rules anymore;

she was making her own. As these thoughts stormed over me, I saw Hermes' car pass in front of me. I knew where he was going.

CLEAN-UP

I found Michael in the office. I had to find out about Pepe. I was also anxious to know when the new drugs would be coming in from South America. It would close the case with a grand finale of more killings. Michael and I met in one of the private conference rooms. He got right to the point.

"Someone almost got killed yesterday. This is the second time you fucked up. Silkey was on stakeout outside the Medalleys' Brooklyn apartment. Pepe tried to kill him. Dewey took him down, shot him about four times, all the way across the street. Dewey's unbelievable with that gun of his. How would Pepe know Ed Silkey? You told Ed to beat him up, didn't you? You're endangering the case; people are starting to get hurt."

"People are starting to get *hurt*?" I laughed. "Michael, you want *every*body dead! I thought I was doing the right thing. I had to save Leah's life."

Michael just glared at me in disbelief. "Listen to me, they're all going down – Hermes, Leah, Regina, the whole family, *all* of them. Do you understand me? Who the fuck gave you the job of saving the lives of these murderous dope dealers?"

"Michael, when is the shipment coming in? I want this case to be over with. I can't stand it. I have to get out."

Michael shook his head with disgust. "You hang around the Medalley pool all day long; you don't even know what's going on. The shipment came in four days ago. Dewey was right, the dope comes in at night and they throw it over the side. We got word from the Feds in South America. We waited and watched them fish it out of the water and deliver it to Brooklyn, just like Dewey said. We anchored a three-mast sailboat right in front of the Brooklyn shore. Then Dewey hung huge beer signs on trees along the shore so they couldn't see anything from Staten Island."

"You got the drugs? That's great, how many kilos?"

Michael shook his head with more disgust. "Why would we do that? We don't *seize* drugs. That's nonsense. That's the bullshit you hear from Pike and Blanker. *Cops* seize drugs. Have you ever read the charter for 90 Church? We are charged with the responsibility of curtailing the flow of drugs by stopping major dealers by all means possible. Besides, haven't you read the newspapers? The Medalley case is already over. We killed four major dealers, and seized eight ounces of coke – never mind that it was your cocaine for your services around the pool, trying to fuck their daughter. While you were trying to get laid, we set up surveillance on the Brooklyn apartment and busted everybody that carried anything out of it. We have cases on everybody: Regina, Leah, Pepe, Sprague, everybody. Now we're going to pick them up.

"Dewey was right, there's nothing special about these people. They just wear fancy clothes and cheap jewelry, and shake each other's hand all the time. Anyone who is still alive is an informant for us now. Dewey's already got them organized, ratting out people all over the city. You wouldn't believe the shit – murders, robbery, everything. So much for their bullshit family code of honor. Dewey's little file clerks are working around the clock. Speaking of Dewey, why do you think he's buying all those suits?"

When I didn't respond, he added, "Don't go to the Medalleys' tomorrow. We're going to pick Hermes and Regina up in the morning, along with your little girlfriend. She's a coke dealer just like the rest of them. She was with Chevy, trying to sell dope to Louie, remember? We got Hermes for killing McDermott's son. Dewey took the prettiest girl we caught carrying dope from the Brooklyn apartment and gave her a choice, fuck Hermes and get him talking on tape about killing McDermott's kid, or go to jail for ten years. You wouldn't believe what Hermes said in bed. He did it, alright. He and Pepe. We got two others who were there. We cut a deal with them too. Hermes is going down for murdering a federal officer. He's going to fry in the chair, and McDermott's going to be watching."

And with that, Michael walked out of the room. I was shaking with anger. I tried to sit down, but there were swatches of cloth on the chair, left behind by Dewey's tailor.

I felt bad about endangering Ed and Dewey. I asked them to meet me in the conference room and told them I was sorry for almost getting Ed killed. Neither seemed concerned, and then Dewey said, "Look, Pepe had just killed Sprague, so we were going to have to pick him up anyway. It worked out just fine."

"Lieutenant Sprague, the dirty cop?" I asked. "When did he get killed?"

"Yesterday," Dewey replied. "Pepe went to his house in the morning when he was getting ready to go to work, slugged his wife when she answered the door, walked in and shot Sprague in the bathroom while he was shaving. Pepe's a tough guy. He was on crutches and could hardly breathe when he blew Sprague's brains out, all over the bathroom. That's a tough guy, killing people while he's on crutches and gasping for breath. I like that! I really like that!"

"But why?" I asked. "Why?"

"Don't you read the papers? Michael made arrangements for Sprague to get a big promotion in the police department. Michael gave him all the credit for the Medalley case – the four spics we took down in Queens – hung it all on Sprague so he would get promoted. One of the little bastards we took down was Pepe's son. Pepe Click-Click thought Sprague got his son killed and his promotion proved it. Just like Michael always says, when you're guilty you assume the worst about other people. Michael could never forget a dirty cop. No need to go to court; what a mess that would be! Sprague died a hero. Pepe was just cleaning up early. Pepe was too hot-headed to have been any use to us anyway. Besides, did you see how ugly he was? I couldn't stand to look at him."

It was all over, the big case that was really a small case, but really a big case. I had lost count of all the dead. Nothing had gone as planned, except that first night of the sting with Louie the G. That had gone like clockwork, but it set in motion a series of events that the devil himself could not create. I didn't know Lieutenant Sprague that well, but could imagine crazy, ugly Pepe on a crutch shooting him in the bathroom all because Michael got him promoted. All these people dead...and all my fault.

I had to get "organized," as Dewey would say.

Before I left the office I heard Dewey talking to Pike. Dewey complained that he didn't want to go to the Medalley mansion the next morning to make arrests. It was Sunday and he had to go to church.

Everyone, except Pike, knew this was nonsense. In the end Pike ordered him to go, but gave him his Cadillac to appease him, which was what Dewey wanted in the first place. Dewey was so smart and

Pike so dumb that these pranks came easy. Dewey often tormented Pike and the other supervisors – to the never-ending amusement of the office. I heard Dewey tell Pike that he, Ed and Michael were going to the Medalleys' mansion at noon to arrest them all, and he would take good care of his Cadillac.

HOMECOMING

Michael had already told me to stay home; it was over. Dewey told me the same thing, but I had to go. After all, Regina had hired me to protect her! This I had to do, not just for Regina or even Leah, but for myself. It was my fault that Jerry Ramirez was dead, the same way Mercedes got killed. In my drug-crazed mind Regina was a loving, beautiful woman, a mother who lost her innocent daughter. I had destroyed their home. I had killed Mercedes and ruined their lives. They had trusted me and now this trust was going to put them in prison or get them killed. I wanted to find Leah, tell her I was sorry and join her world, her peaceful, loving, simple world. None of this mattered to Michael. He could have Hermes, but not Regina and Leah.

If I got there early I could get Leah out before all hell broke loose. I pulled up at the Medalley mansion at ten a.m. It was a bright, sunny, Sunday morning. As I drove through the gate I saw Hermes' car parked in the middle of the driveway. The engine was still running. I walked in the front door and saw him slumped over in a chair, his white suit was wrinkled and spattered with blood. He got up from the chair, stared at me with bloodshot eyes. "Do you know what I deed last night? Do you know what I *deed*?" he whispered to me.

"No." I mocked him: "Deed you go out drinking?"

He was not impressed with my humor. "I keeled my brother. I keeled my leetle brother Orlando, me *own brother*."

It was odd that now he had an accent. I walked past him, past the fresh-cut flowers, the beautiful murals, the bubbling fountains – to find Regina.

She was in the living room, wearing a magnificent gold-and-orange designer robe with green jade jewelry. I took her extended hand and we sat down for my "we must leave now" speech. Before I could start there was a horrible sound, so loud it echoed off the marble floor and vaulted ceilings. Over and over, there was a scream – "*woo rahs, woo rahs*" – like some kind of animal caught in a trap and in great pain.

Suddenly the screaming was in the living room. Hermes crouched before us, one of the most frightening apparitions I had ever seen. His skin was completely red and his eyes bulged even redder. He squatted on the floor with clenched fists then jumped up and down like a giant red frog. Each time he squatted, he reached inside himself for all his strength to scream, "*woo rahs, woo rahs*." The tendons in his neck stuck out so much his body seemed to lose shape. It was as if he was trying to lift a great weight each time as he squatted low and leaped up bellowing. Regina did not lose her composure for a second – but I did. I backed away from the screaming, hopping maniac and reached for my gun.

Finally Hermes stopped, fell against a chair, and lay on the floor, looking up at us. He had ruined his voice, but still rasped "*woo rahs, woo rahs*." Then, in a whisper, "Whores, whores, all whores." Through his tearing, bloodshot eyes he glared at Regina. "Whores, they turned them all into whores." He broke down crying, wiping his nose with his shirtsleeve and kneeling on the floor. "We were all proud, honorable, and now I have killed my little brother...then I find that all our honest people have been turned into *whores*, ratting and stealing from each other...turned into *rats*, rats for 90 Church! It's your fault, *you* told me to kill my brother to protect the honor, *you* corrupted everything. Where is the glory now? Why did I listen to you? You are going to die, just like Orlando. I'm going to get a gun; you will die now, *now*!"

Hermes rose to his feet and stumbled from the room, sobbing. He was coming back to kill both of us.

I grabbed Regina's hand and pulled her into Hermes' study. I closed the study door and bolted it with the deadlock. We got behind Hermes' desk and I grabbed the edge and pushed it over. It crashed in front of us on its side so we could hide behind it. Within minutes Hermes began banging on the door, screaming in Spanish. When he did speak English, all he could say was, "You fucking *bitch*! Let me *in*. I'm going to kill you. *No one* is going to protect you."

Regina was calm as ever. I pulled out my automatic and waited. Hermes continued to scream and bang on the door. Sooner or later he would find a way through and I had to be ready. With the extra clip I carried, I had twelve rounds to stop him and whomever he brought with him, but it didn't seem enough.

Regina held onto me like it was the proper thing to do in this type of situation. Then there was silence, a long silence. I thought Hermes had left, or perhaps was going around the side of the house to come in through the windows. I heard gunshots, a lot of gunshots, pistols, shotguns, on and on. Then silence. Regina and I waited in each other arms, waiting and staring at the door with my automatic pointed at whoever might come through it. But there was only more silence.

Then all hell broke loose; the lock of the study door shattered into a thousand pieces, blowing chunks of wood all over the room, as the door banged open. Only a shotgun blast could cause so much damage so fast. I grabbed her hand and we retreated into the back room where I had seen her shadow on my first visit with Hermes. We stood in the sunroom holding each other, waiting for the inevitable. Then a black figure appeared; it was Michael in his floppy black hat and black suit, holding his revolver, dead on, straight at me. I continued to point my automatic back at Michael, and then he said, "It's over. It's all over; she goes down *now*! They're *all* going down. She goes down and so does your little friend!"

"No, no!" I shook my head. "*No!*" And, as if I had sprung a leak in my brain, my mind filled with terrible images: the little boy in the wheelchair, the crying man without a hand at the pool, Hermes screaming and hopping about, Mercedes sitting in the car with her face blown off – the images kept coming and coming. Everything was my fault. I could not disappoint Regina. She was the only thing that made sense! She was the only thing that was decent! Some*how*, some*way* if I could save Regina, all of this would be forgiven and forgotten. If somehow I could stop Michael it would help pay for all the things I'd done. Tears streamed down my face, but I managed to say, "No, I'll kill you first, Michael. You're not going to get her."

As we stood there pointing guns at each other, we heard Dewey in the next room with Hermes and Ed Silkey: "Herman, somebody told me there was a wall safe in here. Why, lookee *here! Here* it is!

Aren't you *clever* to hide it behind a *picture*? Why don't you *open* it for us? No? No! Come on, Ed, let's play catch with Herman."

Through the door I saw Hermes being thrown from one end of the room to the other, crashing against furniture, then the wall. I heard Dewey again, but in a high-pitched effeminate voice, "Look what you've *done* here, you're breaking the *furniture*. Stop it, Ed, stop it." Then there was another huge crash and Dewey's high-pitched effeminate voice, "*Now* look what you've done. You've broken this *beautiful* table lamp. Look at this *fine* furniture. Stop it! Stop it!"

Again Hermes went flying across the room, crashing into more furniture and glass, and then Dewey, in an even higher-pitched, mocking voice, said, "*Stop* it, Ed, you monster, you're going to *ruin* all this *nice* furniture." Then in a normal voice he said, "Take this asshole into the bathroom. Stand him in the shower. Beat him with the barrel of the shotgun. At least we'll be able to save the carpet."

Michael and I just stood there, still pointing our guns at each other. Regina held me tight, so close that her tongue touched inside my ear as she whispered, "*Kill* him; *kill* him now before he kills you. He's not your friend, I have millions; we'll make a deal with the others, you'll have Leah."

Then I heard Dewey's mocking voice. "You see, Ed, now he wants to *help* us! Okay, Herman, if you insist, go ahead, show us what's in the safe. How kind of you."

Then Dewey came into the room. He had a silver bowl in his hand. "You guys have got to try these flavored cashews; they're great." He dipped his fingers into the bowl, ate some and offered them to Michael. Michael ignored him. Then Dewey stepped between Michael and me and looked at my gun, now pointed at him. Still in his idiotic mocking voice, Dewey said, "Saaay, that's a *real* pretty gun, never seen a blue gun that blue before. Where'd you get it? I bet it was expensive. Did someone *give* you that gun? Boy, I wish *I* had friends that gave *me* nice gifts."

Dewey's face changed from a stupid, mocking grin to seriousness, and he said coldly, "Let her go, Michael, she's just a stupid housewife in a cheap outfit. How do you think we're going to report all this? Look what's going on in the next room."

I could see Ed Silkey cleaning out the safe, stuffing money in a pillowcase ripped from the couch.

Still looking at me, but talking to Michael, Dewey continued, "You see, Michael, when we got here we were too late. Regina had cleaned out the safe and run off, leaving poor Herman here to take the heat. She was cheating on him! You can't trust these fancy women; it would be hard to find her in South America...Too bad she took all the drug money. Think about it Michael, it's the only way we can write this up."

There was silence. Then Michael lowered his gun, turned away from me and said, "Okay, she walks." Then he looked at Ed. "Ed, take her to the Idlewild airport, put her on the first plane to South America, buy her a coach ticket, one way."

I looked in Regina's eyes and said, "You hired me for protection."

She stared back at me with disbelief. "I never hired you, Hermes did. He owed you money. I would *never* hire you; you were just another hard-on for my daughter."

Ed Silkey threw the bundle of money over his shoulder, then dragged Regina out of the room, headed for the car. Michael helped Hermes to his feet and followed Ed out through the broken door. Dewey, still eating nuts from the silver bowl, put his arm around me. I could still feel tears streaming down my face. I felt as if I had just awakened from a terrible dream. I wiped my face off.

Outside on the front porch, in the bright sunlight, lay four bodies – the three house bodyguards and someone I had never seen before.

Pike's government Cadillac was in the driveway; the windshield and both side windows were shattered, and bullet holes dotted the hood. I looked at Dewey and said, "What happened here?"

Dewey smiled. "You see, Michael knew you'd try to save Leah. She had you snowed just like the rest of those dumb spics. I staged that little scene yesterday over Pike's car so you would hear us set the time. We needed a schedule. We knew you'd come early. We just waited for you down the road from the house. Then when we heard the screaming, we thought they were torturing you. Ed and I ran up to the side of the house, then Michael drove up in Pike's car, and these assholes started shooting at the car. Ed and I took them all down from behind."

Michael pointed to my car. "Silkey, take her to the airport, off to South America with her."

I tried to comfort Regina. "Trust me, you'll be free. Leah is safe, too."

Her cold gray eyes glared at me. "Trust you? Never! You're a weak fool and a cokehead. You were just a hard-on for my daughter."

Silkey had heard enough. "Shut up and get in the car, bitch."

"How dare you speak to me like that." Regina slapped Silkey across the face as hard as she could.

Ed showed a slight twitch like avoiding the buzz of a fly. Dewey started giggling. With lightning speed Ed gave Regina an upper cut to the jaw that raised her off the ground. She landed on the hood of the car and slid down the fender like a rolling pile of mud. Dewey started laughing so hard he had to hold onto my shoulder. Then Ed grabbed her waistband and dragged her like a suitcase into the back seat. He got behind the wheel and started the car, waving good-bye to everyone, like he was in a parade.

Standing on the porch next to the four dead bodies, Dewey looked at the bullet-ridden government car and yelled to Silkey, "Ed, when you get to the airport you'd better call Pike. Tell him there's been an 'incident' at the Medalley house. No one got hurt, but a government car got damaged. He needs to get some people over here right away. He's going to be pissed when he finds out it was his Cadillac that got trashed. This will be two this month for Pike. The Bureau doesn't like that. They'll probably ground him."

Silkey laughed and waved again. Then Michael, Hermes, Dewey, and I got into Hermes' car and followed Silkey out of the Medalley estate.

Michael was driving and I assumed we were going to the office; instead he turned off on Canal Street and headed toward Greenwich Village, where he pulled up in front of a small restaurant with a breakfast sign. Standing next to the front door I saw Agent Springfield, who had that smug, arrogant look of an FBI agent. When he saw us, he pulled out his gun and let it hang by his side. He talked into his lapel and I saw two other agents, not far from where we parked, react. Michael leaned over the back seat and said to Hermes, "This is where you get out. Someone is waiting. I think he's going to buy you breakfast. Get out."

Still dazed, Hermes got out of the car. He walked slowly up to the restaurant door and Springfield opened it for him. I could see through the front window. Special Agent John McDermott was sitting alone at a table. When he saw Hermes, he stood up and waved to Michael.

I got out of the car, too; I started to walk uptown through the hot Manhattan sun, on a "nothing going on" Sunday morning.

CHAPTER NINE

SMALL-TOWN SPORT

REHAB

The Medalley case left my mind drifting. I couldn't sort out all of the mistakes I'd made. I had no moral compass to guide me anymore. All I knew was that somehow, Michael had saved me... again. And I owed him, but I hated him for it.

Weeks after the Bureau recognized me for my "brilliant undercover work" on the Medalley case, Michael came in early for the Monday morning agents' meeting. Since Michael never came in the office before three-thirty in the afternoon, we all knew something bad had happened. Michael went into Blanker's office; when he returned he was covering his face with a handkerchief, his eyes red and teary. He looked at us like he was lost, then walked out and down the hall to the elevators.

Word spread quickly that Michael had been crying. The mood was like a funeral parlor when the agents assembled for the morning meeting. Blanker walked to the podium stone-faced. There was no "Good morning." Instead, he said, "They shot Danny

Cupp three times in the face yesterday at the boat dock."

Danny Cupp was Lollipop. Lollipop was the best. As Michael's Mafia informant he had the most dangerous job in the world. I met him several times and he was incredibly handsome: blue eyes, blond hair, a great smile. When he worked undercover it was impossible for mob girlfriends or whores to hold back their deepest secrets. Michael encouraged him with this vile charm, so the case files were loaded with the fruits of his labor, harvested by lust and trust. Besides skimming a lot of drug money, no one really knew why Daniel Cupp was an informant or why he so often trusted Michael with his life. Michael always took a dedicated interest in protecting the identity of all his informants, but Lollipop's death was very personal to Michael.

Blanker gasped for breath, holding onto the podium with both hands. "No one volunteers information to us without protection. Do you hear? We have failed. He was killed on our boat, which is federal property, so the FBI's on it. No one knows nothing. He was Michael's number-one guy, responsible for many cases, including the Louis Turko case. Without Cupp, Turko's going to walk." Then he walked out.

The Bureau of Narcotics was on the top of the building at 90 Church, on the sixth floor. Several mornings later I caught a lobby elevator with several other people on their way up to work. In the corner on the floor sat a drunk, his hat covering his face. He was out cold. My fellow passengers gave each other a little smile, trying to ignore the hopeless drunk that had been riding up and down all night. I knew it was Michael. I was alone with this pitiful heap when the door opened for me. I dragged him by the collar of his suit jacket out of the elevator, down the hall, and into the foyer of the Bureau, where he laid face down just five feet from Blanker's desk.

The next morning Dewey and I waited for Blanker or Pike to say something about Michael. Pike's phone rang. He answered it, and then pointed to us. "Go see the boss now." Michael was sitting on Blanker's couch, tears streaming down his cheeks. The man we stared at was not Michael. It was someone else; weak, broken, disgusting, just like the hundreds of wretched addicts and drunks we saw every day in the street. Michael's hands shook as he stared down between his legs, trying not to look at us.

Blanker said, with the sanctimonious tone of a backwoods preacher, "Agent Giovanni here has made a commendable contribution to the Bureau's work and we take care of our own, right?"

Dewey and I just stared at our friend.

Blanker started again, "Well, now it's rehabilitation for Agent Michael Giovanni in a government asylum for rest, reflection, healing and God's word to restore the dignity to his lost soul. We can't have our people riding in elevators all night, can we?"

Dewey could never be serious; he first nodded yes, then shook his head no. Blanker continued, "Michael here wants to help himself. He even chose the hospital and signed an order for forced commitment; isolation for the next six months, so there's no backing out. He's asked you two, and Group Leader Pike, to transport and admit him to the nut house this afternoon."

I drove. Dewey was in the front; Pike was in the back with Michael. We could all smell Michael's bad body odor and liquor. Pike complained, "If it was me or you guys, they'd throw our drunken asses in the street, no fucking rehab for us."

Michael never stopped crying and he kept saying over and over, "I'm sorry, I'm *really sorry*. You guys are my best friends. I'm *sorry*." I had never been to the Jonathan Wilham Rehabilitation Center, but I heard it had a hard reputation. It was a large, three-story brick building, a no-nonsense institution with bars on the windows. They lock you up until all your demons crawl out, and then you're either cured or dead. Pike was sure Michael would never make it and he was probably right. Dewey and I were just very sad.

I pulled into visitors' parking; there was an awkward silence. No one wanted to be the first to open the door. Suddenly a pretty young nurse in starched whites – carrying a clipboard – came to the car. She pulled open the back door, smiled and said, "Let's see...You are either Mr. Bernie Corman or Mr. Michael Giovanni. My guess is that you're Michael because Bernie is sixty-five years old."

Michael tried to smile as she helped him with his bag. The three of us sat there watching the pretty nurse in a white uniform, wearing high heels, grab Michael by the arm and lead him away.

AFOOT

Of course no one had any confidence in the FBI's ability to find Danny Cupp's killer. Weeks, then a whole month, passed without anything. If Michael were back on the street the killers would have been dead weeks ago. I spent the time making low-level junkie heroin buys and Dewey expanded his sports-betting operation to the employees of the Post Office on the ground floor. His desk was littered with betting slips on every conceivable sport, from basketball to dog racing. Still no one had heard anything about Michael.

Finally one morning Blanker called Dewey and me into his office. We could see Michael's file on his desk. He looked up. "Say, do you boys know what tomorrow is?"

Dewey answered with childish delight, "Wednesday."

Blanker smiled. "No. Tomorrow is Michael's birthday. I was thinking maybe the three of you here should visit him. You know, cheer him up, that sort of thing."

"Is that why we're here?" I asked. I knew from his smile he was lying.

Dewey shook his head. "No one is supposed to have any contact with Michael for six months. He's been in there for less than two."

Blanker exploded: "Listen, Paris, Michael has *sway* with McDermott. The Feds *owe* Michael. We need some help here with this Daniel Cupp thing. Louis Turko is out of jail, out on the street, a free man. He's well-connected, knows Aggi Angelici. They're going to gang up on us. God knows how many other cases are going down the toilet. We've got to get Cupp's killers. I know what went down with the Medalley dopers and McDermott's kid. We need Michael to cut things short a bit. You know, just a little work, make some calls to the Feds, get things moving. He can always go back in. Hell, they'll probably keep his padded cell warm for him. Tell ya what, why don't you just go up and talk to him? Maybe he can just give you some inside information and not even have to leave that recreational facility."

That afternoon Dewey ordered a big white cake from an Italian bakery in Greenwich Village. He had them write *Happy Birthday, We miss you Michael* on the top in red letters. They'd have the cake ready the next afternoon.

The next day Dewey wanted to stop at the FBI offices in Midtown before visiting Michael. He hoped there would be progress on the case that would cheer Michael up. I recognized the same wood paneling in the reception area, the backlit FBI logo and the snotty English receptionist who had greeted us for the Medalley meeting six months ago. "Can I be of service to you fine gentlemen?"

Dewey straightened his tailored suit and imitated her, "Why yes. We would like to see Special Agent McDermott. Please be so kind as to tell him Dewey is here. Dewey is a friend of Michael."

"My, I'm sorry, but all our meetings are pre-registered and you're not on the schedule today. Also we do not acknowledge the names of any of our field personnel. However, if you would like to walk down the corridor over there to our public inquiry desk, one of our specialists will be happy to help you file a complaint, or a request for information." She smiled primly.

I started laughing inside before Dewey answered, "Listen, you limey bitch" – Dewey leaned over the reception desk, just inches from her face – "You tell that faggot McDermott to meet me now, or I'll come around there and suck your cunt till your head caves in."

She dropped her fountain pen; it rolled across the desk onto the floor. She rose slowly, staring at him, and walked through a wooden door behind her desk.

Dewey turned to me. "I think she likes me. I'm gonna ask her out. What do you think?"

We waited for about ten minutes until a well-dressed agent came out. "Welcome, Agent Paris. I'm Doug Campbell; it's good to see you. John is in D.C. today. I think I know why you're here. Come with me."

He led us into a small conference room. Cupp's file was on the table. Dewey began leafing through it.

Agent Campbell started the briefing. "Your informant was shot three times, died instantly. The weapon was a nine-millimeter. The rifling on the slugs suggests an automatic weapon, probably an Israeli Uzi, and the use of a silencer. We think the silencer is military because of the smooth metal boring, not homemade. No doubt the killer is a pro. Daniel Cupp was hit standing up while on board a forty-foot cruiser at the boat dock on West One Hundred and Thirty-eighth Street. The boat is 90 Church inventory; it was seized by your people a year ago. I assume that Agent Giovanni used the boat as a safe house for his informants. Since the killing was on federal property, we investigate, but you could give it to the cops if you want."

Agent Campbell handed Dewey a photo of the boat's galley table; on the table was a pair of large binoculars and a blank yellow pad. "We think he might have been looking through the binoculars, but we don't know why. The boat was docked, so there was nothing to see. The pad was blank, but there was a pen lying on the floor."

Dewey continued staring at the photographs and leafing through the file. "What's this?" he asked, picking up a sheet of paper with large numbers scribbled randomly on it.

"We don't really know," agent Campbell answered. "Our people lifted it from the paper tablet. The top sheet was gone, but we were able to pull the numbers from the pen's impression."

Dewey stared at the sheet, mumbling, "Thirty-five, dash, six, two, one, three, nine, four."

Agent Campbell followed Dewey's interest. "We studied these numbers. D.C. thinks it's some type of code, but no one has been able to make sense of it. Even our military people couldn't crack it."

There was nothing else in the file except photos of Danny's face and dead body. Dewey couldn't look at them. Agent Campbell had prepared a duplicate file and handed it to Dewey. We shook hands and said good-bye.

On the way out, the snotty receptionist was back at her desk. Dewey couldn't resist. "Say, honey, we're on our way to have a birthday party at an insane asylum. Why don't you come with us? It would be great fun. What do you say?" She ignored us.

With the cake in the trunk we picked up Silkey and the three of us drove north to Westchester to celebrate Michael's birthday. We wondered what Michael would be like, and felt certain he would not be the same man who had left us.

Silkey started it off, "You know, I've known Michael for eight years and I've never seen him sober."

"You know, I've known him about the same, but being drunk is being Michael," Dewey added. "The trouble is that drying out takes time; it breaks you down day by day, makes you crazy. I've seen it before. If you live through it you're never the same person. Michael is not going to be the Michael we knew. You saw him crying and broken; what do you think he is now? That son-of-a-bitch Blanker. We shouldn't be doing this. We should leave him alone. He was supposed to have his full six months. This isn't right."

Silkey was carrying the cake box when Dewey approached the front desk and asked to see Michael. The receptionist fumbled through some papers, then shook her head.

"I don't care what your papers say. See this?" Dewey pulled out his credentials. "You get Agent Michael Giovanni. Get him now and we want to see him in a private room."

The orderly left then returned a few minutes later to lead us into a small room with a table and chairs. We were all nervous. I unboxed the cake and laid out some plates and forks. Still no Michael. It was unbearable. After about fifteen minutes the door opened and a huge black man stepped into the room. He was dressed in a green inmate jumpsuit and extended his big black meaty hand to me and said, "Hi, I'm Michael Giovanni. How nice that someone remembered my birthday."

Dewey laughed so loud that he sounded like the other nut cases down the hall. Through his hysteria Dewey managed to yell, "Happy Birthday, Michael! Have some cake. How about an end piece?"

NUMBERS

"The shoes, the shoes, the *shoes*," Dewey chanted as he banged his hands on the dashboard while Silkey drove us back to the office.

"What did Michael always tell us over and over? The shoes, look at the *shoes*. You can tell a lot about people from their shoes. When we brought Michael to the hospital that tight-assed nurse was wearing three-inch spiked *heels*. How fucking stupid are we? Michael *chose* the hospital; yes, he's as dumb as a stick, but we should have known better. Who admits a patient to a nut house in the fucking parking lot with high heels and a clipboard? Now the government is paying for rehabilitation for one of Michael's drug-dealing nigger pimps. That's just swell."

I tried to calm Dewey down. "Where do you think Michael is now?"

"Who knows? He's got a two-month head start and another four months to go before anyone misses him, and all paid for by Uncle

Sam. You know he gets sick pay for this. Will Michael's madness ever cease? I have no idea where to begin looking for him."

Silkey tried some humor, "I heard he's been living in elevators. Maybe we should start there. You know, let's go to Wall Street and work our way uptown."

Dewey pointed to a street. "Very funny, but this is serious shit. We need Michael. Turn right up there. Let's go see the boat where they clipped Danny."

It was a blustery day and the docks were empty. A uniformed guard pointed to the crime scene, a boat draped with yellow tape now hanging loose and blowing in the wind.

It was cold and clammy inside the boat. We sat at the stern around the galley table that was in the picture and stared at the binoculars and the blank tablet, still lying on the table. There were brown bloodstains on the floor, walls, everywhere, even on the ceiling. Dewey opened up the FBI file and stared at the sheet with the scribbled random numbers and dashes. He stood up and looked around. Dewey knew boats. He started in the sleeping berth, looked at the sink, opened up the cabinets, read the Captain's log, then sat back down. "Two people were on board. See, two cups in the sink. But why the binoculars? They're high-powered, out of their case. There's nothing to see, no open water, nothing. Everything is so well-kept, why weren't these glasses stored?" He put the binoculars to his eyes and looked down the length of the dock, which was the only open visual path from the stern.

The dock ended about thirty yards away at a walkway on the shoreline. Beyond, a ten-foot wooden fence secured the boatyard. Dewey laid the binoculars down on the table and stared at the sheet of scribbled numbers. In a whisper he said, "Look at this; you see, the numbers are all over the sheet. Wouldn't you normally write a series of numbers in a straight line?"

"Not if you're Michael," Silkey replied. "Michael could never walk a straight line, so he probably couldn't write one either."

"No, he was not here," Dewey answered calmly. "If Michael came here it would expose Danny, besides there's still plenty of booze in the cabinet. The FBI always over-thinks things. These numbers are not a code; they were scribbled on the tablet while looking through the binoculars, that's why they're not in a straight line." Dewey looked through the binoculars again, then he smiled and pointed down the dock to the wooden fence.

I saw nothing. At the end of the dock, bolted to the wooden fence was a pay phone. Then I got it. "My God, he was writing down a phone number while he watched someone dialing the pay phone. He made them. The number is for us."

Dewey smiled. "Eight numbers, two dashes. He couldn't see two of the numbers so he filled in a dash. Let's get back to the office."

The logs for the pay phone were in the FBI file and having eight of the ten phone numbers made it easy to complete the full sequence. It was listed to another pay phone in Green, Louisiana. Pay phone to pay phone, means guilt. Two days later Dewey had the name of Danny Cupp's killer.

Pike hated Dewey, so Dewey had Silkey lay out the case for him to Pike and Blanker. Silkey told them that all of the leads had come from Michael directly to me. Michael was doing well, but needed the full six months of treatment with total isolation, no outside contact. Silkey even told Blanker that before Michael ate his birthday cake he led everyone in prayer.

The killer was Lorenzo Bonnet and he was connected to Louis

Turko. The mood in the office changed instantly. Michael was back, revenge was coming, death was returning from a holiday. No one questioned how Michael got the information, but I knew how Dewey found it. He gathered all of his low-life file clerks for a special assignment. Using the location of the pay phone in Green, Louisiana, the clerks researched the home addresses of the top two hundred suspected Mafia killer leaders and then cross-referenced them with defendants in Danny's cases. Lorenzo Bonnet lived less than a mile from the pay phone. He was part of the Magaddino family.

A FOUL WIND

To hell with the FBI, they didn't care about an informant. This was our case, even though there was no record of Lorenzo Bonnet ever being connected to drugs of any kind. 90 Church was on a mission of revenge and was being guided by a sober Agent Michael Giovanni who had found Jesus and now prayed over his meals.

Lorenzo Bonnet was a bad guy – murderer, smuggling, extortion – but he was smart; no drugs. In fact, Bonnet had never been arrested or charged with anything, but his name was mentioned hundreds of times in case files by informants, wire taps, confessions, and speculation. He was a Mafia political fixer well-known to the unions who had long since been infiltrated by the mob. There was also another side. He was a family man, active in Louisiana politics, a well-respected business owner and Mayor of the town of Green, Louisiana.

Mayor or not, he was going down and a Task Force was

assembled, headed by Pike. I was chosen first because Silkey told
Blanker that Michael had given the information directly to me. I
then chose Dewey because he helped me the first week on the job.
Dewey chose Ed Silkey because Ed liked to drive, and so our revenge
Task Force was complete. This absurdity made planning for any
serious undercover operation a dangerous farce. Nevertheless, the
four of us – Pike, Dewey, Ed Silkey and I – headed for Green,
Louisiana, population 1,250.

Green was green. Although named after Nathan Green, a Civil
War hero, the town still deserved its name because of its color.
It was lush and well-manicured, flowers everywhere. There were
no "other side of the track" type neighborhoods or trash along the
road. The center of the town was a square park with a gazebo in the
center. City Hall was a small red brick building at one end; shops
and restaurants with bright colors and gingerbread trim completed
the square. Four tree-lined roads forked off to accommodate
Victorian-style houses and small businesses. A four-lane highway
with no exits for twenty miles connected Green to Lafayette and
the rest of the world. They called it "Lorenzo Way" because Bonnet
had used his political influence to have it built. The people were
well-dressed and radiated happiness. Posters were everywhere,
proclaiming support for the local high-school football team, with
pictures of the players and cheerleaders. The school colors were
orange and black.

The plan, such as it was, was to contact the Chief of Police and
get his cooperation to introduce me to Bonnet while I posed as
a drug dealer. Dewey's black humor forced him to embrace the
ridiculous scheme while Ed Silkey, not much brighter than Pike,

assumed there was more to the plan than he knew, so said nothing.

The police station was a converted blue Victorian house just two blocks off the square with white trim and a hanging wooden sign. We had no trouble meeting Police Chief Robbie Morganthal, who ushered us into his comfortable office, which was decorated with pictures, banners, and trophies of Green's football team. He stared at this menagerie of creatures from New York City: a fat, stupid man desperate to be in charge; a mean-looking thug with creepy eyes; a giggling, harmless-looking teenager wearing a two-thousand-dollar suit; and me, a long-haired grease-ball punk. Finally, the bewildered Police Chief said, "I got your call from Agent Blanker. Of course I'm willing to help, but boy I'm not sure what you all want to do."

Pike started the first round of embarrassments, "We want to get the skinny on doper Bonee."

"Who's doper Bonee?" Chief Robbie asked.

Pike shot back, "You know who I mean, Bonnetlee or whoever, you know, the Mayor."

"His name is Larry Bonnet; the 't' is silent. Just 'a', Bone-ay. If you are conducting a federal investigation, of course, I want to assist wherever possible, but what is it that you have in mind?"

Pike waved his hands in the air. "We want to do an insertion of an undercover operative into your community. We have a classified covert purpose that's top secret."

Chief Robbie tried not to smile and looked us over again. "Uh, who do you have in mind leaving behind here for insertion into this covert operation?"

Dewey giggled and pointed to me.

Chief Robbie tried not to laugh. "Yes, he looks like he'd fit right in. You know, all three of you look like you were born and raised here. How much thought have you guys given to this plan? Tell ya what…Why don't you get settled in at the hotel and meet me for dinner. It'll give us some time to think things through a little better. There's a great Italian restaurant here that will impress you guys. It's just the other side of the square, one block further, the Half Moon. Seven o'clock, okay?"

Even Pike knew how ridiculous the situation was, although he would never admit it. We checked into our hotel and strolled through the park, killing time before dinner. The townspeople greeted us, but rolled their eyes when they passed. By the steps at City Hall was a glass encasement of photographs taken at the City's events. Mayor Lorenzo "Larry" Bonnet was in most of them – handsome, gray-streaked black hair – smiling and hugging. There was a picture of Mayor Larry Bonnet holding a trophy in one hand while his other arm draped around the high-school football coach, Police Chief Robbie Morganthal.

The more we saw, the more we realized how impossible it would be to reach Bonnet. He was protected by good townspeople who loved and respected him.

The Half Moon was not what we expected. It was a replica of the mob joint in the Bronx: big oak bar, great food, and white tile floor. The waiters were all Italian and wore starched white shirts with black ties. Chief Robbie ordered Chianti and constantly waved or smiled to other tables. After a few sips of wine, Chief Robbie unveiled his own plan: I would pretend to be a graduate college student working on a thesis about small-town government and its law enforcement. As dumb as it was, at least it would give me an excuse to snoop around for a couple of months and no one had a better idea. Even Dewey, who had forsaken the wine for vodka martinis, fell silent.

Dewey had already knocked down three drinks and was fingering his olive when he stared around the room. Suddenly, as I dabbed my chin with a napkin, Dewey snatched it from my hand and began stuffing it into his mouth. He made gagging sounds as he tried to push it down his throat. It got everybody's attention. He motioned to us that he was okay, but got up and staggered out the front door with the white rag still hanging from his mouth.

They brought me another napkin; our conversation started up again. Pike apologized, "I'm sorry, Agent Paris does love his martinis." Chief Robbie smiled and nodded, but I wasn't so sure. I looked across the room where Dewey had been staring.

Sometimes innocent little things can kill a whole town – a pond that goes stagnant, breeding disease, or a raging tornado from an innocent breeze, or a bearded old man cleaning the tables in a small restaurant. You could hear a soft rattle of plates as Michael Giovanni's quivering hand struggled to stack the dirty dishes on a serving tray.

I tipped the "busboy" at the Half Moon as he slipped me a note scribbled on a paper napkin: *Fuck Lucille*. That's all it said. Dewey said that I should take Michael's instructions literally, otherwise Michael would have given the note to Silkey. Dewey and I were the only two that knew. Eventually Silkey would be the only one told. I was not to make any contact with Michael. Dewey would wait for Michael's orders and then call me. Meanwhile I should find Lucille and fuck her.

LUCILLE

The next morning Pike, Silkey and Dewey left, leaving me feeling like a stupid kid being dropped off at college by his parents. I hung around the police station and met the entire Green police force: a cop named Ken whose uniform was three sizes too big. Day after day I pretended I was writing a thesis paper on local government. I tried to sell my cover by asking stupid questions of everyone I met. Days passed and I developed a habit of spending my afternoons sitting on the same park bench, staring at the pay phone that never rang. At night I would drink and snort coke in my hotel room and then the next afternoon return to the same park bench and wonder if I would ever find Lucille and what terrible scheme Michael was hatching to destroy this innocent town.

After three days of sitting on the same park bench I finally looked up at a five-foot sign in front of me, hanging on the biggest store in town. It read, 'Lucille Bonnet's General Store, everything you need or want with a smile.'

She was about fifteen years older than me, with crow's feet at the edge of her eyes, but she had a runner's body and a great smile. Meeting her was easy, I just walked in and told her I wanted to learn about Green and invited her to dinner at the Half Moon. Michael even cleared our table, but never looked at us. Lucille Bonnet was a widow with a teenage son and a young daughter. After dinner we went for a walk and she teared up while telling me about her late husband. "Bobby came home from Nam cold, cold as a popsicle. He was a war hero – ribbons, medals, stories and Army buddies – but he was ripped inside. Bobby couldn't let go of the horror, the killings. I fucked, kissed, sucked, hugged...

but I couldn't reach him. Bobby's dad, Lorenzo, made it worse, you know the family business. Bobby finally shot himself in the woods and that was that."

I acted clueless. "What family business?"

Lucille shook her head. "Christ, everybody knows what Lorenzo does, but Bobby had seen too much. He didn't want to be part of it. This whole town accepts Larry's mob reputation and union connections. When unions have a problem he fixes it. It's not so bad to just take it in small bites, there's no crime of any kind in Green. Whatever goes on outside of here, well that's someone else's problem. Larry's a good Mayor, a good politician – how do you think we got that four-lane highway they call Lorenzo Way that connects us to Lafayette? – and a good grandfather. Bobby was his older son. He loved him more than life itself. Larry has been good to me and his grandchildren. If you love and care about people, happiness is easy; just forget about everything else."

She leaned over and kissed me.

I spent the next day with Lucille and that evening I moved into her two-story house on the edge of a beautiful small lake surrounded by weeping willows and bellowing frogs at night. I was in the bedroom when I overheard her explain me to her son Bobby Junior and her daughter Jamie. She told them that she had a life to live too and wanted some period of happiness. Besides, I would be fun to have around the house.

Lucille was a great mother, a successful business owner, a member of the city council, a jogger and an affectionate lover. She wore a spicy perfume and we slept like two spoons stacked in a drawer. I never let her see me do coke and she ignored my six to eight drinks of vodka in the evening. My blue automatic remained hidden in the bottom of my suitcase.

Bobby Junior was the high school's starting quarterback. Every afternoon when Bobby came back from practice I would work with him in the backyard. I had played ball in college and could see that his passing strength and accuracy would soon be on a professional level. Lucille was already courting football scouts for a scholarship at Tulane.

Every other weekend I would go back to New York to "consult with my professors and get my mail". Pike had gotten all the agents to sign a get-well card and sent it off to the Jonathan Wilham Institution with a box of candy. The candy came back with a note prohibiting outside food being sent to the institution. The guys in Group Six ate the whole box. Dewey had been in a car wreck while in New Orleans. I wondered why he was even driving, since Silkey always drove him around.

I met Silkey at a bar in Midtown. "What the hell is going on?"

Silkey ordered his usual Black Label. "Michael called Dewey, gave him the name of a guy in New Orleans, told Dewey he had forty-eight hours to go down there, go undercover and get all the information cause the guy was leaving town, going back to Europe; you know, gone, gone for good."

"New Orleans, that's where Dewey had his wreck? Was he hurt?"

Silkey laughed. "Are you kidding? Nah, Dewey got a baby crib mattress from the hotel and put it between him and the steering wheel before he crashed. Totaled both cars. The other guy was banged up, so Dewey went to the hospital to, you know, meet the guy, apologize and all that. How else you going to meet the guy, keep him from running off to Europe? Dewey brought him some flowers and some coke to snort. Turns out he's got a brother named Albert who's a wise guy that's connected. Anyway, Albert gets drunk and brags about helping to get Danny killed. It seems that Albert has an in with someone at the Justice Department who got into Louis Turko's file. That's how they found out about Danny ratting them out. Michael was afraid that would happen, that's why he told Danny to live on the boat for a while. Somebody in the inside told them where to find Danny. Danny gets clipped, Albert hides out and Michael is mad."

"So, Albert, the mob guy, killed Danny?"

Silkey sipped his scotch. "Jesus, no. Albert may be mob but he's just a mope. Danny got clipped by a pro, direct orders from Bonnet. The killer's name is Glass, Sergio Glass."

"Silkey, are you telling me that Dewey crashes into a guy, gives him some flowers and a taste of coke and learns all of this?"

Silkey shook his head, losing patience. "No. Dewey made friends with him. The guy bragged to Dewey about his connected brother Albert and where he's hiding in New Orleans. It was big Albert who told us."

It was bad enough to imagine Dewey and Silkey driving around New Orleans crashing into people, but I had to know more. "Okay, Silkey, how did Dewey get Albert the brother, the wise guy, to give up Glass?"

"Dewey says we had suspicion so we should go and arrest the mope. We waited outside Albert's house. When Albert comes out Dewey yells at him all the way from across the street that he's under arrest for murder. Big Albert panics and pulls out his gun."

"Oh God, I think I know what happens next," I said.

"No, you don't. Dewey only winged him. Dewey's not as good as he used to be. Usually, it's Come meet Jesus with a tight cluster to the chest. This time Dewey just sent a forty-five round through the guy's kneecap. Albert laid down screaming and bleeding. I had to go over and help him."

I had seen all of this before, but still I had to ask, "You went over to *help* him?"

"Yeah, his knee was really bad. I had to stop the bleeding. You know, apply pressure; stop all of the blood coming out. You know what I mean, but I didn't want to use my hands with all that blood, you know, so I used my foot."

"Okay, I think I get the picture, but let me guess: Albert volunteered the information about Glass while you were helping to stop the bleeding with your foot, right? Did you even call an ambulance?"

He shook his head. "Nope. Dewey said we didn't know which hospital to call. There was some lady screaming her head off down the street so she probably called them. The fucking mope was lucky we didn't take him in. But, there's something more. Albert is hooked into Aggi Angelici, who supports Judge Carl Wineburg's campaign and Wineburg is the judge on Turko's case and had the file."

Before I left New York to return to my quiet life I skimmed some coke from the evidence lockers and met with Pike and Dewey. Dewey was restricted from driving any government vehicle for six months because of his wreck in New Orleans, so Silkey, who regularly wrecked cars, drove him around as usual.

Pike was pleased to learn that Chief Robbie was helping me with my cover. "You can trust him," Pike said. "Robbie is a cop, he's one of us."

Dewey let out a high-pitched giggle.

NYMPH

Early in this period of my small-town domestic bliss I had a bizarre vision. Lucille's upstairs bedroom balcony overlooked the lake. The whole area was isolated except for a small house next door. Lucille was always the first one up to get the kids off to school. Very early one morning as I tried to resist waking, I heard a lyrical musical sound, like a flute. At first I thought it was the radio. I staggered out onto the balcony to face the morning fog rolling off the lake and shrouding the weeping willows covering the ground like deep gray snow. There, standing on a branch of an oak tree in the yard next door, was a naked teenage girl playing a flute. Her long blonde hair touched her breasts, which were still budding and stood straight out. Her fingers danced up and down a long bright silver flute. The music was classical, complex, and passionate. She leaned and bobbed as she sent her magical sounds against the fog. When it ended she did a complete somersault out of the tree and struck a perfect landing, then walked inside the little house.

Lucille interrupted my vision. "So you've met Alice?" She led me back in like I should not have been out there in the first place. "They tried to teach her music at school, but all she wanted to do was to learn how to read notes. She learned the flute completely on her own. Most of the time she plays her own original music and teaches her songs to the other kids. She's pretty good, isn't she? She's our head cheerleader."

The Bonnet household accepted me as one of their own. After my brief encounter with the Wood Nymph I did something that I could never tell Dewey or Michael; I went to church on Sunday night to a Christmas music recital, even though it was still a couple of months before the real holiday. An early Christmas show was a tradition in Green. Alice and Lucille's daughter Jamie were on the program. Alice played her long silver flute, Jamie played saxophone, and a little fat boy named Howie played the drums.

The preacher introduced them and their song, "Silent Night." The group started out traditionally, beautiful and soft, then Howie seemed to snap. He went into a loud snare-drum roll. Alice joined in, whipping her flute up and down, blazing notes to match Howie's drum rolls. Little Jamie hopped to the center of the stage, spread her legs, and wailed away on the sax. It was still "Silent Night," but the jazz version was as good as anything I had ever heard at the Half Note in Greenwich Village. I wished Daisy was here to see this. She would have been impressed. The church rocked. The startled preacher leaped to the stage and pulled the amplifier plug, then dragged fat Howie off his stool. Jamie and Alice stopped and glared at the frantic preacher, who announced to the audience, "I regret this sacrilegious spectacle. I'm sorry about this, folks, but this concludes the evening's performance."

Jamie spun around, bent over and flipped her dress up; written across her panties was a day of the week. Lucille was next to me and I heard her say, "Oh my God, Tuesday, and today is Sunday."

There was an awkward silence in the congregation, and then Lucille stood up and yelled at the preacher, who was leading Alice off the stage, "Reverend, that was an original composition: maybe it was a surprise, but these kids worked hard and did it for us. I agree with my daughter, you can kiss my ass."

On the way out I recognized Lorenzo Bonnet sitting in the back row. He hugged his granddaughter as we passed. Next to Lorenzo was a thin man dressed completely in black. It was Sergio Glass, Lorenzo's bodyguard and Danny's murderer.

VINNY

Coach Robbie made me his assistant football coach. Lucille came to one of our practices to see how Bobby Junior and I were doing. Alice, the Wood Nymph, was there practicing cheerleader routines with the other girls. She was terrific, doing backflips, cartwheels, and hip grinds. In the stands was a small group of rowdy boys howling and whistling. One of them, older than the rest, was fixated on Alice. He stared at every move she made, like a thirsty dog on a hot day, with his mouth open and tongue going in and out. His obsession was obvious to everyone.

"Who's that kid?" I asked Lucille.

She knew exactly which one I meant. "Vinny, Larry's youngest son."

Police Chief Robbie finally got a "perpetrator." While I was wasting the morning at the police station a man walked in waving a summons and said, "Fuck you, Robbie. I know what you're trying to do with these bullshit charges. You want me to help you. You are not going to screw her and you're not going to win. She's a Valkyrie. A stone-cold dyke warrior and the best football coach I've ever seen. We lose to her every year. This year we lost by three points, but she could have driven the score up to thirty. She didn't want to humiliate my kids. Now either put me in jail or buy my lunch."

"Carl, I've got to beat them," Robbie pleaded. "Everything is at stake. You don't understand. I need your help. The future of this

SMALL-TOWN SPORT | 283

town depends upon winning the game."

Carl rubbed his chin. "Yeah, I heard that business about the bottling company looking the town over and everything. That's really unfair hanging a business deal on a bunch of kids. Is the Half Moon open?"

It was linguine and white clam sauce for Robbie, Carl and me, as agent Michael Giovanni polished the glasses behind the bar at the Half Moon. Carl was the head football coach at Lafayette High School, thirty miles south, and a part-time game warden. Green High was in line to be the state champion, with only one more team to beat, Saint Agnes, an orphanage. The Valkyrie was Edwina, their lesbian coach. The game was only three weeks away and had enormous significance. The two biggest companies in Green – a boat factory and a plastic-molding plant – were going under. However, a privately owned Coca-Cola bottling plant was planning to open up a new facility in Green, which would save the town. Its president had already met with the Green City Council and worked out a tax-free land deal. The president was also a fanatical football fan and expected Green to be the state champion. As if this wasn't enough, two football scouts from Tulane and Auburn were coming to see Bobby Junior. Michael cleaned off our table before we had our tiramisu and coffee. Then Carl agreed to help us prepare the team.

That night there was a knock on our door. Lucille let in a middle-aged woman who covered her eyes with her hands. It was Betty, Alice's mother. I had seen her before, working in the yard. She was the type of person who looked like it would be easy to make her cry, like a frightened lost child. She looked to everyone for help at every smallest bump or turn in her life. Alice was the only thing that gave any purpose to her existence.

This time it was serious. Alice had been injured and was in the hospital. Lucille and I put her in the car and we sped down the winding road to the county hospital. Robbie was there to greet us outside Alice's hospital room. "She's alive, but don't go in there just yet," he said to Betty, who was already shaking. "Your daughter was beaten and raped and somehow her face made contact with an electrical box in the maintenance facility behind the school. Both her upper and lower lip were damaged."

Covered with a sheet all the way to her neck, Alice's blonde hair framed a macabre skeleton mask. The electricity had cauterized the wound so there were no bandages. A black-bluish line went from one corner of her mouth to the top of her nose and back down to the other side; the flesh was gone, exposing all of her upper and lower gums and teeth. Betty's little nervous tics disappeared. Her whole personality evaporated, completely traumatized into a cold trance, waiting for somebody to tell her to wake up.

The thirsty dog, Vinny, was in jail. The janitor saw him run from the maintenance shed, found Alice, and called Robbie. Alice was clutching a piece of cloth. It was the torn pocket from Vinny's shirt.

GAMEBALL

Three weeks later, on a cool clear night, Green High met Saint Agnes in the biggest football game in the town's history. I have seen a lot of grotesque things in my life, but nothing like seeing Alice lead the cheerleading squad. Completely oblivious to her horribly scarred face and exposed teeth, she backflipped, did her bumps and grinds, and cartwheeled across the field as the crowd cheered. Betty had never recovered from the hospital visit. She sat motionless, staring down at her feet, unable to look at her skeleton-faced daughter jumping up and down on the field.

The whole town was on our side of the field. There were only about fifty people on the other side, supporting the orphanage. Ironically, our school colors were orange and black, while Saint Agnes's color was green. We were ready for them. The bottling-company president was in the stands with his mousy wife and Lorenzo Bonnet. The two college football scouts were seated mid-field watching Bobby Junior. Robbie, Carl and I had worked with the team for the past three weeks. We were all pumped.

On the other side of the field, Edwina the Valkyrie coach ran out first. She was over six feet tall, with short blonde hair and a muscular build. She carried a pole with a green flag on top and stood at attention in the middle of the field with the pole at her side like the front guard of a parade. She jerked the flagpole smartly across her chest. Her football team came running out in sync, forming a straight line facing us. There were only about fifteen of them, all sizes and shapes. There was even a girl. Their green uniforms were homemade with different-sized numbers. Robbie and I tried to figure out which one was Bumper, their quarterback. Carl had said that he was as good or better than Bobby Junior.

The Saint Agnes team stood in a line at midfield, extending their hands. Then our boys took the field, and the audience jumped up and screamed. We let the orphan kids stand there with their hands out, looking silly. When Edwina realized we were not shaking hands she flipped her hand pole and the team returned to the sidelines. Saint Agnes kicked off first. They didn't even bother to chase the ball as their girl kicker sent it through the goalpost and into the end zone. On the first play Bobby Junior burned them for ten yards with a short pass. Saint Agnes's scrawny little players could not move our offensive line. We were bigger and stronger. The mismatch was obvious. Robbie began sending in his best plays and we marched down the field, passing and throwing until we were at the ten-yard line. Robbie and I cheered but Carl said nothing. I looked across at Edwina, who was flanked by two girls, each of them scribbling frantically on clipboards. We stalled on the ten-yard line and settled for a field goal.

We kicked off and they downed it at the twenty-yard line, then Bumper came out. He was just average-sized, with big feet and big hands. First we shut down his running plays and then on third down Bumper managed a short pass for ten yards. Saint Agnes never huddled, instead they looked over to Edwina, who would wave the pole flag in different directions to signal in plays. In the next series of downs we saw how accurate Bumper really was, but his passes would bounce off the chest of his receivers, who spread their hands out, afraid of our tacklers. Their series stalled and we got the ball back. Bobby Junior marched the team down the field with pass after pass. Five minutes before halftime Bobby Junior had completed sixteen passes out of sixteen throws. Bumper was three out of twenty-one throws. The Valkyrie continued to wave her flag even though everyone could see it was going to be a blowout. At halftime the score was thirty-one to zero.

The whole town was happy, except Carl, who had been continually arguing with Robbie. Finally Carl said, "Robbie, you've lost the game already. Can't you see what she's doing?" We ignored him. Everyone could see that we were going to win big.

I looked across the field at Edwina, still flanked by her two little secretaries scribbling on their clipboards; she was smiling.

When the halftime buzzer sounded, both teams trotted off to their side and the whole stadium stood and cheered. I looked across the field at the small group of Saint Agnes fans bravely waving their little green flags, and suddenly all my hope for success and happiness for the town of Green popped like a cheap carnival balloon. Sitting next to one of the nuns was Agent Dwight Paris, wearing a green shirt and waving a pompom. He saw me and put his arm around the nun. I had serious doubts that his sports-betting operation had brought him all the way to Green versus Saint Agnes. Michael's dark, evil conspiracy was going to hatch soon.

We kicked off the second half and a little kid caught the ball as we charged down the field to crush him. They formed a flying wedge to protect him; but instead of trying to run he pitched the ball backwards to Bumper. As we began to break through to get Bumper, he leaped in the air and threw it back all the way across the field to a lone receiver, who gathered it in and sprinted eighty yards for a touchdown.

Carl looked at Robbie with a told-you-so look. The first half had been a set-up. Edwina had her two assistants record every one of our plays and knew our weaknesses and strengths. Now she was ready to play football. Now she was going to turn Bumper loose. There was no longer a little green flag on the end of the flagpole. It had been replaced by another flag, one with our school colors, orange and black.

As before, the girl kicked the ball out of the end zone so we started on our twenty-yard line. Their defense no longer challenged our players man-to-man, but instead shifted quickly to a group and stormed through all together at a single point. We were gang-tackled every time we had the ball. Edwina knew every play we called. The size of our players no longer mattered. Bobby Junior went down for a twelve-yard loss on the first play. Two downs later we punted, giving Saint Agnes back the ball on their own five-yard line.

This time Bumper came out wearing a silver helmet and the offensive line had their hands taped in a fist so they could not be penalized for holding. There was no running game, only passes. Edwina knew that her little players were no match for our crushing line and strong tackles. Her receivers caught the ball and fell immediately to the ground, rather than risk being hurt. With short dart passes, Bumper moved his team down the field, constantly watching his coach wave and jerk her flagpole, signaling in plays and weak spots in our formation. They scored with a series of short-yardage plays.

We got the ball back and went three downs and out. The mood of our fans changed. Our grotesque, skeleton-faced cheerleader jumped in the air and did sexual hip grinds to lift everyone's spirits. At the twenty-yard line Bumper finally called a running play. As he handed it off, the kid ran five yards and made a lateral pass back. Bumper snagged it with one hand and zipped it thirty yards to a lone receiver – who did not fall down but sprinted to the end zone.

Even when we got the ball back, we could only run it for a few yards. Saint Agnes knew every play that we called and controlled the game. By the end of the third quarter the referees started to make bad calls to help us out. Saint Agnes was called for holding; even though their players had their hands taped closed. Then they were called for off-sides when they were clearly not. Then they lost yardage because of an illegal formation when only Bumper was in the backfield. Despite all of this, nothing could stop Bumper. He picked apart our defense. His receivers, who had refused to catch the ball in the first half, now never dropped a single pass. By the fourth quarter the score was twenty-seven to thirty-one. Everyone was scared. Something had to be done. Robbie called for a time-out and pulled his biggest defensive players into a huddle. Lucille, Bobby Junior and I were there too. "Listen," Robbie told them, "Bumper's got to be stopped on the next play. He's got to get hurt. Do you understand me? Do it. Don't worry about the penalties, we've got to win." Lucille and I stood silent.

On the next play Bumper took the snap five yards back and caught it with one hand. He wound up like a baseball pitcher and threw it twenty yards to a waiting receiver. The play was over. He was looking at Edwina when three of our players hit him in the back, knocking him down. By the time the referees pulled them off Bumper had a mangled hand and blood dripping from his mouth. Edwina rushed out on the field, scooped him up and carried him back to the sidelines. She cried as she pulled him to her breast. The referees charged us with a fifteen-yard penalty for unnecessary roughness and gave Saint Agnes an injury time-out. The first-aid people gathered around Bumper as he lay on the ground. Edwina stood up, wiped her tears and glared at us across the field. Then she did something I shall never forget; she lined her orphan players up in a line then slapped the first kid, almost knocking him down. He regained his balance and slapped the kid next to him, who then in turn hit the next kid, on down the line; even the girl kicker got it.

Now, Saint Agnes was ready to play football. The team wearing the color of the name of our town rushed out onto the field like a pack of wild dogs. Some didn't even bother to bring their helmets.

When they got to the scrimmage line they looked over to Edwina for instructions. Her teary eyes burned red with anger. She took her flagpole and snapped it over her knee like twig. All hell was going to break loose. Saint Agnes no longer cared about winning, they wanted to hit, bite or scratch everyone for the rest of the game. There was no more scoring, only chaos until there were only two minutes left to play. The score was still twenty-seven to thirty-one. All we had to do to win was to hold them off. Bobby Junior drove the ball down the field to the ten-yard line. One more play and it would all be over. Robbie called for a time-out. Lucille, Robbie and I huddled with Bobby Junior.

Bobby Junior was shaking and kept looking across the field at Bumper still getting first aid. Lucille hugged him. "I'm proud of you. You have to pull this off." He just stared at her without saying a word.

Coach Robbie touched his shoulder. "Just hold onto the ball, unless you see a good opening, we can wrap it up without another score. Take the downs. No chances. Do you understand?"

Bobby Junior looked at his mother and then again across the field at Bumper. He grabbed his helmet and trotted back out to join his team. It was first down with only ten yards to go. The snap was perfect, Saint Agnes screamed and clawed but our line held. Two receivers were wide open in the end zone, then suddenly from the far side a single Saint Agnes player got through. It was the girl kicker. Bobby Junior could have swatted her off like a fly, but instead he held out the ball to her. She stopped in front of him, ripped off her helmet, took the ball and ran eighty yards.

THE SHERIFF

That night Green lost a hell of a lot more than just a football game. While everyone was watching Green High School lose the state title to Saint Agnes, someone broke into the police station and stole all of the evidence incriminating Vinny. They also stole Vinny. His cell door was wide open and his black Corvette was gone, but things were just getting started. The president of the bottling plant, who was such a football fan, told Lorenzo the game was a disgusting spectacle. Not only was the deal off, his company would not be coming to town, and he wouldn't even fly over Green in his plane. Somewhere between the skeleton-face cheerleader doing bumps and grinds and the biting and scratching of the wild orphan dogs, and the great Bumper stomp, the president's mousy wife had thrown up.

Betty slipped a suicide note under our front door. It said that Jesus loved her but wanted her to come home now. Robbie called later to report that they had found her body floating in the lake by the docks. No one could find Alice, but I did that night. Lucille was sleeping, but I lay awake thinking that the streets of Harlem and the killing fields of the Medalley mansion were more peaceful than Green, Louisiana. At about two a.m. I walked out on the balcony to watch the moon color the lake a bright silver. Betty's house next door was dark, but I thought I could see something in the oak tree where I had first seen the beautiful wood nymph named Alice playing her silver flute. I put my pants and shoes on.

As I approached the tree from the side, I looked up through the branches at the moonlit skeleton-face, teeth glowing in the soft shadows. Alice was standing on her branch, naked, just like she had done before. Her arms and legs and chest were covered with deep bleeding cuts where she had been scratching herself. Her arms were raised as her fingers danced up and down on an imaginary flute.

"Alice, honey, let's get you down."

She refused to hear me.

They brought the thirsty dog Vinny's dead body back to town the next day. He had escaped in his black Corvette and crashed, killing himself, while speeding on Lorenzo Way.

That night I sat in a lawn chair on Lucille's balcony with a bottle of vodka and my little bag of coke. I had been undercover for more than two months and had accomplished absolutely nothing. I knew when I saw Michael cleaning off the tables at the Half Moon that the little town of Green was doomed. He was like Typhoid Mary: bad things happened when he was around. I woke up, still outside in the lawn chair, with a black crow pecking on my knee and the noon sun burning down on me.

I turned to see Lucille standing over me. "Who would think," she said, "that a college student could fuck a lonely middle aged widow, wreck a whole town, and bring down a Mafia leader?"

"You give me a lot of credit," I answered.

"You deserve it. I know you won't understand this, but you gave me strength. You restored my dignity, my self-confidence. You helped me face life so I wouldn't end up like Betty."

"Lucille, I never gave you any advice. I was never any help and I never told you what to do."

She ran her hand gently down the side of my face, pushing back my long dirty hair. "Strength and judgment never come from the outside, they only comes from within. Sometimes it takes a young man loving an older woman for it to come out. You're like a mirror. I can love you and see myself, and like a mirror I can make corrections, look better and do things, things I never thought I could do before. I had a long talk with my children last night. They love me, and we're going to have a lot of fun for the rest of our lives. They are better than me, better than I ever was or will be."

I smiled and kissed her. She was already dressed or I would have dragged her into bed. She looked into my eyes. "I'm going to be gone for a while, why don't you mow the yard?"

"Where to?" I asked. "I think it's really best to stay away from town for a while, don't you think?"

"No. Robbie and I are going to arrest Lorenzo the Mayor, Larry the mobster, Larry who broke his son out of jail last night and stole evidence. This whole town is afraid of him so it's up to me. I have to do this. I have his grandchildren, I'm his only family, and only I can bring Lorenzo Bonnet down. He's not going to get away with trying to protect Vinny. I just hope Robbie and that chicken-shit Deputy Ken will stand up...There's still some coffee left."

Bobby Junior came out on the balcony and said to me, "You've got a phone call; it's the coach."

I took the call. Chief Robbie was desperate. "I need you. Ken is scared to death. This whole town is. I'm going to arrest Lorenzo this afternoon with Lucille. I need another gun. Are you with me?"

Lucille was curious. "What did Robbie want?"

I whispered in her ear, "I need to find my suitcase."

Robbie and Ken were waiting for us at the police station. Deputy Ken was completely void of any self-confidence; law enforcement was the worst profession he could have chosen. His greatest pride and ambition in life was to be Robbie's Deputy, but he was so afraid that his hand was shaking worse than Michael's. He kept mumbling about Larry and Sergio Glass being killers and shouldn't we call for help, like the State Police or the FBI. Nevertheless, the four of us drove to Lorenzo's mansion. As expected, it was beautiful, the driveway lined with flowers and trees. We pulled to a stop in front. Before we even got out I knew that this was going to end badly. I wished that Dewey were here. He would be laughing by now, making everyone feel safe.

Sergio Glass came out to greet us. He stood on the top of the front steps, about six feet from where we stood. He looked down on us. "You all come at a bad time. Larry has just lost his son. Come back tomorrow. No, come back never."

Ken hid behind the car. Chief Robbie reached through the squad-car window and got his pump shotgun and held it to his side. "You see this lady here? She's the new Mayor. The City Council voted her in this morning. Larry's out. See my uniform here, and my badge? I'm the Police Chief. Mister, I don't know who you are, but we're here to get Larry for breaking into my office and stealing evidence against his son Vinny and letting him go. Mister, you're in harm's way."

Glass started to place his hands on his hips when a shot rang out. He tumbled down the steps with a red hole in his chest and lay at our feet. It was crazy Deputy Ken, scared out of his mind, still shaking. "I'm *sorry*, I'm *sorry*, I thought he was reaching for a *gun*. I'm *sorry*."

Suddenly Lorenzo appeared at the top of the steps. He was probably thinking it was a mob hit. He had a black revolver in his hand. Instantly Robbie leveled the shotgun and blasted him off his feet and into a house window.

After a moment of silence, I couldn't resist. "Well, this went well...I'll see if there's anyone else who would like to talk to us."

I pulled my blue automatic and climbed the steps. Inside the door, hanging on a coat hook, was a thirty-eight revolver in a shoulder holster. I picked it up and walked back outside, laying it at the top of the steps where Glass had been standing. "Stop crying, Ken. Looks like Glass was going to kill us. Look what I found," I said, pointing to the gun. "You're Wyatt Earp and you have the Mayor and Police Chief as your witness. It was him or us. Robbie, Deputy Ken saved our lives, he needs a raise."

GOOD-BYE, GOOD-BYE

Police Chief Robbie Morganthal knew the State Police, so it was more family talk than hard investigation. As I read the report, I had that same feeling that I had felt many times before. A secretary was on duty the night Vinny escaped while everyone was at the game. She said a thin masked man came in and told her to open up the evidence locker. He didn't have a gun.

The man then told her to lock herself in the bathroom, but she could still listen through the door. She heard him say to Vinny, "If you're innocent, stay in your cell and trust justice. If you're guilty, drive away as fast as you can. Your car is outside."

The police report said no one was chasing Vinny when his tires exploded and crashed, killing himself on Lorenzo Way. It is likely that his tires were over-inflated and gave out at high speed, but there was no way to be sure.

That afternoon Lucille told me our relationship was over as we sat on the bedroom balcony. She never asked about the gun; she only said thank you and that I should go back to New York City and continue my education. I had nothing more to learn in Green. She said I was smart and didn't belong in a small dying town with an old widow. She knew that she was the only one in town that could have faced Lorenzo and now as the new Mayor she had to rebuild Green.

It was a sad, quiet, personal moment, then I ruined it. "Dewey, Dewey and Michael, *Michael* and *Dewey*!" I yelled. "Why was *Dewey* at the game rooting for the *orphans*?"

"What?" she asked. "Who's Dewey?"

"Never mind. Please never ask," I said calmly. The phone began ringing and she left to answer it.

It would take two people to rob the police station, one inside, and one outside. I could never explain to her or anyone else that it was Michael and Silkey. Dewey made sure everyone stayed at the football game. If it was Glass, like everyone believed, why would he say to Vinny, "If you're innocent, stay and trust in justice, but if guilty drive away as fast as you can"? The *over-inflated tires*! Dewey!

Michael had wisely chosen Lucille to stand up against Lorenzo, and sent me to give her courage. Michael had to wait for the right spark to set off the powder keg to blow Lorenzo to hell. Vinnie was the spark.

Lucille came back outside. "That was Dewey. He sounds like a kid. He said they'll pick you up in half an hour."

I kissed Lucille as a white Cadillac rolled up in front of her house. There were two men in the front; another was asleep in the back with his hat over his face. I got in the back seat with Michael, who was snoring and smelled of booze. Instead of heading for the highway, Silkey drove to the Half Moon. It was mid-afternoon so the restaurant was empty. Silkey went in and started talking to the bartender. I watched him through the restaurant front window. After a few minutes the restaurant manager came into view and extended his hand. Silkey slugged him so hard he went up in the air and crashed on a table and slid to the floor. Silkey began kicking and stomping him, then dragged the man to his feet and banged his head against the bar. He fell back on the floor like a wet rag. Silkey walked out, got in the car and we drove away. Michael was still sleeping. I asked, "What the hell was that?"

Dewey whispered, "Michael's boss at the restaurant. Michael told Silkey to say good-bye."

CHAPTER TEN

LAW AND ORDER

HEAT

Michael and I came back to 90 Church the same day. I arrived in the morning and Michael, as usual, at 4:30 in the afternoon, smelling of booze. Incredibly, no one commented on our long absence. Since there was never a drug investigation in the first place, Blanker told the agents that the 'local sheriff' had killed Sergio Glass and Lorenzo Bonnet in a gun battle somewhere in Louisiana.

Then came news about an Irish agent, Thomas O'Toole. He was a young, good-looking, enthusiastic street agent who, for some reason, ended up one night in an after-hours bar called Little Egypt, on the West Side, in the lower 30's of Manhattan. No one was sure how things got started but the bar was filled with Puerto Rican and Colombian drug dealers who found out that O'Toole was an agent. He was stripped naked, stabbed seventeen times and thrown in the street. By the time the Bureau learned about it the next morning, O'Toole was in a critical condition after lying in the street for almost four hours.

That day the police precinct captain came to the Bureau and told Blanker and some of the group leaders that they had conducted an investigation and none of the patrons would cooperate. No one saw anything. Since O'Toole was assigned to Group Two, we were all called into Blanker's office. Dewey as usual missed the meeting; he was collecting gambling bets in another part of the office. Blanker stood up from behind his desk, his face red. After a rambling, incoherent speech he said he had come to New York City from Georgia because he "knew this was a Christian town." Blanker said, "the forces of evil have broken through, like a filthy sewer main spewing shit into the street, and Group Two is to go and plug it up." He said a "saint" was lying in the hospital mortally wounded and we were to "find the evil devils responsible and serve justice." Everyone knew that, once again, all hell was going to break loose. Worse, Pike was going to be in charge.

Michael argued that it was stupid to have a "white boy" agent in one of the most dangerous bars in New York City without backup. We were as much at fault as the drug dealers. Michael said he would give the case to Dewey and his people would find out who was responsible in a week. Then he would send Ed Silkey to talk to them. Blanker and Pike were infuriated. They hated Dewey, who didn't even attend the meeting. They demanded that it be handled "high profile," to teach the drug dealers a lesson and "restore dignity to the law-enforcement community."

So the next day at about 4:00 in the afternoon, Louie the G and three hookers went into Little Egypt and began to party. Twelve hours later, at about 3:30 in the morning, four agents walked through the doors – Pike, Silkey, Connors, and Greenway – carrying sledgehammers and crowbars. Dewey and Michael took sick leave. They wanted nothing to do with the case. The girls put their drinks down and got off the customers' laps. Then Louie and the girls went around the room, pointing to customers one after another, and then walked out the door. Pike said to everyone, "If they pointed to you, stand up and leave the bar. Don't pay for anything. Don't say anything. Stand up and get out."

Most of the customers fled. Agent Greenway closed the door.

I waited outside in the street; I had seen enough of these kinds of things. They broke everything in the bar, every glass, every plate, every bottle, every light, every table, every chair – and every body. I knew the police wouldn't come and they didn't. There had been five unanswered emergency calls. The next day there was an article in the *Daily News* of a "gang war breakout" on the lower West Side of Manhattan. Five people were critically injured and the police were investigating two Puerto Rican gangs that had come down to Manhattan from the lower Bronx to cause trouble.

My life had become a huge pile of contradictions of all shapes and sizes. I loved my wife and son more than anything in the world, but betrayed them to be with the treacherous mistress of a drug-dealing killer. I worked in the most dangerous environment in the world, but my greatest fear was that I didn't have the courage to shoot anyone. I fought a war against drugs twenty-four hours a day, but couldn't live without my daily line of cocaine. I wore expensive suits, but looked like a manager of a pizza stand from the Bronx. I believed in the law all my life, but now it had no meaning. I had always been a leader, but now hid in the shadows. I was the most productive agent in the Bureau but had not developed or managed one single case. I knew that the United States Government was the greatest force on earth, but drunks and buffoons ran it. I wanted a normal life, but couldn't stand to even look at everyday people going to and from work and raising their families. Money came to me every day, but it had no value. I believed in the truth, but lied all the time. I dedicated my life to the justice system, but knew it didn't exist. I had seen the worst horrors imaginable, but knew they were nothing compared to what lay ahead. I was proud to be an agent, but kept remembering the tape recording played on my first day of work that called us "the most evil people on earth." Every day I did what I thought was right, but knew that someday, someday soon, someone would come and tell me it was wrong.

ANDY

Monday morning is the only time that most agents are in the office because of the weekly meeting to discuss major cases and objectives, and to recognize achievements. A special memo was sent to all agents, ordering them not to miss this meeting. That Monday, I took the subway to work and as I came up to the street level, I looked down Church Street and saw press cars and trucks parked along the curb all the way to the next block. Even television, channels Seven, Two, Five – a sure sign that something big was going on. Everyone in Group Two was trying to figure out what the topic would be to draw so many news people. We hadn't closed any big cases in weeks.

Earlier that morning Pike had called Agent Cleo Brown into his office. He said Blanker had asked him to take his gun but he didn't know why; perhaps he was being transferred to another office. Brown looked more bewildered than scared, but gave up his revolver. Blanker normally presided over the Monday meetings, but this time a stranger took his place at the podium. He introduced himself as Andrew Flowers, lead investigator for a special Task Force of the Justice Department assigned to the Federal Bureau of Narcotics. Two marshals came from behind the room and arrested Brown and another agent, John Winkler. They stood stone cold while the marshal cuffed them and led them from the room in front of the news cameras and bright lights. Flowers said Brown had sold marijuana and Winkler was being arrested for theft of personal property. Winkler had arrested a suspect with a gun, a felony in New York. He should have turned the defendant over to the police; instead he kept the gun and did not file charges. Winkler had hoped that the suspect would be grateful and provide information in the future.

Except for the presence of media and the stranger at the podium, the scene would have been a typical opening for the Monday morning meeting, that always began with an outrageous joke before going into who got killed, wounded, or beaten. But this was not a joke. Flowers announced indictments of two New York City policemen. Everyone had heard about the cases because one of the detectives, rather than implicate his fellow officers, had committed suicide. Despite enormous resentment by the NYPD over Flowers' investigation Flowers said he was proud of these arrests, that they were just the beginning. He ended the press conference and asked the people who had press passes to leave.

After they dragged their cameras out of the room, Andrew Flowers continued, "I know what's going on. I know about the drug money being skimmed, the dope you give to junkie informants, and the drinking on the job. Most of you are going to the penitentiary. I have all the files. I know who your secret informants are. I intend to interview every one of your informants, and take his word over yours. As far as I'm concerned, you are all evil thugs, worse than the Mafia itself." He then glared at everyone and said, "My agents are secret and we're going to get every one of you. I dare anyone to try to stop me. It would make my work that much easier. Now, are there any questions?"

The room was stunned silent, but Dewey couldn't resist, "Yes, I have one, Agent Flowers; how many of your secret agents will be attending this year's Christmas party? I'll need a count by next week."

Flowers glared at Dewey. "Agent Paris, isn't it? I know you well, you smart-ass son-of-a-bitch. You're first on my list."

No one said anything; we just left the room to return to our desks. While we were attending the meeting, some of the desks in each group area had been searched; Michael's, Dewey's, and mine. Lying on the desks were copies of a search warrant. Altogether, ten desks had been searched in just one hour while we were attending the meeting. It was more amusing than alarming; no agent would ever leave anything incriminating in his desk. Incredibly, work went on as usual, as if nothing had happened.

The charges against Winkler were so outrageous that most of us thought it was a camouflage for something more serious. Winkler was an extremely popular, brave agent who had been shot twice in the line of duty. He also conducted training for new agents and represented the Bureau to other agencies on joint investigations. Brown's charges were just as absurd. An informant had pleaded with Brown to give him a bag of pot taken from a drug raid. Normally, small amounts of pot are thrown away because they just create additional paperwork and complicate the more serious charges of trafficking cocaine and heroin. The informant was wearing a body wire. When Brown gave him the pot, he insisted on paying him. Brown at first said it was a gift and refused the money, but the informant stuffed $20 into his coat pocket and made sure it was recorded on the body wire he was wearing. The story appeared in the *New York Post* and the *Daily News* the next day. It said that a federal agent was caught selling drugs.

Although things appeared to return to normal that day, Michael, Dewey, and some of the others whose desks had been searched met secretly that night at the Heidelberg. No one was really sure if Andrew Flowers was just another dumb bureaucrat or a serious investigator. Kyle and some other New York City cops who knew about Flowers' earlier investigations came to the meeting to help us. We learned that Andy Flowers was very religious, a dedicated family man who had a strong opinion of what was right and wrong. As Kyle put it, "To Flowers, there is no difference between cheating on your expense report and murdering somebody. Wrong is wrong."

Kyle told us that when Flowers was investigating the police, one detective refused to rat on the other cops. Flowers threatened to send him to jail, where he would be beaten and raped. When the detective killed himself, Flowers bragged about it. He said that it proved that the cop was crooked, and that, one way or the other, justice had been served. Dewey learned from Blanker's secretary that she overheard Flowers say he had been investigating the Bureau for six months and was already prepared to ask for criminal indictments on at least six agents. He had created a list, dividing the agents at 90 Church into those that had the guts to stand up to the investigation and the others who were weaker and would probably cooperate. He was thinking just like us. But Flowers's first job was to get rid of the incompetent or lazy agents. Everyone knew Dewey was on the top of that list.

Later that night I visited some of my informants to see if they had heard anything. Charles DeWitt, the greatest trumpet player I ever heard, was as kind and gentle as ever and said a man in a suit had approached him, asking about me. He said he wouldn't give him the right time of day, but the man kept asking him if I had ever given him any heroin. He said he told them no, but the man offered him a deal: the government would not try to put him in jail if he found out something bad about me and reported it. I told DeWitt to remain loyal to me, to say nothing, to sign nothing.

The next day I went to see Tony Degaglia, my Mafia informant, at his mother's house. She said he hadn't been home in a while but called often to see how she was. Tony called me back later and I saw him that evening in a bar. He didn't look well. He was a heroin addict and was shaking. "I'm strung out pretty good. I need something to keep me going. You're all I've got, but I've got something moving, it could be sweet, but you don't want to know about it," he said as he laid his head on the bar.

"Tony," I said, "has anyone contacted you about me or Michael? You know the kind of person I'm talking about – a suit."

"Are you kidding? No. If anyone like that talked to me I'd tell you. My life is in your hands. We've got to protect each other." Then he started to cry. Tony used to be a smart, tough guy, but now he was broken. The others in the bar turned their eyes away, but I put my arm around him. Then he said, "Please, I need something to get through this, please!"

"Life's not easy, we'll stick together. Here, I've got some smack for you. Good stuff. It'll hold you over." I then reached in my pocket and gave him a bundle of nickel heroin bags that I had taken from an earlier case.

His teary eyes lit up with gratitude as he stuffed the bundles in his pocket. "Thanks," he said. "I know you're not supposed to do this, but I'd be dead without it. I've got another problem; Brimstone knows it was me that set him up. The cops busted him last week. He's going to kill me."

"Tony, George Brimstone is a vicious drug dealer who would not hesitate to kill anyone he suspected of being an informant. How did you get into this mess? We don't have anything on him. How did the cops get him?"

He hung his head and looked away.

"I get it, why don't the cops protect you since you're working for them too?"

Tears rolled down his cheek. "Because," he stammered, "Brimstone's going to cooperate, they don't need me anymore. But if Brimstone kills the informant on his case then he skates without being a rat."

His hand was shaking badly and saliva dripped from his mouth. "You can't stop him. I'm going to die."

I thought a minute, then said, "Do you know Heyman?"

Tony shook his head. "No."

"It doesn't matter, I know him, I'll tell Brimstone it was Heyman and not you. You'll be off the hook. Trust me, Heyman will be dead in a week."

Tony smiled and wiped his eyes with his sleeve. I knew he would stay loyal.

Later on, at about 2:00 in the morning, I saw Brimstone at an after-hours club in Harlem where he hung out every night. He was still out on bail. Brimstone looked like a banker, no fancy pimp clothes for him. He was good-looking, smart and dangerous. He knew who I was and even about the investigation. I offered him a deal. "Hear you got in a little dust-up with the cops. Need some help?"

He waved everyone away, then said, "Why?" He was interested.

"Because, George, I need you. If Flowers or his people come to you, you know nothing and don't make up anything. Do you understand?"

After a bit of silence and studying the bar to see if I was alone, he said, "Why?"

I had his interest. "Don't ask why. What do you want?"

He lit a cigar. "Only one thing you can give me. I want the rat."

"Of course you do; it's all I can offer. Is it a deal?"

"Done. Who?"

I kept remembering what Heyman's bouncers did to Gabriel's father. He only came to get his teenage daughter out of the whorehouse and take her home. They broke his arm and threw him down the stairs. I remembered standing there watching and I did nothing, but I could do something now, just like Michael would do. I whispered in his ear, "The Jamaican guy who runs a whore-house in Spanish Harlem, always says 'hey man,' he's on our payroll."

Brimstone nodded, he was grateful and he believed me.

DEWEY GOES DOWN

Andy Flowers set up a small office in 90 Church, just himself and one snotty secretary. No one talked to either one of them. Everyone knew Flowers had another secret, much larger office, filled with agents who were all trying their best to put us in the penitentiary – or worse, get us killed. I was the first agent on Flowers' list. They announced my name over the office P.A. to meet with agent Flowers in one of our interview rooms. Everyone looked up at me as I walked down the hall to meet the man who was trying to put all of us in jail.

Flowers was smiling and very friendly. He reminded me of a country preacher. He said he had a tough job and that he would like my help. He knew that I was a good, honest agent and, in fact, the most successful agent in the Bureau. He surprised me when he said, "You are not the target of this investigation, but you work closely with two agents that for the sake of the Bureau must go to jail. You and I know that they have taken government money, falsified cases and killed people." I knew he was talking about Dewey and Michael. He continued, "I know you know the difference between right and wrong and I'm counting on you to do the right thing. I need you to guide my investigation."

I noticed he was smiling. Michael had warned me that smiling people never attack from the front. I said I would help him, but I didn't have any firsthand knowledge about any illegal activities by either Michael or Dewey. He just gave me a big grin. Then said, "I would like you to come back at two o'clock this afternoon."

I went back and told Dewey and Michael what had happened. Dewey said Flowers' secretary had also told him he was supposed to meet Flowers at two o'clock. Things were getting very serious. That afternoon I saw one of the lawyers from the Justice Department who had come over to help Flowers interview Dewey. He was bright, young, and enthusiastic. He reminded me of Tyler Springfield from the FBI.

Flowers pulled me aside before the interview. "Dewey Paris is our first target. He's going to be indicted and I want you to see how we work. I'm going to expose these people and I want you to understand and help me." He patted me on the back and then went into the small conference room while I watched outside through a two-way mirror.

The eager government lawyer and the crusading special investigator were all ganging up on Dewey, who just sat there looking like a well-dressed teenage kid. Dewey wore a grey pin-stripe navy blue suit with a starched white shirt, and a gold tie. He sat straight in the chair, military style. His nails were buffed, and he wore a pinky ring with the head of a gold snake, biting down on a round piece of bright green jade. The full force of the United States Government was coming down on Dewey, and the government didn't stand a chance.

Flowers started in: "Agent Paris, you're a fuck-up, aren't you? It says here that you've been with the Bureau for eight years and you're still only a GS Sixteen. You've been denied six promotions. With this kind of record what kind of advice should I give you?"

Dewey looked at him. "Is that what this meeting is all about? Giving me advice? Higher aspirations for my career?"

"No," Flowers said quietly. "You're not fooling anyone. In the past six months you've been listed as a surveillance agent in only two cases and, six months prior to that, only one. You've participated in only three cases in the past twelve months. You've not conducted one meaningful interview or developed any useful information to further a single case. You're not fooling anyone," he repeated. "But there's something worse. You're a cold-blooded killer. In the past year you've killed eight men. One of them, Bobby

Moon, you shot in the face."

The government lawyer sat there trying not to smile as Flowers waited for Dewey's answer.

"I believe the New York City Police Department filed a report on this incident. It was part of the Domenic Scarluci and Charles Moon case," Dewey answered calmly. "When you take the time to read it, it will say that there were several witnesses. The suspect reached for his gun. I had to angle the shot down so it would not ricochet and hit an agent. I called the police for clean-up and left my number for them to call me. They did. Now what's the problem?"

"What do you mean, 'clean-up?'" the government lawyer asked.

Dewey smiled. "Sweep the trash off the street."

Flowers now seemed unsure of himself. "That does not excuse your actions."

"The man was homicidal," Dewey answered calmly. "He had already killed four people. This is not the Wild West, where they get to draw first. He reached for his gun and I clipped him. I'm not aware of a fair-fight policy in the agent's manual; perhaps you could show it to me so we can move this discussion along."

Flowers tried a different tack. "Dewey, there's nothing personal here. You know what we want. We want Michael Giovanni."

"You just called me a killer. That sounds pretty personal to me, and if you want to talk to Michael Giovanni, I think he's still in the office."

Flowers exploded again. "You're a *killer*, and you don't give a *damn* about authority. You don't obey your superiors. You have no respect for them. You're a rogue killer agent. You've killed more people than anyone else in this Bureau."

"Actually," Dewey replied, "I think that Silkey has a higher head count, if you like to keep track of that sort of thing. And I do respect my superiors – when I can find them."

Flowers ignored the insult. "I'm curious…What kind of a gun does a killer rogue agent like you carry? Let me see it."

Dewey reached his arm up his back and pulled out his forty-five automatic from his custom holster and laid it on the table. It was dull black with bright red cherry-wood grips and a flat straight trigger.

Flowers started in again, "That weapon is not even government issue."

The Justice Department lawyer interrupted, "Uhm, I think it is…This is a standard forty-five automatic with a brushed dull finish used by naval officers, issued for covert operations. It is non-reflective, hard short-pull trigger for rapid fire." The lawyer was proud of himself, to be able to volunteer such technical information.

"Unload it," Flowers ordered.

Dewey popped the clip and placed it on the table.

"And the one in the chamber," Flowers said.

Dewey then did something unbelievable; he picked up the gun and yanked back the carriage, ejecting the bullet with such force and at the precise angle that it ricocheted off the wall, bounced off the ceiling and soared directly to Flowers' face. In one powerful snatch, like catching a fly, Dewey caught the bullet in mid-air with his fist and froze his clenched hand in front of Flowers' face with the green-snake pinky ring just inches from his nose.

Flowers jumped back, almost falling from his chair. He was visibly upset. "I thought I could deal with you reasonably, and just accept your resignation, but I can't. I'm informing you that I'm filing a federal indictment against you this afternoon. We have evidence that you have taken illegal payoffs from underworld sources."

"Since, as you say, I've not been deeply involved in any cases for the past two years, what are you referring to?"

Flowers ignored the question and looked to the young Justice Department lawyer. The lawyer reached in his briefcase, pulled out a file and laid it on the table.

"Dewey," Flowers continued, trying to be nice, "we've audited yours and Maggie's bank accounts for the past year. You've spent ten thousand dollars more through your checking account than you've earned from your government pay. Your wife is unemployed and you did not declare any extra income. We've got you."

I was stunned. In the first meeting, they got Dewey.

Immediately Dewey bowed his head. He began pulling on his gold cufflinks and said, "It's been hard working here. I don't want a lot of publicity. I would like to go on record right now. An indictment won't be necessary. I would like to give you my statement, my confession."

Flowers beamed. Dewey could bring everybody down. I couldn't believe my own eyes. The young lawyer was smiling with satisfaction as Dewey hung his head in shame; with a straight face he confessed: "About a year ago, I was out bouncing, drinking on the East Side, and I met a stranger. He had too much to drink so I brought him home with me. He slept in the guest room, but the next morning when I woke up he was gone. I think he left in a cab. He had some luggage with him but he left behind a small bag. When I opened it there was ten thousand dollars in cash. I didn't know what to do. I thought he might come back, but then

I couldn't have the cash lying around the house, so I deposited it in my account and then over time I spent it. I spent it all. I know it was illegal, improper at the least. I took his money. I should be punished for it. He has every right to file charges and he will probably work with you to charge me. I remember his name. His name is José. He never told me his last name, but he did say he was from Cuba. He lives somewhere in Cuba, shouldn't be too hard to find. Let's write it up."

I started laughing so hard I thought they could hear me on the other side of the glass. The young government lawyer sat there staring into space. Dewey looked at Flowers and said, "Unless there's a point to all of this, I've requested to leave early today."

As if things weren't bad enough for Flowers, the Justice Department lawyer picked up Dewey's black gun and read aloud the inscription etched on the barrel, "Presented by Captain Maurice Castlemann to Lieutenant Dwight Paris for heroic and dedicated service – " Dewey took the gun out of his hand before he could finish reading, reloaded it and stuffed it in the back of his pants and walked out without saying another word.

Flowers sat frozen and silent. I'd noticed earlier that he had an odd mannerism. He would remain very still, then jerk his head or hands to a new position like the movement of a large bird or reptile. Now he folded his hands on the table like he was praying and his head jerked up and down and sideways as he stared into space.

The next morning, at about ten-thirty, an announcement came over the public-address system in the office. The agent on duty announced, "There is an urgent and very important phone call for Agent Dwight Paris from José. He's calling collect from Cuba, will you accept charges?" For twenty minutes the whole Bureau laughed.

At one-thirty in the afternoon someone made the same announcement again, and the laughter started all over. Finally Blanker put a stop to it.

TO TELL THE TRUTH

A week later, one of Dewey's informants told him he had been approached by a Task Force investigator, promising to "lose his file" if he wore a body wire and set Dewey up. The plan was to try to get Dewey to admit that he had given the informant money taken from an earlier drug raid. It was laughable to think Dewey could be set up so easily. Dewey told the informant he could "lose his file" too if he would double-cross the investigators and set them up. The informant feared Dewey more than the investigators.

Dewey told the informant to tell the Task Force that Dewey knew he was working with Flowers and was coming to kill him this afternoon. The informant then went to the investigator for protection.

The next morning Dewey told Pike that the informant had not been producing enough information and that he was going to arrest him and bring his case to trial. Dewey, Ed Silkey, and Agent Greenway went to the Bronx, supposedly to arrest the informant.

The informant was sitting on the front steps of a brownstone on Tremont Avenue with two Task Force investigators waiting for Dewey and the others to arrive. Dewey jumped out of his car, grinning and waving his black .45 automatic. Ed Silkey waved his shotgun in the air when he saw the informant. The two Task Force investigators panicked and started firing. Dewey pinned the Task

Force agents down behind a stone porch with rapid fire from his .45 automatic. Finally, police cars surrounded the block and got control of the situation.

In the investigation that followed, Pike had to admit that the agents were en route to make an arrest and were justified in approaching the informant with their guns drawn. They had no knowledge of who the investigators were or why they were with the informant. The newspapers carried the story: "Agent Against Agent; Confusion Reigns at Federal Bureau of Narcotics." Michael complained to Pike that Dewey was a lousy shot and should be re-qualified at the pistol range. This got the office laughing again. Of course, everyone knew that if Dewey had wanted to kill the Task Force investigators at the shoot-out, they would all be dead.

Still, no one expected anything to end soon. Letters were written by Customs, NYPD, and the Secret Service, protesting the outrageous, amateurish, investigative techniques used by the Task Force. They praised the Bureau for its cooperation and the endless supply of valuable information coming from its Library. They said the Bureau was a major force in the fight against drugs and organized crime, and asked that the Investigative Task Force be dissolved.

But Andy Flowers' Task Force only grew more aggressive. The next Monday morning when we were all in the office they started to use surprise polygraph tests. First they called Michael in, sat him down to a chair, and strapped the wires to him. Afterwards, the polygraph tester said he had never seen results like this before. It was almost a straight line on the sheet. Michael had no reaction, one way or the other, to any question. The results were similar to those of people in deep depression. The joke around the office was that, after all, Michael was a vampire; he'd been dead for years. What did they expect?

Dewey's was next. His test was just as bizarre. It indicated that he was lying to every question asked, except for his name. Even his answer to the test question "Was he an agent for the Federal Bureau of Narcotics?" indicated a lie. Now the joke in the office was that the only thing they proved was that Dewey was lying when he said Michael Giovanni was still alive.

I didn't think they would grab me, but they did. Flowers was nice about it. He said, "We must do this, it's just a formality. You said you didn't know about any criminal activity, but I've got to be sure. You understand, don't you?"

I was terrified as they strapped me into the chair with wires on my arm and fingers. The first questions were easy – my name, family members – in order to get a baseline for the truth. The next question was about the case I had made several nights earlier. It was a small case against a junkie that went according to procedure. After a series of questions I knew I was registering the truth, but then came the unexpected question that was not "just a formality." Flowers asked, "Have you ever stolen any official government advance funds assigned to you or anyone else to purchase heroin or cocaine from suspected drug dealers?"

I thought for a moment, then I answered truthfully, "No."

Flowers was both surprised and pleased. He pulled off my wires and patted me on the back like I had just won some type of award. "Thank you. I believe you. You are a good agent. You've never taken any drug money, unlike the rest of your friends. I know what's going on. You must help me find the truth."

We shook hands and I left.

GRAMERCY PARK

For the next week or so things quieted down and, oddly, Michael began to take more of a personal interest in me. Perhaps it was because I passed the polygraphs and everyone knew Flowers had nothing on me.

Of all the things that I had seen – killings, mutilations, strung-out junkies – nothing horrified me more than something Michael showed me one night just for fun. We had been talking to an informant in a hotel room on the West Side. He had not been contacted by Flowers, so, at least for now, things seemed to be at a standstill. It was about midnight and, incredibly, neither one of us had had a drink all day. Michael suggested we go downtown to a special club in Gramercy Park. It was a big three-story mansion with leaded-glass windows and a heavy oak front door. Michael knocked on the door and a man in a butler suit answered. Before we could say anything, he said, "I'm sorry, gentlemen, but this is a private club. Members only."

Michael came out of the shadows so the butler could have a better look at him.

The butler closed the door quietly and we just stood there. After a few minutes the door opened and a woman motioned us to come in. Tiffany lamps, fringes, wood stairways, crown molding, and crystal chandeliers gave the place an old Victorian look. The woman who greeted us was in her fifties and dressed very stylishly. Her reading glasses hung around her neck on a gold chain. She led us off to the side of the foyer into a small office, and then through another door to a larger office decorated with books and vases of orchids. She sat behind a desk and stared at Michael. Then, in a trembling voice, she asked, "What do you want?"

Michael grinned. "We thought you might be a little short-handed tonight, so we came to help you with your clients."

The color drained from her face. Wherever Michael went, people reacted as though they were meeting the devil himself. She was too frightened to even answer.

Michael saved her from further embarrassment. "My friend drinks vodka straight, no garnish, on the rocks. I drink scotch the same way."

Her hand was shaking as she picked up the phone and ordered bottles of vodka and scotch with a bucket of ice and two glasses. Almost instantly a young man arrived carrying a tray, set it down on the desk, and walked out without saying a word. Michael and I fixed our drinks and sat down facing the woman across the desk. Michael pulled on his drink and watched the poor frightened woman like a snake would watch a mouse. Then he said, "Things should be getting started soon. We don't want to participate, we just want to watch." This bothered the woman even more. She kept quietly repeating, "Please, please, please." Michael tried to put her at ease a little bit, raising his glass with approval. "Not bad. Thank you. Single malt. Very good." And then he said, "I don't care who your clients are, we just want to watch. This is my partner and I'm training him. Who knows, someday you may need him, or worse, far worse, someday he may need you."

She picked up the phone again, asking whoever was on the other end to "find Robin and send her to the office right away."

Within a few minutes a black girl came in, wearing a white nurse's uniform with a folded white cap. The older woman looked at the nurse and said, "Robin, these are special guests of mine. They don't want to meet anyone. They're not here for therapy. Take them with you. They're just here to observe. Let them see some of the stations. Please be careful; I will be waiting here in the office."

Michael and I followed Nurse Robin out of the office into a smaller one where she stopped, walked up to a blank wall and pushed on it. It opened up to a dark hallway and she led us in, closing the secret panel behind us. With the exception of little lights along the floor, it was completely dark. We went through a narrow walkway and down a small flight of steps to a landing. She stepped back and waved to Michael.

Michael chuckled. "I've seen it all before. Let him look."

I walked over to the black wall and put my eye up to a small hole. I could see a room of rough stonewalls. There were steel rings anchored every four or five feet, waist high. A fat, naked, bald, white man was tied to one of the rings by his wrists. He knelt on the floor screaming and crying. Then I saw why. A woman came into view; she was dressed in high-heeled black leather boots, a wide belt with studs around her waist, and a black leather bra that exposed her nipples through large holes in the center. She wore a black mask that covered her face, but allowed her long black hair to flow down over her shoulders. The man was already covered in blood, but she stepped back and hit him again with a short whip. He screamed and whimpered like a dog. She hit him again and again, and he screamed and cried. Then she walked over and grabbed his head and pushed it between her naked thighs. She threw her head back and stared at the ceiling.

I couldn't watch any more. I stepped back like I had been poked in the eye. Michael had been watching me, smoking a cigarette. He told Nurse Robin to go back to the office and get the vodka and scotch, and meet us at station two.

As Michael and I groped through the darkened corridors I saw tripods and camera equipment. Michael said, "You haven't seen anything yet. Just remember sex is at its best when it's forced perversion."

Michael looked through the second peek-hole first, and then said, "You'll like this. This one is special. Even I haven't seen it before."

I peeked through the hole at station number two. There were two men on the floor, on their hands and knees. They were wearing leather masks and had a steel bit, like a horse bridle, jammed in their mouth between their teeth, and a wide dog collar around their necks. One man's harness was red; the other blue, matching the outfits of the girls who tortured them. They were wielding riding crops. There was some type of weird competition going on. The girls made the men roll over on their backs and raise their legs in the air, and then they struck them on the groin with the riding crop. Whoever screamed and cried the loudest seemed to win. Then they lifted the horse bits from their mouths and made them lick each other's crotch to ease the pain. When one of them was not licking hard enough, a girl would whack him on the buttocks with her riding crop. The men licked each other's cocks and sucked each other's testicles until finally the women separated them. Then the two girls began beating the two men all over again.

I pulled away from the peephole and looked at Michael. He was smiling at me over the rim of a fresh glass of scotch. I think he wondered if I was aroused. Then he said, "I brought Dewey here, too. He loved it."

I knew if I didn't leave soon I would throw up. I turned to Michael. "I can't stand this. I gotta get out of here."

Nurse Robin pointed us to go back the way we came, but Michael said, "We're going out through the locker room. My friend doesn't like the golden shower."

Nurse Robin shook her head no.

Michael smiled at her and repeated, "We're going out through the locker room. I want my friend to see who these people are."

"No. I'm sorry but that's not authorized, and I can't permit this."

Michael just stared at her.

In this situation, I could imagine Ed or Dewey decking anyone who stood in their way, but I had never seen Michael hit anybody, ever. There was just something about Michael, something unnatural and terrifying. It was as if he could read your mind, but only the bad things, the weaknesses, the perversions, and of course, the lies. He just gave her a moment to think...and without another word, she led us forward to a wall at the end of the corridor where she stopped and peeked through, then unlatched a door and let us into another small office containing medical equipment. After closing the secret passage behind us she led us through another smaller room into the kind of locker room used by professional athletes – carpeted benches, shelves, hangers, shiny wood, chandeliers. Each locker space had clothes, shoes, coats, shirts, and ties, neatly folded or hung on the padded hangers.

Michael nudged me and said, "Remember what I taught you," and he pointed to the hanging clothes.

I couldn't remember a thing Michael had told me that related to what I had just seen. The first locker held a silk suit, expensive shoes, and a diamond-studded watch. The next locker stunned me. Above the black suit, black shoes and socks sat a priest's collar.

Michael said, "In six months he'll be the next Archbishop of

New York." He gave a little chuckle and we moved on to the next locker, to more expensive suits, expensive jewelry, and then there were women's clothes, elegant silk underwear and designer shoes. Then Robin said, "Each of our guests is attended to by at least two escorts to ensure their privacy and take care of any special needs they may have after their procedures."

"That's always good to know," Michael said.

Robin then led us to a small foyer, not as elegant as the one we had come in by. She opened the outside door for us and Michael and I walked back out into the cool night air. Michael laughed. "Dewey set the nurse up. He tried to tip her ten dollars and she threw it on the floor. She was so insulted and busy throwing the ten dollars on the floor she didn't see Dewey steal a riding crop as a souvenir. I think he wanted it to use on the snotty advertising bitch he keeps on the side, or maybe she was going to use it on his pasty white ass. Dewey's a funny guy, but really tricky."

We were about three houses down from the front entrance when Michael volunteered what I wanted to know. "They have to turn down requests for membership. They can't handle all the business. Do you know how much it costs just to go through one hour of their therapy? Anywhere from two to five thousand dollars. They have to know what they're doing to avoid serious injuries, and of course everything is confidential. I don't know what the initiation fee is, but these are the kind of people that don't worry about such things."

He pointed up and down the street at four limos waiting with their engines purring.

"Why?" I asked. I felt like Ed with his dumb questions at our meetings at the Heidelberg. "Why do they do that?"

"Because they have to." He looked at me and must have realized how truly naïve I was, because he continued in a more understanding tone. "These people have lost their souls. It's a terrible thing to lose, because you almost never get it back." Michael sounded like he was Lucifer, explaining how he made a living.

"Okay, Michael, how do you lose your soul?"

"Easy," he said. "You just start by caring more about saving yourself than anyone else. You see, all of those people in there have one thing in common; they're all high-powered, ambitious, and very selfish. They inflict pain and cruelty on people all day long, at their jobs, in their families. Why, these business people and priests are so ruthless they make what we do look like a church picnic. They have to do something like this to make themselves *feel*, just to feel *anything*. They get so wound up inside themselves that the only way to feel anything is with pain. Pain becomes pleasure. It's the only window left to them to be alive. At least they feel something, and that reminds them that they're not dead. They humiliate themselves – and like to be whipped – as a private payback for what they do every day to others. To them it seems to balance the scale. They beat up on people during the day and they get beat up in a fancy club at night. It's the only way to live when you've lost your conscience, or if you prefer, your soul."

To the underworld, to the Bureau, to most of the law-enforcement community, Michael was known as the cruelest, most ruthless, and most evil agent on the planet. But now I saw a different side of him, and for the first time, I looked at him as a human being. Before he hailed a cab, to go wherever he went late at night, he gave me a warning: "If you hurt people long enough and hard enough, I'll get you a membership to that club, a membership all your own."

For some odd desperate reason I began to think about Daisy and my son. Stranger still, I looked at all of the insanity pouring into my life and began to understand the pleasures at Gramercy Park.

DINNER WITH A FRIEND

I met a model named Cookie at the bar in Maxwell Plum's, one of my nighttime haunts on Second Avenue. At first I thought she was a hooker, and she certainly looked underage. Cookie was intrigued with what she called my "air of mystery" and soon we were kissing. She felt the gun tucked under my armpit and I could tell that it excited her even more. She had a nice apartment in the 80's on the East Side so I decided to stay there for a while. Daisy's temporary move to Chicago to live with her parents had lasted months and I doubted that she and Mark would ever come back. Every day I expected to see divorce papers in the mail. I hated going home to the dirty, empty apartment. And now, at least I had a sex life.

Something else good happened after I met Cookie; Del Ridley invited me to dinner. We had trained together in Washington with Jerry Ramirez, but he didn't like Michael and Dewey, so he transferred to Group One. At the Heidelberg meeting that week Michael had put Del Ridley on the top of the list of agents who would probably cooperate with Flowers. Del had even started to dress better – with shined shoes, starched shirts and dark suits – after the investigation began. I suspected that the invitation had something to do with the investigation, but I was lonely and glad to accept.

I brought Cookie because I knew Del's wife Sarah was a model too, so they could talk about their vanities. Del and Sarah's apartment was nicely furnished in a rent-controlled brownstone on the West Side. Although Cookie couldn't string two coherent sentences together, she talked all the time. The evening started out as a lot of fun. It was the first normal thing that I had done since joining the Bureau, but then, like everything else in my life, there was a strange turn. Sarah asked Cookie to go for a walk. Walking was the last thing Cookie wanted to do, since she was wearing spiked high heels. Sarah insisted and they left, leaving Del and me alone to talk. I sensed a set up.

Del got right to the point. "I'm helping Andy Flowers. Surely you can see he's right. You know what's been going on. Dewey, Michael, Silkey, Greenway, they've all been stealing drug money, killing, and giving heroin to informants. They're all going to the penitentiary for at least twenty years. You can't believe what Andy's investigators have found out. Andy says you're an honest agent, but if you're not careful, you're going with them. You know they've got to be stopped. Michael is evil. He's the mastermind, and Dewey Paris is a killer."

I wasn't surprised at what I was hearing. "Dewey Paris is not a killer. He may have killed a lot of people, but he's not a killer. There's a difference."

"Yes, he is. What about Bobby Moon? He was shot twelve times. Do you call that self-defense?"

Now I was annoyed. "Bobby Moon was going to shoot *me*. I was making a buy of seventy-five thousand dollars from the Scarluci family. He tried to rob me. Dewey and Ed Silkey saved my life. Moon would kill anyone who just looked at him funny. There are police reports all over the place. The killing was justified. Now you and Flowers want to change that? Why? Look at what Dewey and

Michael have accomplished. The list of Mafia leaders, drug dealers, murderers, the list is endless. Doesn't that mean anything?"

Del shook his head. "Their names are not even on most of the reports."

"That's it, isn't it? Numbers, paperwork. Answer me this: have Dewey, Michael, or any of the others ever lost a dollar of government money? They don't even cheat on their expense reports. Michael hasn't filed for reimbursement for his travel expenses in years. It's all about the paperwork isn't it? What about the war on drugs? What about this country?"

Del was still determined. "Flowers asked me to talk to you. He respects you very much and he needs your help. Flowers knows what a good agent you are. He knows you've never taken any money and won't lie on a government report. He knows about your first case. You proved to everyone that you'd rather lose your job than lie. They wanted Dewey first; he's incompetent and weak. Flowers thought getting Dewey would be easy."

"*Incompetent, weak?*" I almost laughed. "Jesus Christ, you have *no* idea. Flowers is an idiot, a bureaucratic idiot. Dewey and Michael are the toughest, meanest, smartest agents in the Bureau."

Del said, "These people are evil. They're wrong. I'm sorry you can't see it. Michael doesn't scare me. I'm not afraid of them."

I looked back at him. "You should be."

"I'll tell Andy about your threat."

"Threat? Jesus Christ! We're in a war, can't you see that?"

He just shook his head and looked away.

"Thank you for dinner," I said, "but I'm out of here. You and I see things differently." I walked out of the apartment without saying another word. It took me a few minutes to find Cookie hobbling along after Sarah. I thanked Sarah and hailed a cab.

The next day I met with Dewey and told him about my conversation with Del. Dewey was not surprised and said, "Del Ridley has never been on one single case that would be of interest to Andy Flowers. The sad thing about Ridley is he thinks he's a street agent, but he isn't even a decent paper pusher. We also know more about Flowers' Task Force; they're FBI, they're IRS, they're Justice Department, a mixture of elite agents – all of them with clean records and all of them are absolutely sure they know the difference between right and wrong. I think they're very determined and Michael is worried. Now they want you; you'll be their first target because you're the weakest and you can bring the rest of us down."

I had a bad feeling. "Never."

Manchester, our international informant from the Moon/Scarluci case, was the first to go. Flowers' investigators didn't like the way the case was written up. They said it was "a little too staged" and "too convenient for the wiretap" so they interviewed Charlie Moon in prison. Everyone knew Charlie Moon was still running things from his cell, but that didn't concern Flowers and his investigative agents. They told Charlie Moon that Manchester was an informant and that Michael and Dewey had killed his son Bobby. The police found Manchester in his apartment garage, slumped over the steering wheel of his Cadillac with a bullet in the back of his head. The office was filled with stories of the same type: informants running for their lives, being murdered. Flowers was building a reputation to scare people into cooperating, but he was still a bull in a china shop, except he was breaking real people.

A PLEA FOR HELP

The office's anger grew. Supervisors like Pike and Blanker, who never understood the cases in the first place, listened patiently but said there was nothing they could do. I knew they really didn't care if a few drug-dealing informants got killed. For the first time, Michael was called in for an interview with Flowers. Again, Flowers asked me to watch through the two-way mirror. After the fiasco with Dewey, I wondered why I was invited to watch again. Michael came in and sat down and Flowers started in on him. "We've already interviewed Agent Dwight Paris; now it's your turn. What do you think?"

Michael smiled at Flowers. "Agent Paris is weak. It was a good place for you to start."

The Justice Department lawyer nodded with satisfaction, but Flowers knew better. "You're the mastermind behind all of this, aren't you?" He glared at Michael. "I'm going to get you. I'm going to send you to the penitentiary for twenty years. You'll have lots of friends there."

Michael said softly, "Is there a point to all of this?"

"You know what I'm doing in the street? Do you know what my people are finding out? Finding out about you?"

Michael lit a cigarette, and I noticed his hands were shaking. He said, "I know that six people are dead because of you. Six people who trusted this office. Six people who risked their lives to give information so we could put drug dealers behind bars and solve major cases. Six people who trusted me...and they're dead because of you and your stupidity."

The Justice Department lawyer sat there blinking. Flowers turned red. "My people are conducting an *investigation*! We have a *right* to interview everybody! We are led by one of the most prominent federal judges in the country – Judge Carl Wineburg. He's newly appointed from New York so he knows what's going on."

I remembered meeting Judge Wineburg when I had lunch with Regina Medalley.

Michael shouted back, "Wineburg was appointed by senators who got elected by union block voting and teamsters and longshoremen's money. Who do you think controls the union? Angelici, Louis Turko, that's who! Did you give Wineburg Louis Turko's files so they could find and kill Danny Cupp? Or how about Manasso's file so they would find out about Agent Jerry Ramirez and kill him?"

Flowers exploded. "You're a corrupt agent. You've taken money from the underworld. You've lied in government reports. I'm going to put you behind bars and I'm going to do it in a fair and honorable way, not with lying informants and illegal wiretaps, but with sworn truthful testimony and evidence gathered by the law and presented fairly in court. Judge Wineburg is an honest man; you will not smear his name. By law he had to give Turko's lawyer the file. It's too bad Cupp's name and where he was living was in it. It was an oversight, a mistake, that's all."

Michael shot back. "It could have been withheld until trial. Wineburg knew that. You got Danny killed. And what about Manasso, did his file go to the Mafia too?"

Flowers was visibly shaken, but managed to say, "I'm not afraid of you like the rest of the people here. What do you think of me?"

I knew that was the wrong question for Flowers to ask. Michael, with his cigarette bobbing in his mouth, replied. "I think you are an ambitious, sanctimonious, little man who has been given too much power. I also think you're very dangerous because you really have no idea what you're doing."

The young lawyer sat there blinking. Flowers said nothing. Michael got up, picked up his cigarettes and walked out of the room.

Before I could go back to my desk Flowers pulled me into a small conference room. "Please help me," he said as he grabbed my arm. "I know you know right from wrong. I'm trying to clean up things here. I'm sorry about Cupp and Agent Ramirez. I believe Judge Wineburg is honest, we didn't realize, but I will look into Wineburg's mob connections. We just want justice. But you must choose. If you work with me, things like that wouldn't happen again. You like Michael and Dewey, don't you?" He reached into his pocket and handed me a photograph, a mug shot of a woman. I recognized her immediately; she was at the bar in the Manasso case. She was supposed to be waiting for Michael, yet she didn't know Michael.

"They suckered you on your own case, the Diplomat case, remember?" He smiled.

"I've seen her; so what?"

Now Flowers was enjoying himself. "You gave her nice presents from Saks Fifth Avenue, didn't you? All wrapped up pretty. They were presents from Michael, weren't they? Right under your nose, Michael played you."

"What are you talking about?"

"Think about it. Michael's little scheme in the street with the cab running over the luggage and Dewey finding five kilos of heroin in the diplomat's suitcase, just like Manasso had said. Except it wasn't heroin, was it? No, it was talcum powder. Michael knew Pike didn't trust Dewey and he knew Pike would grab the evidence *himself*. You and Pike and the Bureau would look like fools when there was no evidence at all, just talcum powder. I'm going to tell you what really happened. Michael knew Manasso was too smart for you, Michael knew all along we could not make a case against a diplomat and the heroin would be wasted."

I was completely bewildered. "What the hell are you *talking* about? Michael turned the case around and we got Belonconi with a search warrant the next *day*. It was *my* case!"

Flowers put his hand on my shoulder and talked close to my ear. "When you call me an idiot, think of this: Dewey carried five bags of talcum powder to the Sherry Netherland Hotel and when the cab split open the suitcase Dewey planted the talcum powder and *pretended* to find heroin. Pike seized the five phony bags and told Dewey to carry the broken suitcase down to the Bureau, but the heroin was still in the suitcase. Then Dewey walked a block down to Saks Fifth Avenue and had the five kilos of heroin gift-wrapped. Michael told you to take the pretty little presents to the woman at the bar. Who is she? You didn't know her, did you? I'll tell you who she was – she's Lollipop's girlfriend. And what did she do? She sold the dope to Belonconi. She told him she worked for the diplomat and was delivering the dope, all neat and clean, and everyone makes money."

"This is bullshit." I said, pulling away from him.

"Is it? I'll tell you how we know, because we followed you, we saw you give the pretty presents to the girl, we saw Dewey go from the hotel to Saks. It took us a while to figure things out. We're watching you." He smiled again. "Dewey baited poor stupid Pike to take charge of the phony evidence. Michael knew you didn't have control of the case. The only thing we don't know is how Manasso knew when the diplomat would be checking out of the hotel. Who told Manasso? Only you and Pike and Ed Silkey knew when he would be leaving the hotel to fly back to South America. We know Manasso killed the diplomat. We have ballistics. It was the same gun that Manasso used to try to kill you, but how did Manasso know? Did you tell Manasso? Was it Michael? You know what's going on here; please, I'm begging you to help me."

My guilt started to choke me. I tried to stop my face from turning red and my throat from drying up. I knew how Manasso knew when and where to shoot the diplomat – the same way Manasso knew Jerry Ramirez was an agent.

"You can't prove a thing."

I started to walk away. Then I heard him say, "Not now, but you know I'm right, and sooner or later you're going to help me get these killers. You know what is right and what is wrong. You know I stand for justice."

CHAPTER ELEVEN

A GUILTY CONSCIENCE

DADDY'S GIRL

About a week after Flowers' meeting with Michael, and his talk with me, Flowers' fifteen-year-old daughter was busted in Queens with drugs. She had met a new friend, smoked a joint, then he gave her a bag of pot and cocaine for free. She said she had never seen the man before and only knew his nickname, Zipper, because he carried a leather pouch with a big zipper on the top of it. The arresting officer had gotten a tip that she was working for Zipper. She was charged with intent to sell and transferred to Women's Detention at the Tombs in Manhattan.

Despite Flowers' efforts with the police department, it took three days before he could get his daughter released. She had been imprisoned with whores, lesbians, and junkies who had beaten and sexually assaulted her. She was in a state of shock and couldn't speak. When Flowers collected her personal things, there was a copy of his memo to Judge Wineburg recommending that charges be brought against agents Winkler and Brown stuffed in her purse.

No one took any pleasure in what happened to Flowers' daughter, but everyone knew it was war.

Dewey said that setting up the daughter was stupid, that it would only make Flowers enraged and more determined. It would be better if Flowers remained arrogant and confident, since he would be easier to manipulate and predict. Eventually the ridiculous illegal-gun charges against Winkler were dropped. Agent Brown pleaded guilty to the pot charge and got a suspended sentence with probation. But both agents were fired from the Bureau and their careers ruined because of Flowers.

The tragic incident with Andy Flowers' daughter was a mistake. I knew that neither Michael nor Dewey had anything to do with it, but Flowers was sure they did. Dewey believed that it was the work of the police department. They had reason to hate Flowers as much as we did. The memo to Wineburg put the blame on 90 Church and away from the cops. Michael agreed, but the end result was that Andy Flowers changed dramatically. He no longer wore the starched shirts and pressed suits. He was obsessive, irritable, silent, and moody. He shouted and accused Blanker, Pike, and the other supervisors of not helping him. First to go was his snotty, tight-ass secretary. Flowers became just like Michael; he even began to look like him – dark wrinkled suit, unshaven and seemingly shy. Everyone – even Blanker, Pike, and the supervisors – feared him. The body count of dead informants continued to rise as Flowers' men threatened to expose them unless they cooperated to set up the agents.

The Investigative Task Force tried to make cases on the weakest agents first, then turn them into informants to get the more experienced agents, especially Michael and Dewey, who were their real targets. Their strategy was exactly like the one we used in the street. All they wanted to know was which agents took drug money. Flowers had been promised he would head the New York office if he was successful, but what happened to his young daughter changed him and how he did his job. He didn't care about a promotion; all he wanted was revenge for his daughter. I remembered how he begged me to help him. It was too late now. Finally he got the weakest agent.

Flowers visited Tony Roma, "Tony from Roma." The shy, quiet, Agent Roma who became my friend while I was recovering from my LSD trip. He spent all of his time in the Library, doing research on international crime. He was the best connection to the CIA, Interpol and foreign law enforcement. After the darkest, coldest, most tragic night of my life, I took the three-by-five card from the file that read "Twigs" and gave it to my friend Tony Roma. All I said was, "Find her." I knew he would never stop until she was located.

Flowers told Roma that the Bureau was tired of protecting him and if he didn't make a case on Michael, Dewey, or me, they would force him into a high-publicity case and the Mafia would know where to find him. "Tony from Roma" – the shell-shocked agent from years undercover in Europe – went to his little one-room apartment only five blocks away from the office, slit his wrists and bled to death in the bathtub. On the day he killed himself I found the file card on my desk. There was an address scribbled on the back. But for now, Rachel would have to wait.

Soon after Roma's suicide, Del Ridley openly joined Flowers. None of the agents trusted him; he was too religious and too idealistic. I warned Del at his dinner party not to get involved with the investigators, but he said he "wanted to do what was right." He met with them and volunteered information that he had overheard in the office, but none of it was of any use. Flowers' investigation came to a halt, and his Task Force got desperate.

Pike became a frightened stooge eager to please them, obeying every order and agreeing with everything they said. Blanker became a helpless drunk. His secretary would often find him asleep on his desk in the morning, having gotten too drunk to drive home the night before.

There were no new cases being made. The Bureau was coming apart and everyone knew it. Like Michael had said, they had no idea what they were doing. Every day, informants called Dewey or the other agents, afraid for their lives. I wasn't worried about my informants – I only had a couple – but I saw a look of worry on Dewey's face. He worked day and night trying to hold things together, trying to save his people. Since there weren't any cases being made I didn't have much to do, except sit back and watch Pike and Ridley and the others become more and more desperate, trying to find information to feed Flowers before he turned on them.

THE RUSSIAN

In the midst of all this, Tony Degaglia, my Mafia informant, called and said he had set up a buy for me. He said it was the Russian Mafia in Brooklyn. They were ready to deal for ten thousand dollars and had good-quality heroin. I was anxious to get back to work, if only to restore some sense of normality to my life and the office. I requisitioned the cash and Tony Degaglia and I drove to Brooklyn. Degaglia said he knew the dealer well. The three of us met at a bar in Coney Island. The Russian was big, strong, smiling, and wore an expensive open-collar shirt. I told Degaglia to wait in the car so we could get better acquainted.

The Russian told me he had five ounces of excellent-grade heroin. He wanted ten thousand dollars cash and was prepared to deal immediately.

After many undercover buys, and Michael's teachings, I thought I had pretty good instincts. Something felt wrong. I began studying the Russian. He had very good teeth – unusual for anyone coming from Europe. He carried his handkerchief in his back pocket like an American and he kept asking me if I wanted to try the heroin to be sure it was good quality. High-quality, uncut heroin is instantly lethal. I studied his shoes and the way he walked; one pant leg was longer than the other, so he had a gun on his belt. When I showed him the money he didn't have the excited expression on his face that I had seen so often. He never once looked me in the eyes. I said I wasn't interested in making a buy today. I wanted to think about it, but would call him later, one way or the other. I left the bar and Degaglia and I drove back into Manhattan. It was a set-up – and I knew my informant Degaglia had arranged it.

Back in the office, Pike asked me how the buy went. I told him it didn't go well and he kept asking why and whether there was a chance we could go back and try again. Pike had never cared about any other case I worked on. If it didn't go down, it didn't go down. I met with Dewey and Michael and told them what had happened. Incredibly, Michael opened up his briefcase and pulled out a notebook of photographs. Most of them were headshots like the kind used on government credentials. Michael said, "These are from McDermott." On the third page, I picked out the Russian.

His name was Jake Bellows. He was an investigator for the Justice Department. He had to be working with Flowers. "They've got Tony Degaglia," I said, "and I think they've got Pike."

Michael laughed. "They've had Pike for months. Flowers has sent someone to get inside of one of our cases to see if we lie on the reports, or skim money, or make strange deals with the informants or suspects. This is how they get cops. They put someone in the inside and wait for you to do something wrong."

The next day, Degaglia called me again and asked if I was ready to deal with the Russian. I said I had thought about it overnight and wanted to go through with it. I then told Pike that I was going to buy the heroin from the Russian in Brooklyn. He seemed pleased.

I met Degaglia in Midtown and we drove to the bar in Brooklyn. On the way, I again asked him about the Russian. I said I was almost certain that he was carrying a gun, and appeared very dangerous. Degaglia said he had known him for a long time, that he did carry a gun and was dangerous. I met the Russian at the bar and asked him if he had the drugs. He pointed to a duffle bag next to his chair. I reached over and grabbed the bag, pulling it to my chest as if I was going to run with it.

The Russian pulled out his gun and pointed it at me. "You don't touch anything until I get the money. Put the bag down!"

There were other people at the bar so he tried to keep his voice down and hide the gun. Degaglia kept pleading for us to calm down. Then I yelled, "He's got a *gun* on me, he's got a *gun*, he's going to *shoot*! *Please* don't shoot me!"

Before the Russian could put the gun back in his holster, Ed Silkey came up from behind and picked up a chair and hit him with it. He fell to the floor. I leaned over close to Degaglia and started yelling again, "He has a gun! He's going to *shoot* us! He's going to shoot us! Look *out*! Look out! Oh my God, oh my *God*!"

Dewey, who was also at the bar, came over and kicked the Russian too. Ed and Dewey kicked and beat him until they found the gun and he lay on the floor in a pool of blood. I kept yelling, "Be careful, be careful. He's going to shoot!" The bar had cleared out and it was just the Russian and us.

I grabbed Degaglia and threw him against the bar and ripped open his shirt. There was a recording device strapped to his back with a wire running down between his legs and up to the top of his chest. I ripped it off. We handcuffed the Russian, opened up the bag, and found the heroin. We then put him in the back of the car and drove to the Bureau. Silkey had broken the Russian's nose and he was bleeding down the front of his face.

Once at the Bureau, all hell broke loose. Pike just kept pacing up and down and muttering, "My God, my God. What have you done?"

The "Russian" sat in the interrogation room, bleeding on the floor. In his coat pocket we found his Justice Department credentials with his name, Jake Bellows. Michael called the U.S. attorney's office and asked for an attorney – adding that we had collared a Justice Department agent trying to sell heroin. Dewey called one of the newspapers. The U.S. attorney came over, the same stupid kid who had tried to help Flowers interrogate Dewey. He confiscated Tony Degaglia's body wire, and interviewed us. The body wire clearly indicated that Tony – a reliable informant – had warned me that the man was dangerous and carried a gun. The tape also revealed that the Russian pulled a gun on me and the surveillance agents acted to save my life. We had a solid case against Jake Bellows and we were justified in beating him. Flowers was then forced to admit he set up the buy to see if we skimmed money or heroin or would take a bribe, and had taken heroin from the evidence lockers and forced Tony to wear the wire.

The embarrassment to the Task Force was enormous. Flowers was not fooled by what we did, but there was nothing he could do about it. They tried to keep it quiet but it was in the newspapers, *Double Cross Gets Double-Crossed*. We knew the reign of terror was not over. Twice we had embarrassed the Task Force so we were starting to even the score.

Then things took a disturbing turn. Tony Degaglia told me Flowers had told him to try to skim some of the heroin and plant it in my car. The paranoia in the office grew. Flowers was just like us.

A REUNION

I got a phone call from Elliott Goldstein, who I had completely forgotten about. Crying, he said that Ridley and Flowers had met with him. They threatened to expose him to the people he had ratted on unless he signed an affidavit accusing me of inflating the amount of money I paid him for the coke in his case. He said he had refused, but now one of the people he had informed on seemed to be suspicious. He needed my help and I agreed to meet with him at the El Hambra Bar, where it all started. I waited two hours for Elliott to show up and then gave up and went to Cookie's for the night.

The next morning there was a message from Dewey asking me to pick him up after lunch, at about two. He was having lunch at the Peacock Alley in the Waldorf Astoria and I should wait for him in the street, Park Avenue side. I found a parking space, but rather than wait in the car, I decided to go into the hotel. I was curious. I looked over the room at all the elegant people, the flowers, the vases, and it reminded me of the Medalley mansion. I saw Dewey; he had his back to me. He was having lunch with an older man, someone I had never seen before, but yet seemed familiar. I went to the bar to wait and chose a stool as close as possible, not more than eight feet from their table, hoping to overhear some of Dewey's conversation.

I sat there and studied Dewey's lunch guest. At first he looked like any other businessman, but I knew he was not. He had short white hair in a military cut, but flat. He was dressed in a tailored blue suit, as well-dressed as Dewey. His shoes were expensive Italian loafers. His piercing blue eyes were hypnotic. He was handsome, but he looked as dangerous and mean as Michael. I could not imagine who this man was. I tried to listen to their conversation. Whatever they were saying, they were laughing and joking with each other. I had no idea what they were saying, but knew it was Russian. Then the man got a little serious and started to speak in a second language. It sounded like it could have been Chinese. Dewey answered in the same language. I couldn't believe what I was hearing.

Then someone came up and sat beside me and said hello. He was about my height, with a military haircut waxed so it stood straight up, a cheap suit, pot belly, spit-shined shoes and, most interesting of all, one pant leg longer than the other. The way I looked, no one would ever come up and start a friendly conversation with me, so I played along. It didn't take long before I began to realize that he was the bodyguard for Dewey's guest, and he had caught me trying to eavesdrop. The man tried to be nice, engaging in a friendly conversation about the bar, weather, anything to distract me from listening.

But I could still hear them talking and now I heard Dewey speaking in Spanish. I couldn't understand anything, but then I heard Dewey say, "José from Cuba." I looked over at the older mystery man as he put his napkin to his face to hide his laughter.

I got up, patted my new friend on the shoulder and walked out of the hotel to wait in the car. As I sat there I saw the man who had talked to me at the bar leave the hotel and walk down the street to a dark blue car. He opened up the trunk and got a briefcase, then walked back into the hotel. I was sure he worked for Dewey's mystery guest and now I knew what car they were driving. I got out and walked up to the dark sedan. It was definitely a government car. It had blackwall tires; the government would never approve the added expense of whitewall tires. I tried the door and to my surprise it was unlocked. I looked in the glove compartment, but it was clean. The whole car was clean, too clean. I looked under the seats; nothing, not even a registration. But then on the floor between the seat and driver's side door I found a restaurant receipt. It was from Virginia. The name was "Maurice Castlemann." I remembered the name, it was Dewey's ship captain. His name was on the picture hanging on Dewey's wall with the sailors saluting Dewey on the ship. As I closed the car door I noticed that the side windows were bulletproof glass.

About a half hour later Dewey's friend and the bodyguard got into the car and drove away. Then Dewey came out next and told me to drive to the Bronx. He had just gotten a call from Michael. As we drove I waited for the right time and then asked who he had lunch with. Dewey just chuckled and lied, "An old college roommate that I hadn't seen in a while. He was in the Navy too."

Michael had told Dewey to meet him at a grocery store in the Bronx close to Yonkers. It was a hot day and I didn't care where we were going because no one was working on anything. We arrived at a grocery store that had a huge refrigerated trailer in a side parking lot. Yellow crime-scene tape hung around the outside of the trailer. Everything around the store and trailer looked dirty and broken. Michael was sitting on the steps in front of the trailer door, smoking a cigarette and talking to a cop. Michael looked at Dewey, ignoring me, and said, "I didn't know you were going to bring him. I thought you were coming alone. I'm sorry he came with you."

"What's up?" Dewey asked.

"Not much," Michael answered. "Just one of Pike and Del Ridley's little friends. Some of Andy's handiwork." Michael's eyes looked sad as he glanced at me.

All of a sudden I couldn't breathe. I pushed Michael aside and ran up the steps and opened up the door to the trailer. The sun streaked in. Inside, hanging on the back wall was Elliott Goldstein. They'd hung him on a meat hook, through the back of his ribcage, his feet about three feet off the floor. He had scratched the wooden wall all night until his hands were bloody. Elliott's face was frozen in a cold stare with his eyes wide open. Burning tears rolled down my face. I began to scream and hold onto one of his legs. Dewey and Michael dragged me outside into the burning sun. I fought them until they threw me on the ground. I got up and started to walk in small circles, crying and waving my arms. Dewey didn't know what to do or where to take me. Finally I quieted down and asked him to drive me to my apartment in Brooklyn. I lay on my dark living-room floor and cried until I fell asleep.

FRIENDS IN NEED

The death of Elliott Goldstein was a simple report: "homicide of a major drug dealer, unknown suspect." There was no mention of Del Ridley, Pike, or any of Andy Flowers' investigators. If ever in my life I needed cocaine, it was now – and it was there for me in the evidence lockers.

The investigators lost patience with Del Ridley and indicted him for filing a false report. He had signed a case investigation saying he was at the scene of the buy when he was not. The charges were ridiculous, since more than half of all the case files were pure fiction. Flowers felt Ridley knew more than he was telling them. I knew Del Ridley was sincere and had done his best to help the Task Force. He thought he knew or could find out things that would be useful, but no one trusted him. He was too honest and too religious. Flowers demanded a high bail and put him in West Street Penitentiary until he agreed to give them more information, just like we would do. But Del Ridley couldn't tell them anything and refused to sign a false report incriminating someone else to save himself. His wife Sarah called and asked if I could do something to get him out. All I could say was that things would be okay even though I had heard bad things from Dewey. Dewey said that Del was thrown into the general prison population. The inmates knocked out his front teeth, to make him a good cocksucker, and were sodomizing him day and night.

I went to see Del and when they opened the door to the viewing room he short-stepped into the booth as if his ankles were shackled, but they were not. His front teeth were gone. He had a black eye and cuts on his face. He just sat there and stared into space. I tried to talk to him, asked him if there was anything I could do. He didn't say anything, just shook his head no. After about five minutes of trying to talk to him without getting a response, I said good-bye and left. I felt sorry for Sarah. I told him I would go and see her.

Badly shaken, I got high on vodka and cocaine, trying to forget Elliott and Del Ridley, who only wanted to help do the right thing. I should have gone home, but instead I went to Del's apartment to see Sarah. She had been to see him earlier that day. She couldn't stop crying and telling me how horrible the Bureau was and what they were doing to him was wrong. She was crying so much I hugged her to calm her down. But then still holding her, I slow-danced her into the bedroom. She didn't say anything, just stared at me. I laid her on the bed and took off her clothes, then mine, hugging and consoling her, telling her everything was going to be okay. She was in a trance. She would do anything I wanted her to do, and I made her do everything. I loved doing things with her, especially the things that gave both of us pain. I thought fucking and hurting her would help keep her mind off her husband. I had things to forget too.

Afterwards, when I was tired and she stopped moaning, I dozed off and was half asleep when I felt her get up and leave the room. I thought she was going to the bathroom. Then I heard her come back. I rolled over and looked up. She was standing over me with her arms straight up in the air, clutching a kitchen knife with both hands. As she brought it down, I rolled toward her and hit her in the stomach with my fist, but it was too late. I felt the pain in my side. She doubled up on the floor, gasping for breath. I held my side and swore at her. She had dropped the knife but was trying desperately to get it back. I kicked her in the ribs and threw the knife to the other side of the room. She lay on the floor, naked and crying. I got dressed with one hand, holding my side. I left the building and got into my car. I could feel the blood running down into my boot. The closest hospital was Lenox. I went to the emergency room and they stitched up my side. I called the office and told them I had been mugged during an undercover operation to buy heroin, but was all right.

DEWEY GOES DOWN AGAIN

They arrested Dewey in front of everybody at the next Monday morning meeting. There wasn't any press. We had gathered expecting to hear reports of "no progress made in any investigation." Flowers walked into the room with two U.S. marshals, asked Dewey to stand, hand-cuffed him from behind, and led him out without saying a word. You could feel the fear in the room.

Blanker tried to continue the meeting, but then Flowers came back in and, without asking Blanker, took the podium. Flowers looked a lot different from the first time he stood before us months ago to arrest two agents on ridiculous charges. He was unshaven, his eyes were red and glaring, but he managed to start with his "come-to-Jesus-I'm-going-to-get-you" type of speech although he rambled so much it was hard to follow, and halfway through it he began to tear up.

When he finally got down to business, the reason for Dewey's arrest, he was calm, his pride clear. "Agent Paris," he said, "will be indicted tomorrow on many counts of felonies. He's going to spend the next ten years of his life in the penitentiary. Things aren't funny anymore, are they, boys?" Then he pulled out a sheet of paper from his pocket. "I'm going to read you some of the charges: Theft of drug money" – and he named cases that I had never heard of, and continued – "Assault and battery, with robbery, two counts connected to an incident in lower Manhattan at the Little Egypt." Then he said, "This is a breakthrough. There'll be more indictments to follow. I promised you would all be going to the penitentiary and that's what's going to happen. Have a good day, gentlemen." He smiled with his bright, shiny white teeth.

We all filed out in silence and went back to whatever we were doing, except Michael, who just walked out the front door. After lunch Pike told me that Maggie, Dewey's wife, had posted fifty thousand dollars bail, so at least Dewey was out on the street, and would not have to spend time in jail until his trial. Pike confirmed that the charges would be presented to the Federal Grand Jury for a felony indictment.

Flowers was so pleased with the arrest that he distributed copies of the arrest warrant with the reports of probable causes to every Group Leader in the Bureau. Pike gave me his copy. It looked as if Flowers had won after all. If they could bring Dewey down, people like me would be easy. I was scared. I had always hidden behind Michael and Dewey, but now I was alone and didn't know what to do.

I went over to Cookie's apartment to drink and snort a few lines of cocaine. After a while she came home and tried to get me out of my dark mood. She put on a little baby doll negligee and pranced around trying to show me her stuff. She was truly beautiful, but when I could follow what she was saying it was always about herself, how beautiful she was, who liked her, and who was jealous of her, or where she should go next to get her hair done. She got aggressive, and for the first time in my life I was impotent. Embarrassed, I got dressed and went out.

I bounced from club to club and ended up at Count Basie's to hear DeWitt play his trumpet. I sat at the bar, feeling sad for Dewey, his wife and his two sons Maurice and Dwight Junior, who looked just like him. I respected him. I had hit a new low, losing the closest thing to a best friend that I had since I started at the Bureau. Flowers, an arrogant bureaucrat, who had never faced a dangerous situation in his life, had destroyed Dewey. My hatred and frustration boiled as DeWitt began his trumpet set. I reached for my cigarettes and found the copy of Dewey's arrest warrant in my pocket. It was painful for me to read it, but I read it anyway. There was nothing new, except on the back page was a list of people who had signed affidavits supporting the charges against Dewey. I scanned the list. They were his informants. In the middle of the list was Charles DeWitt.

I looked up and saw the old man playing his trumpet. After all the kind things that Michael had done for DeWitt, he had ratted us out. I remembered that Dewey had said you can't expect an informant to stand up. You know they're going to rat you out. As much as I liked the old man and his wonderful music, my anger grew.

After his show I went backstage where he was putting his trumpet away and said that I would walk him home. He grinned in anticipation, no doubt thinking that, as usual, I would give him a little gift of heroin. DeWitt lived about ten blocks from the club and we walked along the dark Harlem streets together until I found an empty stretch with a small alley. I grabbed the old man by the shirt and shoved him down and dragged him into the alley. I pulled out my automatic and pointed it at his face. "You stupid old nigger. Why would you rat out Dewey?" The old man was surprised and frightened. I screamed at him, "You signed a paper, an affidavit testifying against Dwight Paris. *Why*?"

His answer stunned me so bad that I almost dropped my gun. He knew exactly what I was talking about. He said, "*Michael* told me to do it. *Michael* told me to do it."

"*Michael*?"

"Michael says he hates this Dewey fellow. That if I would sign the paper against him, that he was beating up and robbing people in a bar called the Egypt, that I would be doing a good thing. Michael told me to do it. He hates that Dewey fellow."

I was so confused I just stared at the old man. Then I helped him to his feet and said, "I'm sorry, Charlie, I didn't understand. I'm sorry."

DeWitt brushed himself off, picked up his trumpet case and walked away alone, shaking his head. I called him back and gave him a bundle of heroin. He thanked me and continued on again.

Michael set up Dewey! Michael set up Dewey! These words pounded over and over in my mind. Michael, the evil genius vampire, sacrificed his number-one henchman, his apprentice, his protégé, to Flowers! I was lost for sure now. I thought I had hit bottom, but I was still in a horrible free fall. Then something clicked – like a wrench in the gears that were grinding up my life – and everything stopped. I pulled to the side of the street, parked and turned the overhead light on to re-read Dewey's arrest warrant and probable-cause pages. Each of the charges had the name of the person that had signed the affidavit. DeWitt's name was next to the assault and robbery incident at Little Egypt. It also said that they had recovered the stolen property – a wristwatch and gold ring described in DeWitt's affidavit – from Dewey's locker in the office! Then I looked at the names next to the other charges, for theft of drug money.

I opened the door, staggered out of the car, and lay on the hood, screaming with laughter. I rolled off the hood and sat on the curb, tears rolling down my face. What a fool I had been! While the other agents and I ran to our informants and told them to stand up to Flowers, Dewey and Michael set each other up. They knew that no informant could be trusted, so Michael told some informants to rat on Dewey, and Dewey told other informants to rat on Michael. Everybody was happy. The informants were cooperating with the investigators, who in turn would not threaten them by revealing their identity. It was perfect. Typical Michael. Only Michael could think like this. However, what Flowers would soon discover was that Dewey Paris had not been at Little Egypt. He was on sick leave and four other agents, including Pike, who were there at the Little Egypt to beat the hell out of everyone and wreck the place, would discredit DeWitt's sworn statement. Dewey would never be so stupid as to steal personal property and put it in his locker. Dewey planted it there to draw Flowers deeper into the trap, so Flowers would believe DeWitt. As a witness, DeWitt would be totally discredited, but more importantly, it would show the world what amateurs Flowers and his investigators truly were. Dewey *expected* to be arrested. Once the Justice Department began to look at cases and prepare them for trial they would realize the whole thing was a fiasco. Flowers would be destroyed. I got back in the car, drove to Cookie's apartment, and fell asleep laughing.

The next morning I couldn't wait to ask Pike when Dewey was

going to be indicted. Pike looked down and said quietly, "There's been some kind of snafu; he's not going to be indicted. They dropped his bail. It isn't over yet, but he's coming back to the Bureau."

I smiled, turned to walk out, and faced Flowers. He glared at me with his stingy, haggard, red eyes. That afternoon Blanker circulated a memo throughout the office. It simply said the arrest warrant of Agent Dwight Paris had been vacated and plans to present his case to the Grand Jury had been suspended indefinitely. Agent Paris was to be reinstated in the Bureau immediately.

THE COVENANT

There was an eerie calm in the office for the next few days that was finally broken when Dewey came back. The New York winter was over; spring was here as if nothing happened. He came in with his big grin, cracking jokes and collecting money from everyone for the weekend basketball game. I even began to think that Michael had finally beaten Flowers and that the reign of terror was finally over – until Blanker's secretary handed me a note: *Flowers conference Room B 2:00 p.m.*

Defiantly I walked into the conference room at 2:20. The transformation of Andy Flowers was amazing: his dirty black hair framed red, beady eyes, and the strange jerking mannerism of his head and hands had gotten even worse.

There was no Justice Department lawyer. Instead there were two of his agents, who looked like dumb cops. One was fat, with his shirt buttons pulling, and body odor that reached me as I came in. The other looked like a hick, with a cheap plaid sport jacket, high-topped work shoes, and a toothpick at the corner of his mouth. The fat one grabbed me by the lapels and threw me against the wall. I hit with such force I bounced off and fell on the floor. Immediately, both of them lifted me up and shoved me into a chair. I couldn't believe I was being assaulted in a government office. I slumped in the chair and gave everyone a big smile.

There was a tape recorder in the middle of the table. Flowers reached over and gave it a little pat. "You're Michael's stooge. You think you can beat me and the United States of America? You don't know right from wrong, but you're loyal to your friends, aren't you?"

I used a line from Dewey and Michael: "Is there a point to all this?"

Jerking his head from side to side, he said, "All this has been for you, all of it, just for you, we always wanted you first. You have a future with the Bureau and you will give me Dewey and Michael because they are incredibly evil, and you know it. We've been working all this time just for this meeting, *this* meeting, right *now*." He smiled the biggest grin I had ever seen and placed his hands together on the table like he was praying.

"You're an asshole," I said, "and this is bullshit. Who the fuck do you think you are?" The fat agent slapped me so hard I could feel blood coming down the side of my mouth. Flowers glared at me and said, "Who am I? I'll tell you who I am. I represent a Federal Judge, Judge Carl Wineburg, who is leading this investigation."

I was not impressed. "Wineburg's dirty; he got into office because he had union support, unions controlled by Turko and Aggi Angelici. Michael told you not to trust Wineburg. You didn't listen."

"Those are legitimate organizations. You can't smear a judge because his friends accept campaign contributions and endorsements," he said calmly.

"I saw him having lunch with Regina Medalley. I was there. You gave him Turko's file so they could find Danny Cupp and kill him."

Flowers was embarrassed. "We're looking into that, all of it, including the unions and how Agent Jerry Ramirez's cover was blown. Judge Wineburg's background is not important; it's how he conducts the case that's important."

Flowers continued as if nothing had happened. "We need to get on to other things, for this meeting. Del Ridley was your friend, wasn't he? You even comforted his lovely wife in the dark until two in the morning, didn't you? That was nice. Oh yes, we've been following you all the time. How do you think we know about your delivery of the diplomat's five kilos of heroin to Michael's girlfriend? You didn't learn anything after meeting with Ridley; you didn't really care about your friend, you just wanted to fuck his wife. So we tried to reach you with Elliot Goldstein to show you we mean business."

I was hot with anger, and could feel the blood on the side of my lip. "You son-of-a-bitch. You killed Elliott and Danny Cupp."

"Son, this is war. You have to make sacrifices to get things done. Generals sacrifice troops all the time to win the war. We did it to save you. Besides, Cupp was a killer."

His words were so horrible it almost made me laugh. "A killer? I thought you said background wasn't important; it's how he conducts the case. Wineburg's background is not important, but Cupp's is? *Save* me? I see how you save people."

Flowers rubbed his eyes, then said, "You're going to end up like

Agent Ridley or Elliot Goldstein, unless you play the game. Don't you get it yet?" He gave me another smirk. "Now let's get down to business, shall we?"

"Fuck you." I got up to leave, but the fat agent hit me even harder across the face and shoved me back in the chair.

Flowers reached over and turned on the tape recorder. At first there was a rustling noise, a car door closing and talk which was too muffled to understand. Then a man said, "*Please I need something to get through this, please*", then sobbing. It was Tony Degaglia's voice and he was talking to me. I heard myself say, "*Life's not easy, we'll stick together. Here, I've got some smack for you. Good stuff. It'll hold you over.*" Then Degaglia sobbed about being scared of Brimstone and I said, "*I'll tell Brimstone it was Heyman and not you, you'll be off the hook. Trust me, Heyman will be dead in a week.*"

"Let's see," Flowers began. "You got heroin from an evidence locker, sold it to an informant and arranged to kill someone named Heyman. We will find Mr. Heyman; I bet he's already dead. Dealing heroin and murder are serious charges, don't you think?"

I sat, cold as ice, staring into space, not able to speak or think. All three of them sat smirking at me. I was going to be charged with murder for arranging to get "Heyman" killed. Heyman, the lousy pimp who threw the Long Island dentist down the stairs with a broken arm when he came to save his junkie daughter.

"Michael has embarrassed me and my men with his little tricks," Flowers continued, "but now you're going to work for me, you're going to give me Michael and Dewey. Not just your word against theirs; we've already had enough of that and it doesn't work. You're going to get proof, *real* proof that cannot be disputed. When we find Mr. Heyman's body, you'll face at least twenty years, or even the electric chair. We've already got you on a drug charge and we'll get you for the five kilos Dewey gift-wrapped at Saks, and you delivered to Michael's so-called girlfriend."

All of them smirked even more. "Oh, one more thing," he started in again, "we know you worked with Manasso to kill Fernando, the diplomat. Only three people knew when he was leaving for the airport: you, Ed Silkey and Group Leader Pike. Silkey and Pike are covered; that leaves you. You told Manasso when to kill Fernando. You killed two people and we're just getting started – and to make it easy for you, all I want is Michael Giovanni and Dewey Paris. If you help me get them I promise you two things: Michael will not go to prison. He needs help. He's a psychotic drunk who needs to be hospitalized. Only Dewey goes down, he was never a good agent, he's just a killer. Secondly, I will end the investigation – go away. It will all end with Michael and Dewey, unless of course they turn on you. You see, I don't care one way or the other. If they give you up first, that's okay too. You're going to work with us – or die in prison. If you don't take this deal, Michael and Dewey will. We'll let the word out. Every time you go in the street to make a buy, you'll worry about staying alive. Your informants work for us now. Do the deal."

"What deal?" I said quietly.

He handed me a folded paper from his suit pocket; it was an official Justice Department memo from Flowers to me. The subject read: *Unconditional grant of immunity for cooperation and truthful testimony*. There were about ten cc's to the Justice Department staff and one to Blanker. The memo was very straightforward. The government would not prosecute, investigate, or assist any local, state, or international agency on any and all crimes that were committed by me as an agent from the date I joined the Bureau up until a month from today's date – but I had to present evidence against Michael Giovanni and Dewey Paris, and testify in court against them. I began to think of all the things I had done. They would all be forgiven and I could do anything I wanted to do, anything at all in the next month, without ever being prosecuted. But I had no real evidence against Michael or Dewey, only my word against theirs. I began to sweat, and I could still feel the blood running down my face from being slapped.

"We're through here. I think you get the picture. We don't want you; you've made too many good cases. You're the best agent in the Bureau. We want Dewey and Michael. But if you can't deliver them we'll take you. We'll be in touch. We're all on the same side now." Flowers got up and tried to put his arm around me. I moved away. He walked out of the room, followed by his two henchmen.

Flowers didn't have anything on Michael or Dewey yet, but he was relentless. Flowers was going to force me to work with him – or have me killed. I wasn't as smart as Dewey or Michael. The Task Force had me and I didn't know how to fight back. How many other people would die like Elliott because I wouldn't help clean up the Bureau and save myself? I felt sick and dead inside. I had to get Michael and Dewey before they found out that I had turned into a rat or I'd be dead. I put the memo in my pocket and walked out. There, down the long hallway, standing in a corner was a dark figure almost hidden by the shadows. It was Michael.

"They have nothing on me. Big nothing. You've beaten them," I lied as Michael approached me. "Don't worry, Michael, I'm standing up, they're afraid of us."

Michael smiled, patted my cheek, then walked past me down the hall without saying a word.

I went into the restroom to put cold water on my face and looked in the mirror. Michael had smeared my blood across my face. I went into a stall to vomit.

HAPPY HOUR

I normally got to the office at about 10:30 or 11:00 in the morning, which was typical for agents working late the night before. I was surprised to see Dewey huddling with a group of agents. Usually he's in the library, meeting his research clerks.

Pike, Dewey and Greenway were cuing up a tape recorder. They would never have included Dewey in anything unless they needed his translating skills. I knew Dewey spoke Russian and other languages as well.

They played the tape; the foreign language was Sicilian. I couldn't tell if it was from a wiretap or a bug in someone's home or office. Dewey rolled his eyes. "It's two meatball guineas bragging about how they got laid last night. One of them banged up his car and ran from the accident."

Pike started the machine again, but this time we all heard the name Turko.

Dewey translated: "The two wops are talking about how Louis Turko got kicked in the ribs by a 90 Church agent when he got popped – broke his ribs, never healed right. Turko hurts when he breathes hard or lays on his side. They say Turko is really pissed. Hey, guys, I remember that bust; it was in Times Square. I did the buy. Johnny Greenway dragged his ass out of the car, Turko tried to pull a gun. Johnny drop-kicked him in the ribs."

Everyone nodded and the tape started again.

The gibberish went on and on until we heard "Greenway" and an address on Rockaway Boulevard. After a few minutes Dewey turned it off and stared down at the floor.

"They're going to kill Johnny. They have his home address. Turko put a hit out for twenty thousand dollars to whoever does it first. These clowns don't have the balls; they're just passing the word around."

There was a serious silence. Blanker rubbed his forehead. "We can't use this tape. NYPD sent it over from one of their illegal wires. They wanted us to know what we're up against. Well, now we know. Carry on, boys, carry on." Blanker left the room and Pike went back into his glass cubicle.

Dewey looked at Greenway. "You're gonna have to be careful, real careful. They know your address. They must have some kind of inside information. We've got to get ahead of them. The trouble is I don't even know who these assholes are. Maybe I can get some more information from the cops."

Greenway was just staring into space. Finally he said, "They're not going to help me. No one is going to help me. I'm going in there and talk to Flowers."

Dewey went back to the library and I started typing yesterday's reports. About a half hour later Greenway came back and pulled Dewey and me into a private corner in the office.

Greenway shook his head. "They're not going to help me. Flowers said that if I could provide information on Michael, you or the others, he would consider setting up a team and some kind of protective net, but only if I work with him to investigate the office.

I have until tomorrow to let him know if I have any information against you guys."

Dewey smiled in disgust. "So, unless you rat on us, they're gonna let you die on the street. Don't you just love this place?"

Greenway thought for a few moments and answered, "Michael has got to help me with this. The only way that I can save my life is to go back to El Paso. Flowers and Blanker are refusing to give me a transfer back to Texas. They want me to stay in the streets and die – or rat on everybody. This isn't right. Michael will help me."

"No, look at the last time Michael helped you in El Paso," Dewey argued. It got you transferred to here, to this hell hole in New York. Don't you remember the shit he pulled with all the memos and how many people got killed?"

"Listen, Dewey, I got revenge for those sons-of-bitches that killed my partner. Nobody died unless they deserved to die. There wasn't one innocent person killed. Michael will know what to do; he'll help me."

Dewey said, "Michael has got enough troubles of his own. The way he helps does more harm than good. We've got to wait this out. Why don't you move in with me for a while? Maybe this will all blow over in a few weeks or so."

Greenway seemed relieved. "Thanks, I appreciate this. I hope your wife won't mind. I need to think about all this."

I left the office early that day and made my usual rounds of bars and dark alleys, trying to pull some information out of informants about Greenway, but no one knew anything.

Almost a week later I arrived in the office late in the afternoon, still nursing a hangover. Greenway was alone and had that same

shell-shocked look, sitting at his desk. He seemed glad to see me.
I asked him if there was anything new.

"The cops weren't even sure who was on the tape, but they did
tell Dewey it was a bug in a social club in Little Italy, so it could have
been anybody. No one knows how many people were told about the
twenty-thousand-dollar offer."

I tried to do some paperwork, but it was hard to see Greenway
sitting at his desk just staring into space. The cowboy agent with
his string tie, six-shooter, pointed-toe cowboy boots and Western
suit was scared to death.

At about five o'clock, as I was getting ready to leave, Greenway
said, "Would you have a drink with me? Why don't we go down to
the Bull and Bear?"

The Bull and Bear was a small, cozy bar close to Wall Street. It
was a popular place for stockbrokers who cheated on their wives.
It was narrow and only held thirty or forty customers with a long
bar and a few tables at the end. It had only one entrance from the
street. Johnny and I sat at the end of the bar closest to the door. I
tried to make light conversation, but he just stared into space and
stirred his Jack Daniels with his finger.

"Did you talk to Michael?" I asked.

Greenway wouldn't answer. He just looked at me and said,
"Blanker and Flowers don't care if I get killed in the street. All
they want is you and Michael and Dewey. I'm gonna die and I'm
scared to death. All I want to do is go back to El Paso. That's where
I belong. They'd never find me there."

As I was trying to answer, I saw the bartender at the other end
of the bar take a phone call, then put both hands to his face. He
looked around, saw us, and almost ran the length of the bar. "Hey,

you guys are federal agents, aren't you?"

Johnny cocked his cowboy hat and looked up at him. "Yeah, so what?"

"Guys, you have to help me. I just got a phone call, they said there is a bomb hidden somewhere in the bar and it's going to go off in forty-five minutes and I don't know what to do."

Johnny came alive. He gave the bartender a big smile and said, "We're federal agents, we know how to handle this, don't worry about it."

Johnny took a swig of his whiskey and strolled over to the door. It was good to see his self-confidence return. Pushing his cowboy hat just a notch higher, he announced, "Folks, I need your attention here, quiet down. Please no more talking. I need your attention. This is very serious."

The young, hip crowd at first ignored him, but he persisted. "Quiet down *now*. Can I have your attention? I don't want anyone to panic, but I must tell you that we have received a phone call that there is an explosive device, a bomb, that is set to detonate in this bar within the next half hour." There was a soft clamor of women grabbing their purses and guys grabbing their coats. Johnny continued, "Folks, be calm, be calm. As I said, there's a bomb that's going to go off in a half hour. We want to handle this properly." He paused, then said firmly, "No one leaves until we find the bomb."

The disbelief went in waves from one end of the bar to the other. Finally one brave customer broke the growing hysteria. "You can't be serious. This is a joke, right? If there's a bomb we all have to leave immediately."

Johnny was more self-assured and confident than I had ever seen him. "We're going to do this a little different. No one leaves until we find the bomb. Is that clear?"

Customers begin to advance toward Johnny at the door. He pulled his chrome-plated Western six-shooter from his cross-draw holster and waved it at the frightened faces. "Folks, don't panic, start looking. I don't want anyone to get hurt, start looking now."

He cocked the hammer and pointed it directly into the forehead of the spokesman. Everyone froze. Then people began tearing up the bar, looking under their tables, on shelves, anywhere, in a frightened fury of desperation.

Down the bar I saw the bartender on the phone again. One of the men tried to buy Johnny off. "I'll give you five hundred dollars if you just let us through the door. You don't understand what you're doing."

Johnny would not take the bribe and stood steadfast in front of the only exit.

I actually took another sip of my vodka. With all of the insanity that I had seen over the years, somehow this seemed almost normal. It never even occurred to me to stop Johnny from perpetrating this insanity. I sat there drinking my vodka and waiting for the building to blow up. I watched as people began to cry as they desperately searched.

Finally there was an explosion – an explosion of at least five cops crashing through the door and knocking Johnny flat on his face. They cuffed him and dragged him out within seconds.

People scurried through the door like scared rats running out of a drain pipe. Within minutes I was alone. I finished my drink, left a dollar on the bar, and walked out the door through the barricade and the flashing red lights.

It was only a block to the subway so I was home in less than an hour. The madness of this event and the fate of Agent Johnny Greenway numbed my mind.

The next morning I walked in the office and heard shouting coming from down the hall. It was Blanker's voice: "I don't give a fuck who you are, we are the Federal Government of the United States of America. You're not going to tell me what to do. Only the President of the United States of America has authority here and I don't see him."

I saw three men in rumpled suits and wrinkled raincoats walk out of Blanker's office in disgust, shaking their heads. They had to be police brass. I couldn't resist. I found Blanker's secretary and pulled her into the corner. "Dottie, what was that all about?"

"Well, everybody knows what happened last night with Greenway. That was really dumb. The police are very pissed off. They want George Blanker to fire Greenway and the police want to charge him with a whole list of charges – menacing people with a firearm, mayhem, impeding a police investigation. They have a long list."

"Well, what's Blanker going to do?" I asked.

"Everyone knows how Blanker feels about jurisdiction. He told them in no uncertain terms that they don't have any authority over us. We are the United States of America and have jurisdiction. They can't tell us what to do. If we did what they wanted there would be chaos and confusion. They can't tell George to fire Johnny."

"So what's the bottom line? Who's gonna win here?"

"Well, Blanker compromised; he's transferring Johnny Greenway back to El Paso immediately. He's on a flight out of here this afternoon."

Blanker's solution turned me into a raving, laughing maniac just like Dewey. I was able to blurt out, "Sweet Jesus, of *course* that's the only solution. These locals can't tell us what to do. Greenway needs to be punished, and punished immediately! He needs to be sent to El Paso, Texas!"

Dottie didn't see the humor, which made me laugh even more. Finally I staggered down the hall to find Dewey. As expected he was meeting with his clerks in the corner of the library. Business as usual.

"Dewey, do you think this thing with Johnny is another one of Michael's stunts? Was that bartender one of Michael's informants?"

Dewey was indignant. "Why would anyone think that? Everyone knows that Michael is just a hopeless, useless drunk. How could he be involved in something like that? I mean, he wasn't even there. Just ask Blanker, he has control over everything. Although something has to be done about Turko, he is getting out of hand."

SOUL MATES

It was comical that the Task Force was looking for "Mr. Heyman's" body. I wondered how long it would take for Flowers to figure out that "Heyman" was my own private nickname for a Harlem whorehouse master now very dead. Once they figured that out, I would be charged with murder. I felt stupid and alone. I should have never tried to lie to Michael about Flowers. But I was scared, very scared, more than I had ever been in my life, more than when I faced the Medalley family. Michael would never betray me because of our dark secret, but Dewey was different; he owed me nothing.

I had no one to talk to. Without my coke and vodka I would have killed myself. If I didn't rat on Michael and Dewey, Andy would send me to prison. If I tried to rat on them, they'd know and I would be dead. So I did something very strange. I went to the evidence locker and took a kilo of pure heroin from the Manasso file. It would all be destroyed soon anyway, since we had no defendants and Manasso was dead. I had to save myself and needed to know how. Making a case against Michael and Dewey would not be easy. I needed proof.

I put the heroin in a shoebox and took it to the only person left in the world who would help me. I went to the Showboat bar in the Village to see Sally. It was late afternoon, so the bar was empty.

Sally – the ex-CIA agent, the fat homosexual who had been destroyed by his own parties and who Michael had said "knew everything or could find it out" – was at his usual place, leaning against the bar. He wore red shoes, bright blue pants, and a green sport coat with a black silk shirt.

I put the shoebox on the bar as Sally came over to greet me. I could smell his perfume as he hugged me and tried to stick his tongue in my ear. I pushed him away.

"I want some information and I need it now," I said as we both sat down.

"Why you've come to the right place, dear boy." He looked at the shoebox, then, picking it up, he said, "It's too light for money, it only weighs about two-point-two pounds, or, in metric, one kilo. Oh, you *are* a sweet boy. Is it any good?"

"None better, never been cut."

Sally smiled. "Then I shall earn it. Let's get started."

"Is Flowers serious about indicting me?"

"Oh dear, oh dear, I shall never earn the sweet powder with such dumb questions like that. Everyone knows you're going down for killing that pimp you call Heyman. I can't take your pretty present with dumb questions like that; take your lovely box and go."

"Wait a minute. I want to know about Michael and Dewey."

Sally looked away from me and said, "Michael is on a mission, the hardest mission of his miserable life. And Dewey, you don't want to know anything about Dewey – if you like staying alive."

I was angry. "There's a kilo of pure heroin in the box. Start with Dewey."

Sally looked around to see if anyone was watching or listening. With a flick of his finger two drinks arrived, a vodka for me and brandy for him. Then he started. "Did you know Dewey speaks Russian and Vietnamese? He learned them at Annapolis. He looks like a little boy, doesn't he? After he graduated they sent him to Vietnam on a big ship. The ship's captain was given thirty rangers to do a special mission. They were to go into Cambodia and steal documents from a Russian Commander who was training and supplying weapons to the Viet Cong. We knew the Russians were involved and lying to us, but we couldn't prove it. When the rangers got ready to go, their translator got sick. Dewey volunteered to take his place. Thirty men parachuted into the Viet Cong jungle – six came out with Dewey. It was a real bloodbath, but they accomplished their mission. Dewey had over thirty confirmed kills. He presented the ship's captain with a package of Russian orders. It literally changed the course of the war. We knew for sure what the Russians were doing and who was working with them. They couldn't continue to tell the world that they were not involved. That night the Russian Commander radioed Moscow, told them what had happened and asked that the KGB send people to the United States to kill the wife and children of the American commando who looked like a teenager. The Russian said he could identify him. It was amateurism, unprofessional; you don't do things like that. By then Dewey's captain had their codes and intercepted the whole transmission. Anyway, Dewey took his six soul mates back into the jungle and personally shot the Russian. Boy, I'll bet he was surprised to see Dewey again.

"The Captain sent two gunships into Cambodia to get them out – one to shoot the hell out of the camp, while the other got Dewey and his men out.

"Dewey Paris deserved the Congressional Medal of Honor three times over, but they were afraid to give it to him. The publicity would be his death warrant. So they sealed his file and hid him away in another government agency until things could cool off. Dewey is varsity team, he is top management. They're grooming him for big things. But of course he has to stay out of trouble in the meantime. They *need* Dewey, for Christ's sake; don't you know there's a war going on?"

"How do you all know this?" I asked.

"Dear boy, I have just been paid twice for the same information." And he pulled the box closer to him.

"What do you mean twice? Who paid you first?"

He smiled. "Why Michael, of course! You can't fool Michael. Michael didn't buy Dewey's dumb teenager routine for a second. Michael was down here to see me the first day Dewey started at the Bureau, any fool can see Dewey's special – any fool except Flowers, Blanker and Pike. All you have to do is look at his gun, for Christ's sake. How hard is that? He's so cute, don't you think, with that little boy look of his? His big gun. I just *love* it."

"How did you get Dewey's file for Michael?" I asked.

Sally started laughing. "Get his file? You agents are all alike. Why would I read a government file? More than half of what you people put in them is a lie. And then you take all your bundles of lies and put red stamps on them and lock them up. How very, very silly. Young Lieutenant Dewey Paris sailed out on the *Saratoga*. Twelve hundred sailors aboard that ship knew what happened to Dewey in the jungle. Dewey in the jungle, Dewey in the...anyway, I had one of my girls call the Navy and tell them she was helping Castlemann with the next reunion and got a list of sailors; it was easy after that."

"Who is Castlemann?" I asked.

"Maurice Castlemann, Captain Castlemann then, Dewey's captain. Maurice got a big promotion because of Dewey; he's not riding around on ships anymore, he's national security, counterintelligence now. He's a big shot now. Do you know he speaks as many languages as Dewey?"

Sally started laughing again. "Flowers thought it would be easy to start with Dewey, but he got a tiger by the tail, a tiger that's going to eat him for lunch, and that, dear boy, is Michael's mission."

"What's Michael's mission? What are you talking about?"

"Dear, dear, sweet boy, haven't you been listening?" Sally stared into his drink. "How have you stayed alive? Michael has to be protecting you. Everybody, and I mean *everybody*, knows Dewey is a stone-cold killer, with his sweet little face. Michael's mission is to save Flowers."

I was shocked. "*Save* Flowers? What the fuck are you talking about?"

Sally put his pudgy polished fingers on my lips to quiet me, then kissed them for a proxy kiss. "How have you survived? Dewey will kill anything or anyone who threatens him, or his career. There's no question about it. If Flowers continues to fuck with Dewey,

Flowers is going to die. Michael is trying to save Flowers' life by fucking with his investigations. Michael is a professional; you don't kill other agents, so he's been trying to stop Dewey from killing that stupid bureaucrat since the day he started the investigation. Although, quite frankly, I don't know a single person, besides Michael, that wouldn't enjoy seeing Dewey's smiling face shooting Andy Flowers to death with his big black gun."

Sally was enjoying himself. He ordered us both another drink and continued, "Now I'm going to earn the shoebox. You must understand that Michael is pure, absolutely a *pure* professional; he only thinks about winning the war against drugs. Everyone else has side agendas, stupid rules, friendships, their careers, finding right and wrong – so they can't understand Michael. They are just too weak to follow him. Michael is a beautiful creature, absolutely pure, absolutely pure of thought. He'd do anything to stop drug dealers. That's what the government really wants. Fuck all this bullshit about right and wrong. You don't have time for all that shit when you're in a war. You need someone as pure and determined as Michael if you want to win."

"Yeah, but what about Flowers?" I asked.

"Oh dear, do you think someone like Flowers, who is stuck in the middle of truth and justice, could bring down Dewey and Michael? No, they need someone like you who doesn't care about such silly things. Besides, you made all the cases. Didn't you? You got all the glory."

He patted me on the back. "You're number-one agent now, aren't you?" He laughed. "But now you have to rat on Dewey and Michael. I wouldn't want Dewey mad at me, *dear* no! I hope Dewey doesn't know you're here. I just put in a new carpet. Whoever jumps first will save himself at the expense of the others. Michael will give you up. He can't stand the thought of being in prison and away from his precious booze. He's trying to save everyone; he'll give you up to do that. He always makes the smart move. Everyone knows that."

"You're wrong," I said. "Michael will stand up for me. He owes me. He owes me big time. He'll never forget what he owes me. I know things. I saved his life. I can count on Michael forever."

Sally started to laugh. "You're such a fool and everyone knows it. Dear boy, dear boy. What are you *talking* about? You shot Michael's *lover*. He wants to see you dead. Just like Louis Turko, Michael will get you."

My mind was reeling but snapped back into focus. "Louis Turko, why Turko?"

"You don't understand anything. You're just a drunk, a cokehead and a fool. You killed Michael's first lover. Then Turko killed Danny Cupp, his second lover. Michael doesn't have anyone left. Michael will get Turko and he'll get you."

I remembered what Michael had said during the weird sex acts at Gramercy Park, *"perversion is more fun when it's forced on you."* I remembered the handsome young face in the morgue photo of the man I shot. I remembered the way Michael held him, trying to save his life as blood poured from his chest. The boy was holding Michael's gun. Then I remembered how upset Michael was when Cupp was killed. It was all true. I had to hold onto the bar to keep from falling down.

CHAPTER TWELVE

TURNING THE TABLES

BLOOD MONEY

Daisy and Mark had been living in Chicago with my in-laws for about six months now. Mark had even started school there. I missed them both so much that I hated to stay at my apartment because it reminded me of them, but I couldn't stay at Cookie's. She was too dumb and made me feel even worse, if that was possible. Nevertheless, I went home and found an answering-machine message from Daisy. She said she was worried about me and missed me very much. She had found a gig, playing saxophone at a small club on Rush Street. She was sending me an ad for the club. In the stack of unopened mail was a newspaper clipping of a music critic telling how good the act was. There was a picture of a tall blonde wearing a beret with her legs spread wide open, playing the sax in front of a band; it was captioned *Daisy Blue*. I sat on the living-room floor and cried.

The next day I returned to the office and tried to act normal. Incredibly, even when the Bureau was completely shut down by Flowers' Task Force, Michael announced he had a huge case. The news surprised me as well as everyone else.

From a series of police wiretaps Michael had learned there would be a major transfer of drugs from France to Louis Turko. Everyone was excited. Now Michael was going to get revenge. Even Flowers was excited and supportive. It looked like the Bureau was finally going to work together. The deal was ten kilos of pure heroin for $250,000. It became a joint operation between Customs and the NYPD, all under Michael's supervision. Surveillance and wiretaps were established for the Frenchman, aka "The Frog" or "Leonard."

The hotel where Leonard was staying already had wiretaps and we were able to bug the restaurant where he made arrangements with Louis Turko. The transfer was surprisingly simple. It was to be done out in the open, in a small park on the East Side of Manhattan. The advantage of the park was that Leonard and Turko, who would be carrying the mob's drug money, would do the exchange in the open. They could see if they were being double-crossed or if anyone was conducting surveillance on them. Leonard was to leave his suitcase of heroin on a park bench, travel across the park, and pick up a paper bag of money to be left in a trash can by Turko, who would enter the park from another entrance at the same time.

Everything went according to plan. 90 Church agents and the NYPD met a block away, preparing to surround the park and watch all exits, but then an hour before the exchange was scheduled, Flowers showed up with his Task Force of twelve agents. He gave Blanker a memo from the Justice Department stating that his Task Force was to take charge of the case immediately. Michael and

Dewey began arguing with Flowers in the street. Finally Flowers had to tell his agents to put Michael and Dewey in the back seat of a government car under guard more than a block away from the park until the case was over. Then Flowers dismissed the police and stationed his Task Force agents at every exit, with movie cameras to film everyone coming and going.

Exactly on time, Leonard, the Frenchman, brought the suitcase of heroin into the park. Then Louis Turko came into the park from the other side, carrying a paper shopping bag. Five minutes later Turko came out of the park carrying a suitcase. Flowers immediately arrested him and seized the ten kilos of heroin.

But something went wrong. Leonard, who by now was supposed to be carrying the paper bag of Turko's money, left the park empty-handed. He was arrested anyway. Flowers was dumbfounded over the missing money. His agents, now assisted by the police, converged on the park, searching it foot-by-foot, emptying every trashcan and looking into every conceivable place that could conceal a bag of money. It was impossible that anyone could have stolen it and left the park unnoticed with all the surveillance and cameras. Although there were no government funds involved, Flowers was desperate to find answers.

Finally he ordered all the agents to return to the office to watch surveillance films of the entrances. It took over an hour to develop the films so whoever had the mob's money was long gone. Leonard and Turko refused to make any statements and were held in isolation. The surprise and speculation grew to such a point that finally everyone just stared at each other in silence.

Everyone was under suspicion – everyone except, of course, Michael and Dewey, who were under guard in a government car more than a block away during the exchange. I had seen all of this before. I knew to expect the unexpected. Dewey tormented Flowers with stupid questions: "Andy, what do you think *really* happened?" and "From your experience in dealing with the Mafia, Andy, do you think he *really* carried the money in, in the first place?" and "Andy, maybe the Frenchman still has the two hundred and fifty thousand dollars on him. Do you want me to search him again? Did you check all of his pockets?"

Flowers' head jerks got worse.

Blanker gave the case back to Michael. Michael didn't like conspiracy cases because they took too much time to prove in court, and so he let the Frenchman go. Turko, however had a previous arrest and now had been arrested with ten kilos of heroin, a major felony with a minimum of twenty years in jail.

Things got much worse. Judge Carl Wineburg handled Louis Turko's arraignment. The same judge that Michael accused of leaking information to Turko that got Danny Cupp killed and who everyone thought, except me, got Jerry Ramirez killed too. Flowers was furious. This demonstrated to me, at least, that Flowers was trying to bring justice to the case. But Michael told Judge Wineburg that there was a vendetta by the government against Turko from a previous case and that he would personally vouch for Turko's character. Turko paid a five-thousand-dollar bond and walked out of the courtroom.

Flowers was livid and began calling his friends at the Justice Department to investigate everyone, including the judge. He said bail should have been one million dollars because of the crime and prior record. Five thousand dollars was outrageous. He accused Michael of being part of the Mafia and ruining the case. For once I understood. I knew what the low bail meant. Like Michael always says, "When you're guilty you believe the worst in people." Turko had lost two hundred and fifty thousand dollars of Mafia money on top of the fifty thousand he had lost in the Charles Stuckey case. The low bail was all the proof the Mafia needed to convince them that Turko had turned into a rat for 90 Church. The next morning when Turko was picking up the morning paper he was shot and killed. By the end of the week there were four more murders of Mafia thugs as they tried to imagine who else besides Turko was "cooperating" with 90 Church.

While the Italians were busy killing themselves, we sat studying the surveillance films hour after hour, watching people come and go on a sunny afternoon – men, women, children, pets, strollers with babies. Michael just sat in the corner of the conference room, smoking a cigarette, not saying a word. Then, as I watched the film for at least the fifth time, I saw it! I lost my breath; I couldn't stop my reflexes that now were going to get me killed. I looked across the room to Dewey and he was staring back at me. It was too late; he knew that I knew. Fear gripped me like electric shock. Dewey was going to kill me! The agents could watch the films for the next ten years and not solve the mystery of who took the money out of the park – because it was Dewey! Up on the bright screen, people coming and going, was a young boy riding a bicycle wearing a baseball cap, with a knapsack. His face showed to the camera only a second, but it was enough, it was Dwight...Dwight Paris *Junior!*

COUNTRY BOYS

Now I had a solid case against Dewey and Michael and they knew it. I could never survive against them, but I was *not* going to go to jail for the rest of my life for murdering a pimp and giving a few bags of smack to a strung-out friend. No one talked to me in the office. It was as if I didn't exist.

A few days later, I found a plain white envelope in my mailbox at the office. The return address was handwritten: Albert Hall – the apartment I had lived in with other new agents during our training in Washington, more than three years ago. The enclosed note read: *2:30 today. First and 67th* and was signed *Steve*. Agent Steve Doll worked in the Atlanta office. He, Jerry Ramirez, Del Ridley, and I had all roomed together at Albert Hall during our training.

I met Steve on the corner. He hadn't changed a bit, but he hardly recognized me. He just stood for a minute, shocked at my appearance. "Pick a place that's private," he said. "I know what's going on in the Bureau. Nothing is safe anymore. Wherever you want to go is fine."

We walked about two blocks and I chose a cheap hotel at random. We walked in, registered, and went upstairs to a room. He was carrying a briefcase and set it on the bed. Inside was a tape recorder; he took it out and plugged it in. I asked if he was here on a case, and he answered, "No one knows I'm here."

He played the tape. Between the thick Southern accents of two men talking to a third and the background bar-room noise, I could hardly understand what they were saying. But I heard them talking to the third guy, who they called Caldwell. He was very angry with the other two and kept screaming at them, *"Why? Why?"*

The two voices argued, *"We don't give a shit if he was a Fed. You were the one who told us about him. You said your spic Frenchman told you he was coming."*

Caldwell responded, "*I didn't tell you to kill him. No one was to be killed. The drug deal was off because we had to put the stuff off on someone else. Now those people are dead, too, because of you assholes. I told you to take the money, not to shoot him. You just don't shoot a federal agent.*"

Steve then turned the tape off. I looked at him. "I don't understand."

Then he explained: "The two hillbilly brothers on the tape killed Jerry Ramirez. Jerry was working with Jack Connors and me to make a buy on a dealer in Atlanta. We were following up on the lead you gave us from the Henri Manasso case. You told us that Caldwell was Manasso's lawyer. We brought in a local informant to help Jerry get close to Caldwell. When everything went bad, Jack and I thought the *informant* had killed Jerry. When we tried to arrest him he pulled a gun on us – so we had to shoot him. We were wrong. The lawyer, Caldwell, set up the drug deal with the hillbillies as the gophers, but there were never any drugs. When he couldn't get the dope, Caldwell set up a heist. He told the hillbillies to rip Jerry off; Jerry had ten thousand dollars for the buy, but when Jerry wouldn't give up the money they shot him in the head, and then we killed the informant who we thought did it. Manasso told Caldwell that Jerry was an agent; but somebody had to tell Manasso. Who?"

I turned cold with fear and shame. "I don't get it." I forced myself to look at the pictures that he had spread out on the bed. "These guys aren't dealers, they're too country. Do you know who the hillbillies are? Do you even know their names?"

Steve pointed to the file, "Sure we do. They're the Weary brothers. Everyone knows who they are and where they live."

I leafed through the file then said, "How could you make such a mistake? Weren't you there when they got the informant?"

Steve looked down. "I was there; I put a bullet in him, too. He was Connors's informant, a bad guy, but he didn't kill Jerry. We even found the gun in his car, but Caldwell put it there. He set it all up. He's smart, and he sent the hillbillies to rob Jerry. When Jerry got shot, Caldwell knew there would be heat so he told us that the informant was double-crossing us and had shot Jerry, then he planted the gun. We believed him at first. Things got even better for Caldwell when we killed the informant. Case closed."

"You don't have any proof," I said. "The tapes are not enough, and you know an informant can turn on you in a second. Besides, Flowers' Task Force already investigated it. Flowers and the Justice Department did a big report; they said it was the informant who shot Jerry. There was no mention of Caldwell or the two Weary brothers. I read it. Why bring this to me? Take the tape to them; they're the government, they're supposed to find Jerry's killer."

Steve shook his head. "You, Michael Giovanni, Dewey Paris and the others at 90 Church are heroes. All you've done – the undercover work, the Mafia – everyone respects you, the cops, ATF, Secret Service, everyone. You're the greatest weapon this country has against drugs and crime."

"That's a nice speech," I said, "but I don't feel like a hero and you have no proof of who killed Jerry."

He dug in his briefcase. "You're too busy on the street to even understand what's going on around you. Here's your proof!"

He handed me a piece of paper. It was a copy of a Justice Department memo from Flowers to Caldwell. The subject line read: *Grant of Immunity*. It protected Caldwell. He would not be prosecuted for the death of Agent Jerry Ramirez, or any other crimes he had committed up until the date of the memo. The immunity was conditional upon making felony cases and testifying against a list of agents. The list included everyone connected to the Manasso case: Steve, Connors, Michael, Dewey, and me. There was also a special paragraph that said Caldwell could work on future cases and be paid for his information.

Steve stared at me. "You just don't get it. This is going on all over. They're willing to let Jerry's killer walk, just to get *us*. Just think of what else they're doing! Where the fuck is the justice in all of this? Where the fuck is the right and wrong?"

Again Steve reached into his briefcase, pulled out a file, and opened it up. There were more photographs of the two Weary brothers and an old broken-down gas station and trailer with a Budweiser sign. "This is where they hang out. It's in Helen, Georgia, outside of Atlanta. Nice, huh? They are really bad guys. Once they raped a local girl and held her captive for days while her husband looked for her. They did everything to her, finally killing her. Everyone knew they did it, but Caldwell got them off. They're animals. We let these people walk around free after they killed Jerry? I can't stand it!"

I looked at him and said, "Why me?"

Steve packed his briefcase, and handed me the file. "Someone has got to go down and stop these hillbillies before they do any more damage. Someone has got to get Caldwell. But Flowers is protecting him. Find out who at 90 Church told Manasso. It's the first place to start. Everyone thinks it was Flowers, but I'm not so sure. Flowers is bad, but not that bad. There is no reason for him to tell Caldwell or Manasso about Jerry."

I stared at the memo. My hands were trembling but I managed

to say, "They're assholes. They can't touch me. I'll wipe my ass with this memo."

Steve could see how nervous I was. "I quit three days ago and took those files, but I'll help you. These people are easy to find. All the information is in there. I have to go now. I have to go home. I'm looking for a job."

When I got back to the office it was buzzing with news. The Task Force was preparing secret indictments against at least six agents. Pike called me aside and said, "All they want is either you or Michael, or Dewey, and all of this is over. If Michael gives you up, he won't do any time. You know he's sick."

"Michael is stand-up," I said. "He'll never give me up. How about the others?"

Pike pulled on his tie and shook his head. "They may have something on Connors; I don't know what, something about the Ramirez killing, leaking information to a lawyer in Atlanta named Caldwell."

It was all coming to a head now; them or me. Flowers was smarter than I thought and he had a lot of perseverance. I was tired and couldn't fight any more. I had to save myself. I had to turn on Dewey and Michael and now with the missing money from the United Nations Park I had a solid case against them. I had to take Flowers' immunity deal.

LOST FRIENDS

Rather than go back to the office for the rest of the afternoon I went to see Charles DeWitt. He hadn't been playing at Count Basie's and I was concerned about him. DeWitt was dying of cancer, and the heroin helped him deal with the pain. I wanted to know for certain that he hadn't told Flowers anything more.

DeWitt lived on the top floor of a broken-down tenement. I knocked on his door but there was no answer. It was unlocked so I walked into a dark room. I could see the silhouette of a light hanging from the ceiling and I pulled the chain. In the middle of the room was a bed. DeWitt was under a white sheet, and the sheet was covered with hundreds of black dots. I heard a strange rustling noise and the black dots scrambled off the sheet and covered the floor completely. They were huge roaches – thousands of them. At the end of the sheet, I could see DeWitt's kind face. He opened his eyes and gave me a weak smile.

I knelt down and asked him if the Task Force had been to see him. He nodded his head yes. I asked him what they wanted and he said, "The usual; they asked me if you helped me with drugs. I said no. They never mentioned that Dewey fellow or Michael, only you."

He closed his eyes as if he couldn't be bothered. He was dying. I reached in my pocket and pulled out a bundle of nickel bags of heroin and placed it on the bed next to him. He looked up at me and said, "Thank you, thank you for saving my life. I can't leave here ever again." I was about to go when he motioned and pointed across the room. He pointed to his worn but shiny trumpet. He wanted me to bring it to him. I picked it up and set it by his side, like a Teddy Bear. I turned out the light and walked out the door.

Next I went to see Tony Degaglia. I called his mother's apartment but there was no answer. I went anyway, thinking she'd be back by the time I got there and could tell me where to find him. When I arrived, Tony's mother was sitting in a rocking chair on the sidewalk. She had been evicted. Tony had taken every dime she had to buy heroin. All of her clothes, furniture, dishes, everything she owned was piled next to her on the street. The family album with Tony's photos was on her lap. She recognized me but didn't say a word. She was probably seventy-five years old, with nowhere to go and no money. I asked her where I could find Tony. She said he was living in the basement of an abandoned building on the corner of 186th and the Grand Concourse. I counted out five hundred dollars of government money and put it in her hand. I had to close her hand on the money or it would have fallen in the street. As I walked away I turned and looked again into her face. She looked back at me with a blank stare.

That night I found Tony where she said I would. There was at least four feet of water covering the basement floor. A small catwalk, barely above the water, led to a wooden platform supported by boxes and tables that were already under the water. Tony was lying there in a drug-induced stupor on a mattress on the platform, only about six inches above the surface of the water. A single light bulb hanging from a wire burned overhead. Tony recognized me and greeted me with a hesitant smile, like DeWitt had given me. "I didn't mean to betray you," he said. "I wanted to stand up. I won't give them anything from now on." His arms were covered with needle marks and sores. "Are you going to kill me?"

"No, Tony, I'm not here to kill you." I reached in my pocket and gave him a bundle of nickel bags of heroin. "This will get you through the night. I'm going to come back tomorrow and put you in rehab. I know that you're going to stand up."

He grabbed my hand. "You're the best friend I ever had in my life. Thank you. Do you forgive me for what I have done to you?"

I knelt down on my knees, hugged him, and said, "Yes, I forgive you, you are better than me. I'll come back tomorrow."

Everything was piling up too fast, I needed a break. After a considerable effort I found a bar on the East Side that I had never been in before. It was small, dark and cozy with normal customers who paid taxes and worked nine-to-five at an honest job. I tried to talk to them, to relax, but soon I was alone with my own terrifying thoughts and downed at least eight vodkas.

I started at the beginning, remembering my first case, Elliott Goldstein, the advertising executive that I turned into a "major drug dealer." The image of Elliott hanging on the wall with his bloody fingers burned in my mind. I knew where all these thoughts were taking me and that liquor and cocaine were the only way out.

By the time I got home it was eleven o'clock and pouring rain so hard I could barely see through it. I was stone drunk and needed a line of coke. As I parked the car, I looked up and saw there was a light on in my apartment. I had been calling Daisy once a week. I tried to tell her what was happening to me, but only in a homogenized, cleaned-up version. The same type of lies that I had been telling her from the beginning. I hadn't seen her in months. The light was a welcome sight. She opened the door for me with a book in her hand. There was no warm smile. "Christ, every time you come home you're drunk. Nothing changes. Who's dead now?"

I wiped my running nose and struggled to be coherent. "Me, I am, Dewey's going to kill me. Elliott's dead."

"I thought Dewey was your friend. Who's Elliott?"

I staggered in and grabbed the back of the couch for balance. "I have evidence against Dewey and Michael. I saw Dewey's teenage son with the drug money. I have absolute proof. All the killings are going to stop. I'm not going to get the blame for killing a lousy pimp!"

She shook her head. "Elliott was a pimp? Dewey's son is a drug dealer?"

I staggered over to a chair. "No. Heyman! Heyman is the pimp, but his name is not really Heyman, I just call him that. Flowers killed Elliott!"

Daisy rolled her eyes. "I'm trying to follow here, I really am."

Now the liquor was starting to take hold of me. "Sooozeee got me on tape, setting up Heyman to get killed; it's all over."

"Who's Suzy? She's got you on tape? You should tell Flowers that he needs to get with Michael and Dewey to straighten things out down there before it gets any worse, and tell Dewey he needs to have a good long talk with his son."

I couldn't take any more, "*Stop it! Stop it!* Dewey and Michael are killers. I'm not going to jail; I'm going to be loyal to my country, just like I always said, truth, justice and the American way."

"So now you've become a patriot?"

"You don't understand. I'm turning Michael and Dewey over to Flowers. I have a case on them. They took the drug money. They're going to jail."

She patted my head. "I understand you're in a war, a terrible serious war. People do things in war."

"Flowers is saving me because I never took any money."

"Flowers, the one that killed Elliott? Right?"

"Yes, but I, I, I – "

She cut me off. "Okay then, now all of this is really just about who took drug money from the mob? Right? Good, because I can't follow who killed who and no one seems to care. It's all about the money, just like everywhere else. I'm going to make you some coffee." She smiled a sympathetic smile and disappeared into the kitchen. Insanity was now taking control. I grabbed my little pouch and dumped some coke on the coffee table. As I was snorting up a line she came back into the room.

"A man, whom I hate worse than all the gates of hell, is he who says one thing, while another lies in his heart hidden well."

I tried to get it back together. "Shakespeare?"

"Homer, it was Homer. You talk to me of war and friendship and loyalty, death, and oh yeah, saving America from drugs, how your friends are killers and incidentally so *is* the government, and incidentally so *is* you."

I felt stupid and pitiful. Her anger was just getting started.

"All this madness and guilt. Then you sit there and snort a line of coke in our apartment! I loved you and your ridiculous suits more than anything or anyone else in my life. I've put up with your drinking and your lies for the past four years because I believed in you, your stupid, childish Superman theme, truth, justice and the American way. I stuck by you because I knew you would get through it and rise to the top. But I was wrong, you betray people, that's what you do every night in the street. Well, now you've betrayed me and your son."

She broke down in sobs, then gained control. "I'm not good enough for you, so how good do your friends have to be before you're loyal to them? Saving your life in the street or being your wife doesn't cut it, does it? *Get out!* I can't stand you. I can't stand myself."

Daisy managed to continue, "Now just because you didn't take money, you think you're better than Michael and Dewey and me.

Well, you're nothing more than a sanctimonious asshole."

She fought to keep going, "And now your guilt is driving you crazy? Because in the end you're just a fucking hypocrite trying to save your own ass, and I'm just a fool who can't stop loving you." She pushed me in the chest and screamed, "*Get out, Get out.*" Then she collapsed on the floor, covering her eyes, crying, "Please dear God, leave, please go. I can't look at you, go, go."

I left to go to the only place I had left to go to – Cookie's apartment to listen to her endless, mindless chatter.

FOND GOOD-BYES

The next day I was in the office early, about 10:00 and hung over. I knew I had to fight back somehow. I thought about Tony Degaglia. I wondered how he was living in a water-filled basement. Maybe I could get him to change his story; after all, he called me his best friend, whatever that was worth.

I headed for the Bronx. There was a rescue unit parked on the street in front of the building Tony was hiding in. Cops were gathered around the entrance to the basement door. I looked down the short flight of steps and could see that – after a night of rain – the water was much higher than it had been. I asked the cops why they were there. One said, "Somebody in the basement was screaming all night long, bothering the neighbors. The screams wouldn't stop, so finally we had to send a unit in. They're in there now."

Two firemen came out of the building, wearing waders and dragging something wet in a white sheet. When they came to the top of the steps at street level, they stopped. The cop asked the fireman what he'd found. The fireman looked at the sheet, which was spotting red, and said, "He was on a platform in the basement with about four feet of water all around him. I guess the water got a little too high last night. There's a walkway but it was under water, and a broken light. He must have been too stoned to get out. Somebody, no doubt, gave him a bunch of dope, just enough to disorient him, slow him down so the rats could get him. His drug dealer probably wanted him dead. Anyway, the rats joined him on the higher ground. They ate him. He was too doped up to stop them." The fireman looked at me. "Do you know him?"

He pulled back the sheet so I could see. At first I couldn't recognize Tony. There were small bite marks all over the body, part of his face was down to the bone on one side. I began to shake. The fireman looked at me and said, "Believe it or not, when we found him, he was still breathing, but he's gone now. Well, do you know him?"

I shook my head no.

A PLAN

I went to Cookie's apartment to snort coke and drink, and I tried not to think about what I had been through. I realized I didn't care anymore. Tony Degaglia, DeWitt, Elliott, not even Daisy or my son. The load was too heavy, I couldn't handle it.

Cookie came home in the afternoon to talk about her nails for half an hour. Then she started whining that she wanted to be part of the undercover operations and that I should take her along when I made my next case so she "could help." She was like a ten-year-old child and it made my depression even worse. My hands were shaking so bad that I had to hold them to my side. I hadn't eaten or showered in days.

Finally I took a nap, waking up at about eleven-thirty at night. Cookie had probably fallen asleep while talking to herself about her haircut. I showered, got dressed and drove uptown to a bar called Harry's Back East. It was always lively and I wanted to call for messages. The bar was filled with people my age, laughing and talking. There was a pay phone on the wall and I called the office.

I had an urgent message. It was from Dottie, with her home number. I woke her up and asked what she wanted. She said, "They came and took your file today." That meant an indictment was coming. "I overheard George say the Grand Jury is in secret session. There's a lot more; Blanker thinks Michael Giovanni is going to testify against you and end the investigation. It's a shame. You're the best agent in the office. Look at all the cases you've made. You even saved Michael's life. I'm sorry to tell you this but I thought you should know."

I hung up and leaned on the wall, still holding the phone to my ear. All of a sudden a tall muscular guy with a military crew cut grabbed my shirt and said, "Enough is *enough*. Give me the phone, you little faggot." He was obviously drunk. He shook me, tearing my shirt. "Give me the phone. You've had it long enough. *Give me the phone!* You dirty little faggot."

All I could later remember was a long, green flash of lightning striking me over and over. When it stopped, I could smell plaster dust. I looked down on the floor and saw the man lying there with a gash on the side of his head, blood streaming down his face. Next to him was the pay phone and part of the plasterboard from the wall. I looked around the bar. There was a strange silence, and no one looked at me. I looked at the bouncers; they turned their heads. I stepped over the guy lying on the floor and walked out the door. I wasn't sure what had happened, but I knew I was now dangerously out of control. I had ripped the phone off the wall and hit a man in the head with it...and I felt good about it.

I walked the streets and thought about the immunity deal. I thought about Caldwell and the Weary brothers. I tried not to remember how Jerry had died.

I walked back to Cookie's and woke her up. "Cookie," I said, "tomorrow is a special day. I would like you to help me with a case."

She rubbed sleep from her eyes. "Are you serious?"

"Yes." I gave her a big smile. "It's a very special undercover case and very dangerous. I need your help. Get on the phone and book two tickets to Atlanta for the day after tomorrow, leave the return open. "

She jumped up and down on the bed like a child. "My God, my God, this is great, this is *great*! Thank you! This is something I've always *dreamed* of! I can't *believe* it. Tell me about the case."

I hugged her and said, "We're going to Atlanta to settle an old score with two hillbillies and a crooked lawyer. You're gonna have a lot of fun."

The idea of bringing a nitwit girl into a hillbilly killing spree made me laugh inside. I was raging out of control and I loved it.

WHAT WOULD JESUS DO?

The next morning I had a line of coke and two Bloody Marys for breakfast, then put on a shiny new blue mohair suit and a red shirt with matching red boots. Cookie kept telling me what a great agent I was and that someday when all the secrecy was over, I would be famous – and besides, I looked great. I couldn't tell her that I was going to rat on all of my friends for immunity so I wouldn't go to jail for killing a rotten pimp and giving a few bags of heroin to a strung-out friend. Her little mind couldn't possibly grasp what I was facing.

I kissed her good-bye and went to the office. It was still too early for anyone to be there. As I walked through the empty halls I saw some things laid out on a table in a small conference room. There was a photograph of Jerry Ramirez, a small piece of polished wood, a brass plate with his name on it and his gun, a blue Walther PPK, exactly like mine. They were getting ready to make his memorial plaque with his picture and gun mounted on it, just like all the others that hung on the wall outside Blanker's office.

After a few moments of sadness I pulled out my gun and laid it down next to his. Then I picked up Jerry's gun, put it in my holster and walked out. Jerry's gun would do the work in Atlanta.

I reviewed the file on the two Weary brothers and looked at the photo of the gas station and bar where Jerry died.

It wasn't long before Ted Pike came lumbering through the office and plopped down in his chair inside his glass cubicle. At first he only nodded, then he waved me in and closed the door. He looked straight through me. "George and Andy and I have been talking about you. You're a good agent. Andy Flowers knows that, but you've got to see what's at stake here. We can't let people like Dewey and Michael run the government, can we?"

"Why not?" I questioned.

His face grew red. "Why? Because they're wrong. That's why.

You see how religious Blanker is. He begins every day with a little prayer to help us. We're the United States Government of America. There's got to be a due process. Do you understand? A due process."

I was quick with my answer. "Ted, there is a due process. There's a due process in the street. You and the others just don't see it."

"That's lawlessness," Pike shouted back. "Andy Flowers is giving you a chance. You could be somebody. He's giving you a chance to forget about the past and to join the team. Are you going to be part of the team or not? To tell you the truth I don't think you have much of a choice." Pike was right.

"OK, I'll give it some thought and meet with Andy again and straighten things out." I knew that I had to give up Dewey and Michael. I needed the immunity deal for what I was going to do in Atlanta anyway. So everything was really very clear. I told Pike I would not be in tomorrow. I didn't tell him I was going to Atlanta. Jerry's death would be avenged and I had to do it.

I decided to go back to Cookie's apartment and rest up for the trip tomorrow. At first I thought she wasn't home until I walked into the bedroom. She was kneeling at the edge of the bed, praying. Her body was taut and focused into her clasped hands as she looked up at the ceiling. I wasn't sure if she didn't hear me come in or was doing this just for my benefit.

"Please, Jesus, help me tomorrow to bring justice and love and God's word to the sinners in Atlanta and help us to be brave." She stopped and stared at me. "I know you think this is silly but it's not. Someday I want you to find Jesus Christ and follow his ways. If you just listened to him, things will become clear and you will be happy. Don't you see?" She pointed to a picture frame on the dresser. In the frame was an inscription that read *What would Jesus do?* She tried to give me a hug. "You see, it's simple; just ask yourself what would Jesus do?"

I stared at the words in the frame then gave her one of those Dewey giggles, "You're right, I need inspiration. I need a new direction. My ways are wrong." I looked at the words in the picture frame again, but now I saw something else; *What would Michael do?* How stupid I've been! I could never kill anyone.

"Cookie, I have to go back to the office. We're not going to Atlanta. You've inspired me, thank you, Jesus, there's gonna be a change of plans. Let's go out somewhere tonight, maybe French."

By mid-afternoon I was back in the office and I was ready to talk to Andy Flowers. He was alone in his office. Andy still had that strange look, a fixed stare and was licking his lips like a lizard. I got right to the point.

"I understand that you have cut an immunity deal with Caldwell, the lawyer in the Manasso case."

"How'd you find out?"

"Steve Doll told me. He also told me some other things that might be helpful to you."

Flowers rubbed his chin. "Yeah, like what?"

"Like the Weary brothers. They are killers and rapists and drug dealers." I pulled out a few papers from Steven's file. "Here they are. They're bad guys. I think you should amend the immunity deal with Caldwell so he gets big-time credit if he makes a case on the Weary brothers."

Flowers studied the papers and then nodded. "Okay, fair enough. He gets a deal if he makes the Weary brothers. I will write it up today." Then he said something creepy, "You know I like you, I believe in you. I'm going to look after you."

I answered, "Andy, I'm still thinking about our deal and I'm almost there; just give me some time."

He rocked back in his chair. "Remember, we stand for justice here, we stand for justice here."

On the way back to my desk I saw Dottie, Blanker's secretary, and walked over to her.

"Dottie, I just got through meeting with Flowers. He wants you to do another immunity deal for Caldwell, that asshole lawyer in Atlanta. Would you type it up for him?"

She nodded.

Several hours later I went back to see Dottie. "Honey, you know I'm working with Andy on the Atlanta case. Can I have a copy of the Caldwell immunity memo that you did on the Weary brothers for my file?"

"Sure." She passed me a copy and I returned to my desk. Just as I expected, Flowers was going to give Caldwell complete immunity if he made a case on the notorious hillbilly Weary brothers. I searched through the files for the address, and then typed an envelope: *The Weary brothers, RFD 942, Rome, Georgia.*

I folded in the immunity paper, licked the envelope and dropped it in the mailbox on the way out to have dinner with Cookie.

I waited a few days, then called the Atlanta office. I told them that we believed that the Weary brothers were dangerous and were going to kill Caldwell, one of our federal informants. They should also alert the local police.

It took about a week for things to come together. The Weary brothers murdered Caldwell a day after they received my letter. The agents in the Atlanta office and the local police killed both of the brothers as they resisted arrest in the investigation of the death of Caldwell.

Cookie missed her big case, but she did take credit for inspiring me on a new way of thinking. What would Michael do?

CHAPTER THIRTEEN

A CAREER MOVE

FORGIVENESS

It's not true that cocaine ruins your sex life, just the opposite. I began with playful little slaps to Cookie's beautiful ass. Then I started tying her up, giving pain with her pleasure a little more each time. There was going to be a whole new dimension to our relationship.

I was feeling pretty good about myself, as I got ready to go to the office. Cookie was still huddled in the corner of the bedroom, silent and naked, like a frightened white mouse that was living with a cobra; although I wondered if she was afraid of me or of herself. She definitely wanted pain in her life. I would shop for a nice, wide, black belt, a belt she could respect. I would teach her not to talk so much.

It was early so the office was almost deserted. I passed the little conference room where they had laid out all the things for Jerry's memorial plaque. I pulled Jerry's gun from my holster and switched it with mine. It was a good idea if there was an investigation; ballistics would have shown that Jerry's gun, not mine, was used. Michael's way was much better. I didn't have to shoot anyone. All the guilty were dead and I was innocent. That's all that mattered. Besides I saved the cost of an airline ticket. I truly understood how things worked.

Group Two was empty except for Pike talking on the phone. He just waved to me. The supervision of agents was ridiculous. They just came and went as they pleased. At the end of the week everyone wrote a silly report on all the hours they spent in the street with most of the cases going nowhere or the arrest of some pitiful junkie.

After lunch I sat at my desk alone waiting for someone to ask me to join a case. I started sorting through my desk drawer until I found the three-by-five index card taken from the file room so long ago on a cold dark winter night. I could never forget the simple words that changed my life forever: *Twigs, Henri Manasso*. On the back of the card was a scribbled address, the last bit of research that Tony Roma from Roma had done before he killed himself.

I picked up the phone and booked an evening flight to Boston. Then I told Pike I needed three days off. He just nodded okay. Rachel was living in Marble Head, Massachusetts. I was glad to get a trip out of New York.

The plane ride and comfortable seaside hotel made me feel a little better. Soon the thought of finding Rachel absorbed me completely. Despite everything, I still loved her. She made me feel strong and smart. None of this made any sense, but I didn't care. I needed her.

I started my stakeout early in the morning. The house was small, on oceanfront property. I parked at the corner of an intersecting street so I could look down the block without being seen. At about eight o'clock the neighborhood started to come alive, people picking up the newspapers, driving to work, running off to school. Rachel's garage door opened at about 9:30 and a white Porsche rolled out and darted up the street past me. It was her. Even with the oversized sunglasses and baseball cap, I could see that it was her.

After a few minutes I drove into a small village that I had passed earlier and found a hardware store. I picked out a small one-inch-wide putty knife. I had the store manager use the metal grinder wheel in the key department to cut a notch halfway through the middle of the blade. The manager asked me several times why I wanted him to grind a huge notch to a new knife. I couldn't think of an answer that he would believe.

Besides the damaged putty knife I bought a roll of toilet paper and drove back to the house, again parking down the street. I unrolled all of the toilet paper and put the brown cardboard cylinder spool in my pocket. I walked up to each house pretending to knock on the door. Anyone seeing me would think I was a door-to-door salesman and hide. When I got to Rachel's house I slipped around back.

Most people feel safe behind their doors with locks and chains. They don't realize how easily a skilled burglar can get through. Rachel's back door opened out with a typical wood frame. When you closed the door the sliding latch would hit the striker plate on the door jamb, pushing the latch in, then letting it spring back into the hole in the door frame to lock. I slid the notched putty knife into the door jamb, pushed down so the notch hooked behind the door latch and gently pulled forward, pushing the latch in so the lock was released. The sliding chain lock was next. With the door open a few inches I jammed the brown cardboard toilet-paper cylinder against the chain, and then carefully closed the door. The cardboard cylinder forced the chain to run along the slider track to the end where it popped out. My street education was starting to pay off.

Rachel's house was very well-kept, decorated in black and white. Dewey would go straight to the refrigerator. I knew why. She lived alone – yogurt, small dishes, one of everything. She ate out at night, no entrée items in the freezer. On I went to the dirty clothes and trash. She traveled a lot. Next the medicine cabinet: it had the usual, aspirin, birth-control pills, and a large jar of Vaseline. Next to the toilet was a vegetable sieve. In the waste basket I found large condoms, double layered, one inside the other. She was still smuggling drugs for a living. No evidence of a boyfriend anywhere. The closet was filled with expensive sexy clothes, but not much for winter. She had another home someplace warm. Her bed was made so she was comfortable living alone. There were pictures of her in a bathing suit with all sorts of people – ugly, fat, dark and pale – with exotic backgrounds of palm trees, mountains and yachts. There was a large picture with Manasso and her, hugging each other.

The garage was neat, with a complete tool bench and a wide assortment of bolts and screws. She had a black, high-powered Moto Guzzi motorcycle ready to roll.

I sat in the living room to think. I had not found the hideaway. All drug dealers hid things. The closets, kitchen, and behind the toilet were all too obvious for someone as smart as Rachel.

There was expensive white pickled wood paneling on one wall next to the fireplace. There were pictures everywhere except there. I pushed each panel, looking for a pressure lock. The third one gave in and sprung open to a series of shelves. The top shelf had a small stack of passports from various countries. Her real name was Rachel Burano. The other shelves were stacked with money and long curved condoms filled with cocaine and heroin. Manasso's black .45 with a silencer was on the middle shelf, still in its shoulder holster. The gun bothered me. Why would she keep it as a souvenir? How did she even get it? This could not be Rachel's gun!

I picked it up. It was loaded. I unscrewed the silencer and went into the garage. I took a drill bit and slid it down inside the barrel. Then I found the right-size machine bolt and screwed it into the front of the barrel as hard as I could. With the barrel spiked, the gun would backfire, blowing the drill bit through the firing pin, into the shooter's face. Manasso's gun would not kill anyone ever again, except maybe the shooter. I replaced the silencer, put it back on the shelf in its holster and closed the panel.

I sucked up a line of cocaine and started looking through the papers in her desk. She had over one hundred and fifty thousand dollars in the bank. Besides clothes, she spent a lot of money at a local restaurant called The Cove.

I sorted through her underwear drawer, all clean white silk. I took one and held it to my cheek, then to my nose – laundry detergent.

I roamed from room to room, still holding her panties to my cheek. Finally I laid on the bed and felt like I was being bathed in warm water. I loved her now more than ever. She knew how to outsmart Michael and Dewey. With her by my side I could face anything. I knew why she had done the things she had done, I didn't care. I even respected her for it. She loved Manasso, but he was gone. She loved me too. When we made love there was such passion that the sheets would be soaking wet. We would hold each other for hours. Now we would ride motorcycles together, travel the world. No more drugs, no more 90 Church. She was part of me and always would be. She lived alone because she could not love anyone else. Now I was back.

I laid my face on her pillow for hours, remembering everything we did together. Finally I straightened up the house and went back to my hotel. It was late afternoon and I wanted to think about how I would contact her. I fell asleep and woke up later at 7:30. I drove back to Rachel's house, but it was dark. I had missed her. I remembered her receipts from The Cove Restaurant. It was easy to find on the ocean front in the small town. Her white Porsche was parked out front.

The Cove was expensive and elegant with chandeliers and waiters in white dinner jackets. I had short hair when Rachel and I were together. It now hung down, covering my face. I sat at the bar and looked into the mirror behind the bottles that reflected a panorama of the restaurant. The Cove was different from most restaurants. Everyone seemed to know everybody else so they stood around in little groups, like at a party.

I saw her right away, talking with a grease-ball hood. She was wearing a long black dress with hidden pleats that showed flashes of red or white. She strolled through the crowd, greeting people. She was alone and avoided anyone who tried to touch her, affectionately pushing them away or stepping back with a smile. As she worked the crowd, laughing and joking, she would occasionally look at me. Her glances began to increase until I saw the shock on her face. She quickly turned away, but her nervous smile gave her up.

Finally after about ten minutes she sat down beside me but looked away toward her friends. "How did you find me?"

With both of us looking in opposite directions I answered, "Through your drug-dealing friends over there."

"What do you want?"

"I want you. I never stopped looking for you. I don't care about what happened or what you're doing. We loved each other, I want it all back. You are my life." I stared into my drink and waited for her answer.

My best hopes came true. She said, "There has never been anyone else after you. How could you ever forgive me?"

"I have to forgive you. I understand what you did. I love you. You can do no wrong. Please, let's try. I need you."

After a long silence she got up and leaned close to me and whispered, "Okay, but not here. That's mob over there. You'll get both of us killed. One mile up the beach going north, there's a small park below the hills. It's the only place you can park next to the water. I'll be there at twelve-thirty."

She strolled back to her mob friends. Her beautiful body and flashy dress again drew every eye in the restaurant to her.

At twelve-thirty I stood on the sand, staring at the rolling ocean and waited. There was no moon so it was very dark. My life had meaning again. I would give up cocaine and find a normal life. Surely she wanted the change, too. We needed each other.

Above the crashing black waves I heard a high-pitched motor, whining slow, then fast. Up above, on the overlooking cliffs I saw a single light darting back and forth. The light disappeared at times but the sound grew louder and louder as the motorcycle made its way down the winding road to the shore.

The light swept the beach and me. Then with a loud click it was dark and silent. I could barely see someone walking toward me. Rachel was dressed in black motorcycle leather and wearing boots with big silver buckles on the side. Even though it was too dark to see her face she was the most beautiful person I had ever known. I wanted to hold her, to kiss her, to feel her tongue on mine. I wanted to cry and have her see my tears.

When she was within a few feet of my embrace, I said, "It's been a long time, never again. I love – "

She opened her leather jacket, reached under her armpit and pulled out the black automatic, Henri's automatic with the silencer, "This is for Henri."

I watched her level the gun with her eye on the sights and pull the trigger.

I never really actually saw what happened to Rachel, it was too dark. I just remember my screams and running to the car. I spent the night at the airport, staring down at the floor and trying not to begin screaming again.

God made darkness for a reason and now I knew why. Michael knows the reason too, that's why he prefers it. Now I hated the daylight, too. From now on I would live only at night.

THE BEACH

The moment I walked into Cookie's apartment I knew she was gone. Closet doors left open, clothes scattered on the bedroom floor. She had taken only what she could carry, abandoning all the rest, along with her whole apartment. No note, just gone for good. This should have depressed me, but it didn't. Considering everything else that I was going through my only reaction was to make a sandwich and pour myself a drink. I was grateful for my wonderful rainbow of addictions. They offered a much better life than my reality. I was proud of myself for keeping my drug and liquor habits secret from everyone, and I knew that from now on my sexual pleasures would probably be found at Gramercy Park.

The next day my cocaine cured a hangover and I went back to the office. Dot, Blanker's secretary, was in the library, eating lunch as she worked on some of the case files. I thanked her for phoning me a warning about my pending indictment. She asked if I had heard anything yet.

I said, "No." Then out of curiosity, or perhaps fear, I asked, "Dot, what's the latest with Dewey?"

She glanced up at me once, then she answered, "They are coming for him soon. I heard Blanker talking to some investigator; he is going to be arrested for multiple murders. I heard at least ten killings."

Trying to keep the conversation going, I said, "I'm sorry to hear that. Didn't Dewey transfer here from Navy Intelligence?"

"No, I'm not really sure."

I was surprised. "No? You don't know where he came from?"

Dot put down her sandwich. "I know this; he came from the University of Michigan, but come to think of it, he was recommended by Navy Intelligence. He had a Master's Degree in foreign languages, so Blanker brought him in to be an interpreter, but he couldn't speak a word of anything except English. Then Blanker found out that he had gotten straight D's."

"Dewey Paris graduated in the top of class from Annapolis. What do you mean got straight D's?"

"I don't know anything about that," Dot replied, "but I saw his transcript from graduate school, not one C, not one F, straight D's in every subject that he took in foreign languages, but he still got his Master's Degree. Blanker thought he was too dumb to be an agent and he wasn't any good as an interpreter, so he assigned him to Michael to get rid of him. Besides, he didn't even look like a federal agent; he looks like a teenager. Blanker couldn't stand him. He was embarrassed to call him an agent."

I was stunned. "Dewey was too dumb to be an agent, so they assigned him to Michael Giovanni to get *rid* of him?"

"That's right," she answered. "Blanker always assigns the dumb agents he doesn't want to Michael." Then she realized what she had just said and was embarrassed.

"That's okay. Dewey was dumb; it was smart to assign him to Michael."

"Dewey didn't make cases like you," she said then. "You have made more major cases than anyone else in the Bureau for the last two years. I don't know why you should care about Dewey. I typed Blanker's personnel report on him. It said that Agent Dwight Paris was a killer and he was disrespectful to his supervisors, and he was never serious about making cases. He was a party boy."

Dewey could always make me laugh and he was even doing it now. He got straight D's in his Master's in foreign languages so he would never be stuck with the dull job of being a language interpreter – and played dumb to get assigned to Michael, so he could learn from the smartest agent in the Bureau.

I thought of the Vietnam War, Dewey's mystery guest he met for lunch at the Peacock Alley, and the picture hanging on his living-room wall of hundreds of sailors saluting him on the deck of a ship. Dot hung her head down. "Flowers and the others talk all the time about you. I'm sorry. They're all wrong about you. You don't deserve this."

I walked out of the library to my desk in Group Two. I wanted to find Flowers and tell him that I was going to accept his deal. I had a solid case against Dewey and Michael. I was not going to jail. An indictment against me was not necessary. I had decided to add one more condition to the letter of immunity: that I stay in my job for the next five years. I was sure he would agree. I hated everybody here at the Bureau. I hated Dewey and Michael for being so smart, and leaving me here alone, but it didn't matter – this was where I belonged. Besides, here I had an endless supply of dope. When I walked into Group Two no one was there except Pike and his secretary. Things seemed normal.

"What's new?" I asked Pike, wondering if he had heard anything about my indictment.

"Nothing," he replied. Then he handed me a memo from George Blanker. It was marked *urgent*. At 1:00 p.m. I was to be picked up to fly by government jet to Texas for a meeting with Johnny Greenway and others from the El Paso office. The objective of the case was to attempt a buy from an international dealer coming in from Colombia. I went to my locker and got four bundles of cocaine and stuffed them in my jacket.

In less than an hour I was the sole passenger on an Air Force jet headed for Brownsville. During the flight, I wondered why I was leaving New York. Maybe they wanted more time to squeeze Michael and the others. Everyone wanted me either dead or in jail

– preferably dead. There was no booze on the plane so I was sweaty and dizzy when I arrived in Brownsville.

Greenway was there to meet me and I asked him if we could get a few drinks. We went to a small bar in the airport. He looked happy, no longer afraid of New York. I didn't mention the bomb scare or his hasty forced return to El Paso, exactly where he wanted to be. We both knew Michael had set the whole thing up. There was no need to talk about it.

He explained the case. There was a fishing camp across the border, on the Gulf, accessible only by boat or plane. Interpol, the Bureau, and the Mexicans were going to show two hundred and fifty thousand dollars in cash to dealers in Monterrey, Mexico. A boat was to deliver one hundred kilos of cocaine, and a plane would bring the money. I was to be the "New York Mafia connection" to oversee the exchange at the fishing cabin. I would fly in first and, once everyone was together, with the drugs, I would signal – and all hell would break loose.

"Why am I going in alone?" I asked.

"You're not. I've got guys already at the camp, waiting for you. I'll be there in about three hours."

"Okay," I said, "let's go."

We headed back to the Coast Guard base. As we pulled up, Greenway said, "Oh, one problem; we have to go through Customs. I don't want them to know who you are. Give me your coat and your gun."

I was searched at Customs but Greenway was not. Greenway walked me to the cockpit of a small single-engine plane, handed me my jacket, which was wrapped around my gun, and left. No good-bye, he just turned around and walked off.

The little plane flew straight south. All I could see was the coast and jungle for miles. The pilot banked a sharp left and I could see a small airstrip cut out of the jungle that ran parallel to the shore. As he maneuvered for a landing, I saw a small house on the beach. The pilot said we were about fifty miles from San Fernando, Mexico, which was west through the jungle. We landed and the plane pulled to a stop. "Here you are," he said.

"Aren't you coming with me?" I asked.

"No, I have to get back to the base. My orders were to drop you and come back. They said there would be people here waiting for you."

I climbed out of the plane and watched it taxi down the runway and bank over the coastline, flying north and out of view. It was very hot so I carried my jacket and made my way to the fishing cabin I'd seen from the air. As I approached the cabin, I sensed that something was wrong. I was alone. The door was open. Inside was a large radio panel but sections of it had been dismantled and taken out. The kitchen was stocked with canned food and there was a little bar with two half-gallon jugs of vodka.

I sat on the porch and tried to relax. This wasn't so bad; at least I was out of New York and out of Flowers' reach, temporarily, so I decided I might as well enjoy it. I reached in my pocket and found my tobacco pouch – a leather bag with a zipper, which I used for cocaine – and set it on the counter. I had all the comforts of home – vodka and dope, plus a beautiful ocean and a sandy beach. I felt tired so I decided to lie down and wait for Greenway to show up with the others, wondering why I was alone.

I woke up after a short nap and fixed myself some canned stew, then poured myself half a glass of vodka. I took a sip. It was water.

I went outside and looked up and down the beach. A terrible feeling came over me. I went back inside and got my leather bag with my cocaine stash, opened it up, and dumped everything on the counter. All my little bags of cocaine were gone.

Then I knew what was happening. I knew they weren't coming for me. I knew I was going to be here alone. I should have guessed from the look on Greenway's face when he first saw me getting off the plane. Sally was right. I was a drunk, a cokehead and a fool, and everyone knew it. And now I was going to do cold turkey – alone – and probably not live through it.

By the end of the next day I had dry heaves, and then I fainted trying to walk up the steps of the porch. I lay on the steps, asleep, and half my body got burned red from the sun. I was talking to myself and beginning to have cold shakes.

At night I ran out into the ocean. The water felt warm. I staggered back to the cabin before I noticed that I had gone into the water fully clothed. I sat down on the bed, took off my clothes, poured water out of my boots, and fell asleep. I wasn't sure of the time, but it was very early morning when I woke up in a cold sweat.

I stumbled out to the beach and began to scream and shake, and then ran along the shoreline. Finally I stopped and just lay down on the sand. When I awoke, the sun was directly overhead and water was splashing halfway up my legs. I was totally naked. There were small crabs all around me, waiting for me to die. I looked up and down the beach and didn't know from which direction I had come or how far I had run. I had no cover and the sun was very hot. I would walk one way for about ten minutes and, not seeing the cabin, I would reverse direction and walk ten minutes the other way. I tried to find my original footprints but I had been walking in the shallow, lapping waves along the shoreline and they were all washed away. The sun was searing my bare skin, and the sunburn from the day before was beginning to blister. I tried to go into the jungle for shade, but with my bare feet the rocks were too sharp. Finally, I just staggered in one direction. I feared that, if it was the wrong way, the sun would bake me to death.

It was late afternoon when I finally saw the cabin. I got down on my knees and cried. I must have walked for five miles, staggering and screaming along the shoreline. If I had walked in the other direction I would have died. I drank some water and fell asleep, but I had a dream, a horrible dream: I saw myself as a child standing on the side of a small stream, staring down into the water at a green frog. Suddenly, from underneath, a snake grabbed the frog in its mouth. The little frog looked back at me with a blank, cold stare, the look of death. The frog became Tony Degaglia's mother in her chair, and then Lisa Marie and Stuckey and DeWitt and Calvin, and the man holding his bloody arm at the Medalley mansion. They were all there, all with the same blank stare, looking at me. I woke up shaking. When morning finally came, I tried to eat, but two hours later I was kneeling naked in the sand, throwing up.

That afternoon I had some luck. Clouds rolled in and it started to rain, at first heavily and then in a light mist. At dusk, I walked along the beach – still naked and hurting from the sunburn. I thought I was feeling better, when all of a sudden I saw the footprints of a child in the wet sand. The right foot was curved inward; I was convinced they were the footprints of my five-year-old son Mark. I followed them along the beach for what seemed to be a mile. How did he get here? I *had* to find him. Then I saw the footprints curve off the sand and into the sea. I looked around, but it was clear; they went into the water and didn't come back out.

As I stared over the water, I saw a large, gray, slimy log about ten feet from shore. I stared at the log and saw that it was bent, almost in a half-circle. Suddenly it moved, making a huge splash, hitting me with water so hard it knocked me down. I looked up and saw the log was actually the body of a gigantic gray snake rising above me. Its head came down; its teeth tore into my leg and held me. I knew I was going to die and I just stared at the jungle and the beach, waiting for the snake to drag me under the water. I knew everything was finally over, and I felt calm resignation. Now I had the same stare I had seen on so many faces, and one by one, just like my dream, all the faces with that terrible calm stare came back to me. So many people were dead because of me, now it was my turn and I was calm too. The snake released me just for a second, perhaps to get a better grip. I scrambled toward the jungle, knowing it could easily follow and get me. I rolled around in the sand and cried, screamed and kicked – and then all was quiet. The snake was gone.

I could hardly breathe. I staggered back to the cabin. There was a mirror in the bedroom and I looked at myself, expecting to see blood all over my leg; instead I saw that I was only covered with wet sand from head to foot. I looked like a cheap cement statue. There was no blood, only the scar on my side where Del Ridley's wife had stabbed me. I lay down on the bed and wanted to die.

Again, I woke up in the early morning. I couldn't face another day, could not face another hallucination.

I found my automatic and went outside to the porch in the hot burning sunlight. I stared at my blue automatic: something was wrong, it was too light. I pulled back the carriage, but nothing ejected. I squeezed the trigger, and again nothing happened. I popped the clip; it was empty. Greenway had thought of everything.

BORN AGAIN

By noon of the next day, my sunburn was so bad that I couldn't go outside; I just peeked out the windows at the blue water and lay in bed. I was able to keep some food down, but couldn't taste anything. By evening, I was able to watch the stars and even venture outside along the beach. I wondered what horror would visit me tonight. But I fell asleep and slept through the night, and when I awoke it was daylight.

I had no idea of the time since I didn't have a watch, and there was no clock or even electricity in the cabin. My head seemed clear and I began to think about things. I spent the whole day inside. *Someone put me here* I reasoned – but to die or to dry out? Greenway could not have done it alone. It could have been Michael or even Flowers, or Dewey with his CIA friends. But why? They were going to kill me in New York, or indict me; either way, sober or stoned... but there were easier ways to kill me than flying me to this beach. Once again I had that sinking feeling that I didn't know what was going on. I guess it didn't matter who or why. What was really important was that someone wanted me ready to face something.

That evening I sat at the edge of the water with the waves lapping at my feet. A calm came over me. I was neither a killer nor a corrupt, cold-blooded agent. It didn't matter that I had not made a single case, despite what all the reports said. I had done my best and fought as hard as I could to save America. That was all that really mattered. I was just a soldier, like the rest of them, fighting a war that society could not comprehend. It was so simple to me that I laughed at myself. I should have seen it sooner. I wasn't here to die. Someone wanted me strong and sober. I didn't regret anything I'd done...except one "heroic act of bravery in the line of duty saving Michael's life" that I would always be remembered for – killing Michael's lover. I tried not to laugh, but it was too outrageous to hold back.

I remembered my first day as an agent. How could I ever forget it? I remembered the tape Blanker played for us in his office that he was so proud of..."*the agents of 90 Church are the most evil people in the world.*" I screamed as loud as I could at the gathering waves as they rolled to the shore, "America be proud! America be proud! America be proud! Be proud of me!" Warm tears rolled down my face. I wanted someone, anyone, to be proud of me.

The next day I still couldn't go out into the sun but I had an appetite, and could eat. I stared at the rolling waves all day, anxious to return – yet afraid of the indictments that awaited me. I wondered about the penitentiary and for how long I would be sentenced and whether I could live through it. I didn't think I could. I was mostly concerned about the embarrassment to my family, Daisy, Mark, and my mother and father. When I thought about Daisy I would start to cry. They were the most important things in my life and I threw them away first. They probably could have saved me from this mess.

I didn't hate Flowers anymore, he was just trying to do his job, doing what he thought was right. Someone else fighting for truth, justice and the American way. Everyone was trying to do the right thing: Flowers, the agents, even Rachel, who tried to save her real true love, Henri Manasso. She was strong and beautiful.

I would always love her. Everyone was just trying to do what they thought was right – except Michael; Michael was just doing what the government told him to do...stop drug dealers. Everyone hated him the most, yet he was the only true hero.

I was part of 90 Church and 90 Church was part of me. We all fought together. We were loyal to each other because we knew how things worked and that was the only way to survive in a war. No matter who betrayed me I would not betray them. It had to stop and it was going to stop with me. Dewey had saved my life many times and Michael forgave me for killing his lover. Why does the government always think it has to be right? The things we did were not as important as why we did them. I knew what was right and how much it was going to cost. The deals with the devil were over. I remembered what Manasso had said, "Mark well your accounts payable." My bills have come due; I must stand up and go to prison for twenty years for causing the death of a lousy pimp and helping a strung-out junkie informant survive. What an outrageous, perverted price to pay.

That evening I made dinner and again sat on the beach, watching it get dark. Since my first day, I had not worn any clothing. I sat on the cool sand, staring at the gray clouds gathering over the ocean. The stars were beginning to come out; as I looked at the brightest ones, I noticed something unusual about them.

There were three stars in a straight line, separated equally. I hoped I was not having another hallucination. I watched them gently rock back and forth, gradually growing brighter, but always in a straight line and equally bright. All of a sudden, there was a loud roar and the stars went from a horizontal to a vertical line. The airplane banked to the left and out of my sight over the jungle.

I couldn't hear it anymore, but then saw the lights coming back to land.

I rushed into the cabin and tried to put on my clothes. They were in a moldy heap. I couldn't find my socks so I put my boots on over my bare feet. One side of a boot was ripped and my foot poked through. I ran down the path to the airstrip to find a long, thin, black plane with small white numbers painted on it. There were no other markings. The pilot lowered a ladder for me to climb and then slid the glass canopy closed. He didn't say a word. The engines roared and he pivoted the airplane, rolled down the runway, and shot almost straight up in the air. The force crushed me against my seat and took my breath.

After leveling off, the pilot handed me an envelope, a memo from George Blanker. It said I was to terminate my activities immediately and report to the Bureau for the Monday morning meeting, without fail. The date of the memo surprised me. I could only remember being on the beach for four days, but the date showed I had been there for seven. After about twenty minutes, the pilot turned to me and pointed down. "That's Houston," he said, and mentioned some Air Force base.

At Houston, a station wagon drove me to the public airport and by 11:00 I was walking through the terminal in Long Island, New York. I saw myself in the glass of the shops and understood the looks that people gave me as I walked past them. I looked like a homeless person, with a stubble beard, long stringy hair, filthy moldy clothes, and my bare foot sticking out of my boot. There was a barbershop getting ready to close but I walked in and asked the man if I could have a haircut. He shook his head and said, "No, no way, I'm closed."

I dug in my pocket and peeled off a hundred-dollar bill of

government money, laid it on the counter and sat in the chair.

"I want it all off, one-inch length, so it lays flat. Cut it all off," I said. My hair was so long it almost reached my shoulders. In twenty minutes I looked totally different and I left, hailing a cab.

MOMENT OF TRUTH

The moment I walked into my apartment I could sense that it had been empty for a long time. The air was stale and a fine layer of dust covered everything. A note lay on the kitchen table. It was from Daisy and it simply read: *If things ever change, let me know, but you'll have to get a job, Love.*

I wanted to cry, but I couldn't. I knew that I had bigger things to worry about tomorrow.

I woke up early. This was my big day. I threw my pimp clothes in the trash, including my deerskin boots. I took a shower and shaved and looked for something appropriate to wear on my one-way trip to the penitentiary. I opened the closet door, turned on the light and looked up at the top shelf at a glorious sight. It warmed me all over and made me chuckle. When Flowers strapped me in to the lie-detector chair he asked, "Have you ever taken or misappropriated government funds?" What he did not ask was "Did I ever skim money from drug dealers?" There in the dim light on the shelf was a wall of envelopes and bundles, all shapes, sizes and colors stacked so high I would need to stand on a chair to reach the top. Every one of them had been handed to me on a dark street, or thrown in the back seat of my car, or counted out at the clinic, and even stuffed in my evidence locker. I was sure there was over three hundred thousand dollars. None of it had ever meant anything to me.

I remembered how they caught Dewey with only ten thousand dollars in his bank account and was sure Flowers had gone through all of my pitiful bank accounts many times. Stacking all this money on the top shelf of my closet was the dumbest, most obvious place to hide it, yet it was probably the last place they would ever look.

I earned every dollar of it – and now it was for Daisy. She would know how to spend it and I would tell her how to keep it secret. Staring at this strange wall of envelopes and packages was the best sight I had ever seen in my dark, miserable, wretched life.

I chose a navy blue, three-button suit, with a white button-down shirt, striped red tie, and the wing-tipped shoes that I hadn't worn in four years.

Then I got on the subway to face my fate. I rode with everyday, honest people living a dull, meaningless life and I envied every wretched one of them. I thought about my disastrous, comical first day at 90 Church and my silly Superman creed "to fight for truth, justice and the American way." I certainly knew what it was to fight for truth and justice, but what was the American way?

I looked like any other businessman going to the office, except I had a terrific tan. As I climbed the subway steps to 90 Church, I remembered seeing the news trucks the morning they arrested agents Brown and Winkler, and wondered if I would see the same sight. I looked down the street. I didn't see any, and was relieved. As I was about to enter the building, a man rushed in front of me, carrying a film camera. I walked to the edge of the block and looked down the side street. There were news cars parked on both sides of the street. I was big time. I was the undercover agent coming in from the cold, being arrested for crimes ranging from drug-peddling to killing "Mr. Heyman." I began imagining all the items on my indictment bill: assaults, theft, selling drugs, trashing government automobiles, murder. I realized that I would be facing a twenty-year sentence and that the combination of crimes and refusing to cooperate would rule out any leniency from the courts. But I was clean, strong, and sober. *I was standing up.* I gritted my teeth.

I got in the elevator and stood in the back. Others got in, then Flowers stepped in just before the doors closed. He looked around but didn't notice me. He still didn't recognize me when we got off together at the top floor. Then he stared at me, and said, "Hello."

I looked back, smiled too, and said, "Fuck you." I walked down the hallway into Group Two. Everyone looked at me like they were seeing a ghost. They didn't know me with my haircut and suit. No one said hello or good morning or anything. They just looked at me then turned away, just like my first terrible day four years ago. I was calm. I sat at my desk, waiting for them to make the first move – and sure enough, Pike's secretary asked me to come into his office.

At first he tried to make light of everything. He said I looked good and then got right to the point. "Blanker wants me to pick up your gun and your credentials."

I laughed. "What do you think, Boss? Didn't they take Dewey and Agent Brown's credentials and piece before they busted them? Or maybe, do you think I'm going to be assigned to a new office?"

He gave a nervous laugh. I went to my locker and got the "toy" aluminum gun, issued me on my first day at the Bureau, the one that I had used to kill Michael's lover. Along with it were my leather-covered credentials with my picture on them, embossed with the United States of America eagle seal. I opened it and stared at a picture of a young man I did not recognize. It occurred to me that in my four years with the Bureau I had never shown my credentials to anybody – not my wife, not other agents, not the police, not to defendants, no one. But the greatest comedy of all was that from the beginning I let Michael and Dewey write me into the reports. No one except Dot, Blanker's naïve secretary, believed that I had made all those major cases. I walked back and gave my "toy" gun and credentials to Pike.

Pike left immediately, carrying them to Blanker's office, like getting them was a big deal. I helped myself to coffee and donuts and waited for the press conference and the inevitable. I hoped that I wouldn't show fear and trembling the way Agent Brown did when they led him out, but I kept remembering my visit to Del Ridley when he was in prison, with his bashed-out teeth and blank stare. It was nine-thirty. Ten o'clock came quickly.

We all filed toward the large conference room past Blanker's office. The press was everywhere. There were three mounted cameras, pointing at the podium. Flowers, Blanker, and three others I didn't recognize were seated in front. I assumed the strangers were from the Justice Department. They looked the type. All of this, just to arrest me and drag me out. How ridiculous – but I was ready. I only felt a deep sadness for my mother and father, Daisy and Mark, but I *would* stand up and the terrible plague of betrayals would end with me. In time they would understand and get over the shame.

Blanker loved the limelight. Press conferences always made him smile and wave his arms when he made his point. First he introduced the press and thanked them for coming. Then he said, "As some of you have heard, Judge Carl Wineburg is retiring. He has been a great friend to the agents and will be missed. Andy Flowers has the details on his retirement party." He paused and grinned over the podium. Then the strangers nodded their heads together in agreement. "The reason you're all here," he continued, "the Investigative Task Force has accomplished their objectives; their final action will to be announced momentarily."

I knew that meant my arrest, their number-one undercover agent and major target. Then Blanker said it. He said my name. Everyone turned to look at me. I grew cold and clenched my teeth, trying not to remember Del Ridley's face when he was in prison. He continued, "This brave agent has made twenty-four undercover buys this year alone, and was responsible for bringing Henri Manasso, Charles Moon, the Medalley family, John Belonconi, and four other major crime figures under indictments. He shot and killed a drug dealer to save Agent Giovanni's life. He was stabbed in the side by a mugger trying to steal government money. Now I am proud to announce that he has been named Head of the Justice Department Covert Operations Division, and will be relocating to Washington. Accordingly, he is being promoted to GS17, the highest jump in grade in the Bureau's history, and of this moment he is no longer employed here at 90 Church. Congratulations, my boy."

When his words hit me, I didn't feel a sense of shock. Instead, I felt like a drunk who has just heard an outrageously funny joke. I started to make a hooting noise, partly to catch my breath, but I couldn't stop. The hoots became louder and louder. I could see the cameras pointing at me, but I couldn't help it. I saw the shocked expressions of everyone. I began to laugh – not a simple laugh but loud maniacal laughter. Every time I looked at someone – Blanker,

Flowers, Pike, Silkey, and poor Michael – I would laugh harder and louder. I stood up and tried to leave. But I had to say it, I had to tell everyone. I almost yelled, "I know truth and justice. Now I understand the American way. I get it. *This is the American way.*" I laughed so hard I was gagging. I started to fall over and reached for a chair. Silkey grabbed my arm and tried to settle me. He said, "Jesus Christ, *stop* this!"

I staggered from the room, into the hall, and down to the men's room. I wiped the tears off my face and looked in the mirror and started laughing all over again...at the short-haired agent in the three-button suit who had just been promoted, and said to my reflection, "Just like Michael always says: When you're guilty you assume the worst." Tears were streaming down my face as I walked out down the corridor to the elevator, and finally, laughing uncontrollably, into the street. I began talking to innocent strangers walking by, "*I found the American way!*"

I was two blocks away from the office before I could stop laughing. The first thing I did was to call Daisy from a pay phone. I stood in the hot New York sun, talking to her for a half hour, still crying. Daisy was crying too, the terrible nightmare was over. I caught a cab and paid sixty dollars for lunch at the Plaza Hotel's opulent tea room. I tried to pretend I was someone important. Then I took the subway back to 90 Church and walked into Blanker's office.

Before I could say anything Blanker said, "You just missed it; they arrested your friend Dewey."

"What? I don't believe it! Flowers?"

"No, three Navy officers, they had a felony warrant for murder, but it wasn't a typical arrest."

I was shocked. "What do you mean it wasn't a typical arrest?"

Blanker looked away from me and answered, "Pike took his gun and credentials and brought him up here, but when he saw the arresting officers they all started hugging and laughing. Then they collected Dewey's black gun and just walked out the door. I could hear them laughing and yelling all the way to the elevator."

I hoped I wouldn't start laughing about Dewey finally meeting up with his Navy buddies. "I'm resigning. I don't want the promotion. All I want to do is leave."

Blanker slumped down in his chair and said, "All of the investigations are over and Michael is on medical leave because of his drinking. The Task Force could find nothing wrong with any of your cases. They thought they could find Heyman's body, but they couldn't. They tried all sorts of ways to spell the name. They're starting a new agency to fight drugs; it's called the DEA. Agents here will have an opportunity to join the DEA if they want to, but I understand all the jobs are already filled. I don't think they're going to take any of us. They're going to do things differently over there. They really wanted to put you in Washington. They thought you were something special. The truth is, they couldn't indict anyone. Couldn't make even *one* case...on the money, the reports, anything. Sooner or later some of Michael's boys in the street would have started taking out the Task Force. Incidentally, how was your vacation? Looks like you got some sun."

I smiled at him, nodded yes, and walked out of his office. To this day I do not know who arranged my Mexican vacation.

EPILOGUE

I resumed a normal life working for charitable organizations, and then later started my own business. As the years passed I began to look back upon my experience with great pride.

After bringing down five Mafia families the Federal Bureau of Narcotics had become the most effective law-enforcement agency in America's history. It had also become very controversial and was terminated in 1968. Its files and cases were taken over by other agencies, including the FBI and CIA, who took credit for the Bureau's accomplishments. In 1972 after years of political turmoil the Bureau was replaced by over 4,500 agents in the newly created DEA with a budget of over a billion dollars.

90 Church succeeded because its sinister network of informants enabled the agents to execute elaborate cases. Unlike the millions of dollars the DEA now spends on cases and paying informants, we were only given $5,000 per case and informants were paid a maximum of $50, including travel, to betray the most dangerous killers in America.

The files could never show that the agents secretly confiscated drug money from overseas and domestic operations to fund their cases and pay informants. It was, of course, this free flow of illicit money and protecting informants that brought 90 Church down. There were only about thirty agents in New York City who made major cases and worked with me. Many of them were indicted for drug trafficking or charged with misappropriation of funds.

Today there is little recorded history of 90 Church except for a large collection of pictures in the files of hundreds of Mafia killers and drug dealers such as Meyer Lansky, Vito Genovese, and Joe Valachi. Under each mug shot is the line: Arrested by Federal Bureau of Narcotics, 90 Church. We worked in an environment of desperation, in a war that threatened to destroy America. The agents did what had to be done.

Years ago in New York City I encountered a man beating an old lady while attempting to steal her purse. There was a short scuffle and the three of us ended up in the NYPD Precinct. A seasoned captain commented that it was odd that a charity worker could disarm a mugger. I told him I used to be at 90 Church. He stared at me for a moment, then turned to the mugger and said "For what you have done, you are going to do five years in prison. But today is the luckiest day of your life. You see I've heard things about the agents at 90 Church. It's a miracle that you're still alive."

There are people who still remember.

SUGGESTED READING

Mafia: The Government's Secret File on Organized Crime
(No Author), Harper, 2007

The Trail of the Poppy: Behind the Mask of the Mafia by Charles
Siragusa, Prentice Hall, 1966

*The Strength of the Pack: The Personalities, Politics and Espionage
Intrigues that Shaped the DEA* by Douglas Valentine,
Trine Day, 2010

*The Strength of the Wolf: The Secret History of America's War on
Drugs* by Douglas Valentine, Verso Books, 2006